ANTONFRANCESCO GRAZZINI

ANTONFRANCESCO GRAZZINI

Poet, Dramatist, and Novelliere

1503–1584

BY ROBERT J. RODINI

THE UNIVERSITY OF WISCONSIN PRESS
Madison, Milwaukee, and London, 1970

Published by
The University of Wisconsin Press
Box 1379, Madison, Wisconsin 53701
The University of Wisconsin Press, Ltd.
27–29 Whitfield Street, London, W.1

Printed in the United States of America by
Kingsport Press, Inc., Kingsport, Tennessee
SBN 299-05590-6
LC 71-106041

To Eleanor

CONTENTS

ILLUSTRATIONS

following page 96

PREFACE

In recent years scholars have given more and more attention to those periods of Italian literature which, barren of truly great writers, had previously been neglected in favor of periods of undisputed merit. For example, while interest has not shifted from the golden age of Cinquecento literature to the ofttimes sterile seventeenth-century Italian baroque, the trend has been toward a reevaluation of this latter period in an effort to recognize its achievements not only for their own value but for what they possessed for future periods. And as the seventeenth century has gained in prestige, greater attention has been focused on the period of transition, the late sixteenth century, when humanistic ideals were challenged and tradition came under the close scrutiny of both skeptics and advocates of change.[1] In order to explain that apparent reversal of Cinquecento decorum which was effected by baroque literature and baroque aesthetics, scholars have had to give greater attention to minor writers of the late Renaissance who, lying outside the humanistic and academic tradition, could provide significant insight into the literary beginnings of the Italian baroque. Not infrequently, unknown or little-known writers have been discovered and their work has been found to merit careful appraisal. Such was the case when Benedetto Croce brought Federico Della Valle to the attention of the literary public in 1929.

Antonfrancesco Grazzini is another of the many figures of the late Renaissance who, until recently, had received little critical attention. For the most part, he has been considered in works of an encyclopedic nature which discuss him together with the numerous writers of comedy and *novellieri* of the Italian Renaissance. The major study of his theatre was conducted at the end of the last century by Giovanni Gentile who, though he provided important material for dating Grazzini's comedies, paid little attention to their literary significance.[2] More valuable critical attention has been afforded the *Cene*, Grazzini's collection of novelle: though studies of the novelle are few, they surpass the studies of the comedies, both for their perception and their consideration of Grazzini's place in the development of narrative style.[3] Grazzini's poetry has remained practically untouched by critics of the Renaissance, although he is considered second only to Francesco Berni in the burlesque genre.

It is clear that Grazzini's work deserves further consideration for its place in the changing climate of late Renaissance literature. Critics of his theatre have indicated its debt to tradition and to the erudite comedy but have also alluded to its novelty: the gusto for clever dialogue and the superiority of its slapstick, the introduction of current speech and humor in an effort to "modernize" and revitalize stereotyped characters and situations.[4] Inevitably, such observations have led to analogies between Grazzini's theatre and the new techniques of the commedia dell'arte. Studies of the prose novelle have pointed to the author's taste for movement and for the picturesque as indications of a narrative form which was tending toward the plasticity and the grotesqueness of seventeenth-century art.[5] Though Grazzini's poetry also reveals his delight in verbal acrobatics, it is most significant for its polemic against pedantry and tradition in support of literary freedom. In all of Grazzini's writings, then, critics have perceived an attempted break with the literary past. No one has yet undertaken, however, a comprehensive study of all his work in order to show, as this book attempts to do, that Grazzini's art was a means by which he remained in constant polemic with the Renaissance traditionalists and academicians and that in his writings he sought to bring renewed life to literature by finding his inspiration in life itself.

Grazzini was, then, not just a writer of popular literature, but, as I hope to show by considering both his writings and his activities as an editor and champion of the Florentine language, a critic of academic traditionalism. In this capacity Grazzini has much in common with sixteenth-century literary bohemianism or *scapigliatura*, and he may therefore be considered an active force in the growing critical spirit of the late Renaissance.

At the same time, however, Grazzini's effectiveness in his role as a critic and literary innovator was limited by his provincialism and his inability to extend his considerations beyond the Florentine world and the mentality of the Florentine burgher. "Modern" literature, as he understood it, was to be a reflection of contemporary Florence and a document of the Florentine language. It is only in a very particular way that Grazzini manifests the sixteenth-century struggle between tradition and innovation in letters: his polemic against the traditionalists was inspired by a desire for a Florentine literature which was, in truth, not new but one which harked back to the popular genres of fifteenth-century Medicean Florence. Grazzini was first and foremost a Florentine citizen, and all his writings show a relatively limited interest in anything which did not immediately concern Florence. For this reason he has always been considered one of the most Florentine of writers.

This study of Grazzini is primarily concerned with the Florentine character of his poetry, comedies, and novelle, and it will attempt to demonstrate that in spite of the antitraditional polemic which dominates his work and the evidence of stylistic change toward a literary "mannerism," all of his art expresses a deep nostalgia for Florence's glorious past. Even within the small world of Renaissance Florence, Grazzini reflects the ambivalence of his age which, while attempting to infuse new life into a culture which had become bogged down in its own traditions, could only with great difficulty shake off the burden of its past.

For his guidance during the early stages of this book and for his example as a teacher, I wish to thank Nicolas J. Perella. I am grateful, also, to Joseph Rossi for his careful reading of the manuscript and his helpful suggestions and to Douglas Kelly for the many times that he has generously given his advice and resolved many problems of style and mechanics. I wish to thank the Graduate School of the University of Wisconsin for providing the funds necessary for completing this study. My greatest debt is to my wife, Eleanor Morgan Rodini, my severest critic and editor.

Note on the Translations and References

All translations from the Italian are mine. In the English version of Grazzini's burlesque verses, I have attempted to preserve the colloquial and idiomatic qualities of the original, while avoiding the excessive repetition which occurs, particularly in the poetry of a polemical nature. In those instances where Grazzini enumerates untranslatable foods, types of fish, etc., I have chosen an appropriate English equivalent or used a generic word to convey the sense, if not the full flavor, of the original. Passages in Italian which are used to illustrate a discussion of style are left in the original with an English version immediately following.

In a bibliographical appendix to this volume is a chronological listing of Grazzini's printed works to 1900. Editions published after 1900 and used or consulted for this study are:

Grazzini, Antonfrancesco. *Le Novelle*, ed. Guido Biagi. Milan: Istituto Editoriale Italiano, 1915.

———. *Le Cene*, ed. Enrico Emanuelli. Rome: Bompiani, 1943.

———. *Teatro*, ed. Giovanni Grazzini. Bari: Laterza, 1953.

———. *Scritti scelti in prosa e in poesia*, ed. Raffaele Fornaciari, rev. ed., Giovanni Grazzini. Florence: Sansoni, 1957.

———. *Le Commedie*, ed. Adriano Spatola. 2 vols. to date: *L'Arzigogolo* and *La Pinzochera*. Bologna: Sampietro, 1967.

ROBERT J. RODINI

Madison, Wisconsin
October, 1969

ANTONFRANCESCO GRAZZINI

CHAPTER I

ANTONFRANCESCO GRAZZINI

Grazzini's Life

Antonfrancesco Grazzini was born on the Via delle Caldaie in the Santo Spirito quarter of Florence on March 22, 1503, one of four sons of Grazzino d'Antonio and monna Lucrezia di Ser Lorenzo de' Santi.[1] Like several members of his family before him, Grazzino d'Antonio was a notary and a descendant of noble lineage which dated back to the thirteenth century.[2] The Grazzini family originally came from Staggia, a small town situated a few kilometers northwest of Siena on the road to Florence, and as late as the sixteenth century, a traveler passing through Staggia could find evidence of the family's ancestral residence. In a sonnet written upon the occasion of a visit to Staggia, Antonfrancesco remarked that he saw his family crest displayed wherever "the eye or the foot wanders."[3] Though a member of a branch of the Grazzini family which had long since taken up residence in Florence, he could rightfully claim that he came of noble stock.

Very little is known of Grazzini's early life. Apparently, as a young man, he assisted a relative by the name of Zanobi di Zanobi Grazzini, the proprietor of a pharmacy which stood across from the Baptistry in Florence, under the "sign of the Saracen . . . at the Paglia corner."[4] Although the Florentine registries of the sixteenth century make no mention of Grazzini practicing the profession of a *speziale*, or pharmacist, in a *capitolo* entitled "In lode dei poponi" ("In praise of melons"), the author provides us with information which has led his biographers to agree that he was at least familiar with the profession.[5] It is likely that Grazzini became an apprentice to Zanobi and then continued to work in the pharmacy throughout his life,[6] supplementing his income with commissions received for various literary compositions. All that we can be sure of, however, is that he was free enough to spend time at the villas of friends outside the city and that he, a man who did not hesitate to complain about his discomforts, found no need to complain about his financial state.

Because we know so little about Grazzini's early life, we are as uncertain of the extent of his formal education as we are of the identity of his profession. Antommaria Biscioni, Grazzini's first biographer, attributed to him a profound and vast culture, and a later biographer, G. B. Magrini, referring to particular poems of Grazzini for proof, echoed Biscioni's opinion.[7] Later critics have shown, however, that both Biscioni and Magrini were overzealous in their praise. The poems which led Magrini to conclude that Grazzini had an extensive knowledge of astronomy were found to have been falsely attributed to him.[8] In truth, Grazzini's interest in astronomy was probably limited to the science as practiced by the fraudulent soothsayers, whom he attacks violently in his poetry.[9] And too often does Grazzini himself admit to his inability to read Latin for us to give credence to Biscioni's statement that he was a Latinist.[10]

Since Grazzini spent his life in polemic against the pedantry of so many of his contemporaries, and yet reveals in his poetry and prose a familiarity with the Italian classics, we can agree with Guido Biagi that he was educated but that his education was such that he could not enter into the lists of Renaissance humanists.[11] Grazzini's ignorance of classical languages indicates that he received a minimum of formal training, but his enthusiasm for the popular poetry of his native Florence, which resulted in his own collection and edition of many Florentine carnival songs (later discussed),[12] the obvious influence on his own poetry of Francesco Berni and the Florentine burlesque poets as well as of Dante and Petrarch, his dedication to Boccaccio and his familiarity with the Italian novella, his ability to incorporate into his own comedies elements of the classical and modern comic theatre attest to a preparation in literature which may have been the result of readings done, not under the supervision of a teacher, but under the influence of the literary groups with which he early became associated.

It is, in fact, not until the formation of the Accademia degli Umidi on November 1, 1540, that we have any definite biographical information concerning Grazzini. He was one of several Florentine burghers, for the most part merchants and artisans, who took for themselves bizarre names—Grazzini was called *il Lasca,* "The Roach"—and organized literary discussions, which they called *tornatelle,* at the home of Giovanni Mazzuoli, familiarly called Stradino for his birthplace, Strada.[13] Although their purpose was to foster the use of Tuscan as a literary language,[14] the Umidi were, with the exception of Michelangelo Vivaldi and Baccio Baccelli, young men of modest culture.[15]

On the whole, the Umidi were not inclined to the formalities of a literary academy. They eschewed the pedantry of classicists and intended that their meetings remain free of the academic stamp: "And because this academy of the Umidi has been created for our pastime, we intend for it to be completely free and will not tolerate annoyance from anyone; it has been founded on these conditions so that it might endure and so that boredom might not infringe upon our honest pleasure."[16] In truth, the Academy was an outgrowth of one of the many *amene brigate* which, after the vulgar tongue had gained new prestige in the early Cinquecento, sprang up throughout Florence to establish the primacy of Tuscan among the Italian dialects, a position to which it had been raised by the great triumvirate, Dante, Boccaccio, and Petrarch.[17] Many Florentines of meager culture, proud of their linguistic heritage, proclaimed themselves champions of the mother tongue and defended it against the classicists who would still uphold the superiority of Latin and Greek. Such were the Umidi. They hoped that by formally establishing an academy they would be able to demonstrate that Tuscan was an effective tool for both scholarly and literary composition. As events proved, however, they were naïve in their assumption that they could remain aloof from the pedantry which had always gone hand in hand with academic life.

For several reasons, the founding of the Accademia degli Umidi in 1540 was a milestone in the history of academic life in Renaissance Florence. As a formally structured literary society with officials and a constitution, the Accademia degli Umidi was the first of any significance to be established in Florence since early in the fifteenth century when Marsilio Ficino's Platonic Academy and the Orti Oricellari had hosted some of the leading political and literary figures of the day. Throughout the Quattrocento in Florence, which was, after all, the seat of humanist culture, academic life continued; however, it fared better or worse depending on the political situation which, during the closing years of the Quattrocento and the first decades of the Cinquecento, was highly unstable. It was not until Florence came under the absolutist control of the duke, Cosimo de' Medici, in 1537, that academies once again flourished. The Accademia degli Umidi led the way for the foundation of many new academies, and, ironically, considering the modest cultural experiences of the Umidi themselves, opened a new era of scholarship—a new Renaissance, as it were—which was to culminate with the Accademia della Crusca, founded officially in 1582.

But most significant is the fact that the Accademia degli Umidi was the first of several academies to develop independent of patronage and without the guidance of an eminent literary figure. In the past, as Marconcini noted in his study of the Academy's formative months, literary institutions had been the domain of scholars who had associated themselves with a humanist of reputation and, often, with a wealthy protector who provided both a meeting place and financial support. But the Umidi initiated an era in which academies "arose from humble conditions, from small and private gatherings of men who were less than secondary figures in the field of letters," and, therefore, without the financial backing of wealthy Florentine citizens. Too, the very nature of academic life had changed. Previously, the academies had been the stronghold of humanistic studies; their members were classicists, dedicated to the philological exegesis of ancient texts. Now, in Florence as elsewhere in Tuscany, academies were founded with the primary purpose of doing battle with humanist traditions in order to restore the *volgare* to its former glory.[18]

During the first few months of their association, the Umidi were without a constitution and they had little in the way of effective leadership. Their Maecenas, Stradino, was a rather bizarre personality, generous and paternal, but incapable of directing the activities of a literary academy.[19] Grazzini, in a capitolo written upon the occasion of Stradino's death, described him as a man who "was so good-natured that he always showed more concern for his friends than for himself; he dearly loved men of letters" (Verzone, p. 483, vv. 91–94). Stradino invited to his home youths with literary interests and he made available to them his library, the famous *armadiac-*

cio.[20] In later years, Grazzini was to recall with nostalgia the evenings spent at Stradino's home in the company of his friends: "What a pleasant group that was! There were so many that I become confused in trying to name them all. . . . And for our gatherings, we used to present a comedy, a *mascherata*, or any number of things to celebrate a holiday" (Verzone, p. 586, vv. 94–102).

Stradino's eccentric manner and dress, which became the subject of many satirical verses, set the tone for the reunions of the Umidi. Conversation was witty and never too serious, the members could freely exercise their fantasy and openly express their opinions, and pedantry was held at bay. The lighthearted nature of the group was reflected, too, in both the name selected for the Academy and the academic names taken by the individual members. The title Umidi, as was noted by an eighteenth-century historian, Marco Antonio Lastri, was chosen "in order to hail [both] vigor and nourishment [because] all the good which comes to man has its source in dampness."[21] And the names of its members—for example, *l'Humoroso*, "The Damp," *il Frigido*, "The Cold," and *lo Spumoso*, "The Foamy"—carried out the "theme" of fecundity in dampness.[22]

Shortly after November, 1540, four new members were admitted into the Academy. Among them was Grazzini's close friend, Luca Martini. The others were Giovanni Battista del Milanese, Goro della Pieve, a local physician, and Giovanni Norchiati, well known for his culture and his interest in the Tuscan dialect. It is possible that the Umidi, anxious to include in their number several men of learning who could organize the literary activities of the Academy, invited Norchiati and the others to join them in a concerted effort to defend their language against the criticism of contemporary classicists. It is quite probable, too, that new memberships were encouraged by Duke Cosimo and that he, an astute ruler who was wont to suspect an organization in which he had no personal interests, recommended to the Academy men in whom he could place his trust.[23] Upon his admission to the Academy, Goro della Pieve was appointed *rettore*, and his duties included private readings of Petrarch.[24] The Umidi then appointed two members to draw up a constitution. Under the provisions of the capitoli, approved on February 11, 1541, there were to be bi-weekly readings of Petrarch's sonnets in addition to readings of Latin authors in translation so that "little by little, all the sciences would appear in . . . [the Tuscan] language."[25] At a later date it was decided to change the name of the Academy to the Accademia Fiorentina and to require of every member a public reading.[26]

These innovations, and particularly the decision to give the Academy a more formal name, met with opposition. Niccolò Martelli, an outspoken man, protested the change of name and was quieted.[27] One member, Grazzini, voted against the capitoli which, nevertheless, were adopted by a majority of twenty-eight.[28] With a membership which had more than doubled since its inception, the Academy found several of its members unwilling to forego completely the informalities of the tornatelle. But few of the dissenters would openly express their disapproval for fear of offending the duke, who had by now offered his services and protection as patron of the Academy: he provided it with a new residence in his own palazzo on Via Larga as well as a device.[29] It would seem that Stradino himself, a favorite of Cosimo, chose not to antagonize a benefactor and set an example for his followers.[30]

On January 1, 1541, Grazzini had been appointed *cancelliere* of the Academy, but he resigned his position when he was denied the office's privilege of drawing up the capitoli.[31] He resented the usurpation of his rights by members whom he considered less deserving than he; and he must have felt, as a reading of his poetry lamenting the reforms of the Academy will show, hurt and slighted. But Grazzini's resignation was based on more than hurt feelings; it was a way of expressing his personal dissatisfaction with the pedantic new members who had changed the purpose of the Academy. It displeased him that a simple reunion of friends had been transformed into a gathering of quarrelsome pedants and that the study of the language which he loved so well had become a pretext for erudite divagations.[32]

In the following year, 1542, Grazzini was asked to do a public reading in accordance with the statutes of the Academy. He was probably expected to present a formal reading of a translation from the classics or to read an original paper, undertakings which, if we recall his limited education and his scorn for academic formalities, were probably of little interest to him.[33] He refused to comply with the request of the Academy; but, contrary to the ruling of the preceding year, he was allowed to remain an active member.[34] Perhaps it was not unusual to violate the Academy's statutes; for Biscioni mentions, too, the name of Piero Covoni, who refused to do a reading and who was a new member of the Academy.[35]

From its inception, the Accademia Fiorentina was plagued by dissension among its members. Grazzini's refusal to address the company, an act which openly defied the statutes, was apparently one of several incidents which, in 1545, led Benedetto Varchi, then presiding official (*consolo*), to say that the slow progress of the Academy was due to "the envy and the maliciousness of its members."[36] In the next few years, the alienation between Grazzini and several members of the Academy grew, and in 1547 it was climaxed by his expulsion from the group for a period of twenty years.[37] The particulars are not known, but several incidents undoubtedly contributed to the action taken against him. One such incident occurred after the Academy had introduced in 1546 a ceremony whereby the consolo was to be presented a silver cup and each of the two censors a gold ring by a young member who would then deliver an oration.[38] In an *ottava* entitled "Agli accademici"

("To the academicians"), we learn that Grazzini was selected to perform the ceremony and that he refused, protesting that he was too old for the "childish office" and that the "courtesy" of those who selected him for the task was really an attempt to humiliate one who opposed the influence of pedantry upon the Academy.

> If you had wanted to do me honor . . . why didn't you appoint me . . . censor instead? . . . I have lived too long to now put myself at the mercy of certain scholarly men who have sugar in their mouths and their breasts filled with rancor and poison. [Verzone, pp. 447–48]

Another contributing factor to Grazzini's expulsion was his refusal to submit his compositions to the censors, who functioned as literary critics, commenting on the language of a composition and censoring critical references to individuals.[39] Grazzini may have feared that the censors would condemn his satirical poetry for the harm it might do to the Academy and its members.[40] Also, since he had hoped to become a censor himself, a position for which he felt "quite experienced and able" ("Agli accademici," v. 39), it is understandable that he might seek revenge for his disappointment by not submitting to the censorship of others. It is more likely, however, that Grazzini, who felt no compunction in criticizing others, was unable to accept criticism of his own work: "I have always tried . . . to make fun of others while avoiding ridicule myself" ("Agli accademici," vv. 15–16).

Both incidents reveal Grazzini to be an independent spirit who refused to comply with the rulings of the Accademia Fiorentina when they threatened to curtail his literary freedom or to harm his well-established reputation as a poet. However, as far as we know, neither incident was directly responsible for his expulsion from the Academy in 1547, although they apparently increased the ill will of his associates towards him. But

Grazzini was not daunted by the displeasure of the Fiorentini, and he continued to criticize and to attack those with whom he disagreed.

Most commentators believe it to have been his vitriolic attack upon Pierfrancesco Giambullari that was fatal to his career in the Academy. In 1546, Giambullari put forth his theories on the origin of the Italian language; he took the position that the Italian language, and more precisely, the Florentine dialect, was not derived from Latin, but from a Hebrew or Chaldean language once spoken in the region of Aram and brought into Italy by the Etruscans.[41] Giambullari and his followers were nicknamed the Aramei. For Grazzini, their theories typified the absurdities of the pedantic mind; consequently the name Aramei became synonymous with the pedantic element which had overrun the Accademia Fiorentina.[42] But when Grazzini broke his silence and spoke his mind, he was personally attacking Giambullari, a favorite of Cosimo.[43]

Grazzini was probably less concerned with Giambullari's theory than he was with the attempts of the Aramei to effect changes in the Tuscan language. He had a very protective attitude toward his native tongue, and he saw it threatened on one side by the empty eloquence of the Petrarchists and on the other by the possible innovations then being discussed in academic circles. He was a champion of purity and simplicity.[44] For Grazzini, the Florentine language could only suffer from change: "Our language so lends itself to the expression of all human deeds that it may be considered one of the two greatest tongues" (Verzone, p. 362, vv. 65–68). Tuscan had reached its perfection in the poetry and prose of Boccaccio, Petrarch, and Dante, but the grammarians continued to burden it with new rules—"Rome never saw so many" (Verzone, p. 361, vv. 9–12). So it does not surprise us that when the Accademia Fiorentina proposed the abolishment of several graphic signs, including the K, Grazzini became the "quixotic paladin" of the threatened victims,[45] and in a *sonetto caudato*,[46] he pleaded in behalf of the K.[47]

It is possible that, to avenge themselves for Grazzini's criticism, the Aramei expelled him from the Academy. For we know that they turned to the duke, asking that he protect them from the "vicious remarks of a man who prizes no one but himself" and from "every malicious critic."[48] In fact, from a sonetto caudato of Grazzini's, also addressed to the duke, we learn that they attempted to have him imprisoned for slander, calling him a "backbiter" (Verzone, p. 69). Since, in the same poem, Grazzini justified his complaints about his expulsion and asked to be protected from the accusations of the Aramei, we can assume, although the chronology is very confused, that the two events were intimately connected.[49]

Grazzini's departure from the Academy in 1547 delivered the *coup de grâce* to the Accademia degli Umidi. He had been the most active and outspoken defender of the original organization, and, without his opposition, he felt that the Aramei and their sympathizers would gain complete control of the Academy. His only recourse was to continue his harsh invectives against his enemies and to become the crusader for complete literary freedom. In an ottava written by Grazzini in 1547, the expiring Accademia degli Umidi, "its eyes turned heavenward, weeping and sighing," calls upon him to save it from oblivion. "Your verses are my only hope of salvation. Lash out against them on my behalf. . . . Others . . . will follow your lead and the Umidi will rout the Aramei" (Verzone, pp. 343–44, vv. 59–88). Elsewhere in this same poem, Grazzini compares the corruption of the Academy in the hands of his enemies to the decadence of the Church in the hands of the wealthy clergy: "Wealth brought with it decay and sterility. . . . The leaders of the Academy have made a trade out of academic offices" (Verzone, pp. 342–43, vv. 25–40).

Had this poem been published at the time it was written, the Aramei might well have had the grounds to prosecute Grazzini, if not for his attack on them, at least for his statement concerning the Church.[50] But Grazzini must have realized that his enemies would use every opportunity to avenge themselves; he was careful with what he wrote for the public, confining his criticism to those individuals who would do him no more harm than to criticize him, in turn, by an exchange of poems.[51] It is not surprising, then, that among the many contemporaries whom he accuses of the most perverted moral and literary crimes, we do not find the name of Giambullari.

Consequently, in 1547, when Grazzini decided to write a poem attacking the Aramei, he chose to write an allegorical mock-heroic poem in which his enemies would be represented by monsters that lay siege to the kingdom of the gods. Grazzini was familiar with a mock-heroic poem entitled the *Gigantea* (1547), also satirizing Giambullari's theory and variously attributed to Girolamo Amelonghi, to Benedetto Arrighi, and to Grazzini himself.[52] His own poem, *La Guerra de' mostri*, continues in the vein of its predecessor; but since it was abandoned by the poet after the first canto was written, and since in these forty-four octaves the references to real situations and personalities are very vague, the few critics who have commented on the poem have shown great caution in explaining its intent. In his dedicatory preface to Stradino, Grazzini does not shed any light on the poem's significance except to mention "the dwarfs and the giants" with which he assumed Stradino to be familiar and which is apparently a reference to the *Gigantea* (Verzone, p. 346). In the third octave, he says that his poem will treat "a vicious horde which has appeared . . . once again," a reference to a group which he does not mention by name but which "torments me night and day." In the remaining octaves, he describes the monsters, one of which is armed "entirely with blotting paper" and another which "knows little of war, schooling as he does monster grammarians." I think it goes without saying that the monsters who are schooled in grammar and who have been the cause of Grazzini's wakeful nights are his enemies, the pedants. Since this poem was written in 1547, there is no reason to doubt that the reference is specifically to the Aramei. This hypothesis is made more plausible by the closing octaves which not only express Grazzini's inability to be more explicit—"let whoever can understand me, for I know what I am about"—but which also look to Stradino, the former patron of the Academy, for help (Verzone, p. 356, vv. 337–52).

Grazzini left the Accademia Fiorentina bitterly resenting his treatment at the hands of the Aramei; but there were several members of the Academy with whom he remained on friendly terms. It was not difficult, therefore, for him to keep well informed of the activities of the group and to participate, via his poetry, in the disputes that ensued within the academic circles.[53]

During the almost twenty years which elapsed between his expulsion from the Academy in 1547 and his reinstatement on May 6, 1566, Grazzini led an active literary life. It was during this period that he published several of his own works and all of the collections of poetry which he had edited. Also, during this period, two of his comedies—*La Gelosia* and *La Spiritata* —were performed for the first time, the former in 1550 and the latter in 1561.[54]

It was actually the year 1540 that marked the beginning of Grazzini's literary career, however; for that was the first time that any work, except for individual poems, came to the attention of the public. *Il Frate*, a three-act farce, was performed at the home of Maria da Prato on the eve of Epiphany, January 6, 1540.[55] Maria da Prato was a young courtesan at whose residence literary figures gathered to while away their free time by playing games of chance, enjoying the latest literary composition of a companion, and conversing.[56]

A description of the circumstances under which the farce was performed was best given by the author himself in the prologue:

> [The actors] thought that, here at the home of the lovely, kind, and generous Maria da Prato, it would be a praiseworthy thing to give the same consideration to the presentation of entertainments, music, and enjoyable games as is given to the serving of good wine and excellent food, so that once the body has been nourished, the soul should not remain fasting. So, in your honor and for your pleasure and satisfaction, they have arranged to provide you with some entertainment in addition to your supper. In truth, when it comes to eating and drinking, everyone can provide well for himself at home, and particularly on this evening, which is the eve of the *Befania* or Epiphany. . . . And so, as best as they were able, [the actors] have undertaken to entertain you with a trifle.[57]

Although the author calls his work "a trifle," the performance undoubtedly increased his hopes that other comedies which he considered of greater merit would soon find their way onto the stage. In the same prologue he stated that he planned, at least, to publish within six months some comedies clearly indicative of his skill.

It was not, however, until several years later—probably 1548—that another work was staged. All that remains of the play is a prologue, and we are as uncertain of its title as we are of its production date. Since, in a catalogue of his own works, Grazzini includes two farces, *La Monica* and *La Giostra*, neither of which has been found, historians have assumed that the prologue belongs to one of these.[58] Gentile, whose dating of the comedies has been accepted by subsequent historians, thought it to be the prologue to *La Monica*.[59] The prologue, itself, makes mention only of the fact that the work was presented at the home of Lorenzo Scala, and that it had also been presented before Duke Cosimo the preceding summer.[60]

Neither the presentation of *Il Frate* in 1540 nor the performance at the home of Lorenzo Scala almost a decade later brought great fame to the playwright.[61] More successful were the productions of his two comedies, *La Gelosia* and *La Spiri-*

tata, which were performed, as Grazzini himself informs us, "publicly in Florence and with the greatest honor, the first during the carnival season of 1550, in the *sala del Papa* . . . , the other . . . at the home of the illustrious Bernardetto de' Medici, at a banquet given by him in honor of the most illustrious Don Francesco, then prince of Florence and Siena."[62] The performance of *La Gelosia* was accompanied by musical intermezzi which Grazzini had originally intended for the play.[63] In the following year, 1551, the comedy was published in Florence by Giunti, but it was not until 1568 that it was published with the madrigals originally intended for the intermezzi.[64]

La Spiritata was performed, first in Bologna, and then in 1560, in Florence.[65] Nothing is known of the performance in Bologna, and there is no evidence that the author himself was present.[66] The second performance, given at a banquet held by Bernardetto de' Medici in honor of Francesco de' Medici, the eldest son of Cosimo, and before a group of illustrious Florentine citizens, must have been a source of great pride for the author:

> If we had thought that our comedy would be presented in such a splendid and esteemed place and before so many noble lords, valiant cavaliers, and honorable gentlemen, and before so many beautiful and virtuous ladies, and, most important, before his most illustrious and excellent prince, we would have tried to rehearse it more.[67]

The performance of *La Spiritata* in 1560 marked the end of Grazzini's theatrical career. In the following years, however, his comedies were reprinted, and in 1582, the Giunti press published the first edition of all six: *La Gelosia*, *La Spiritata*, *La Strega*, *La Sibilla*, *La Pinzochera*, and *I Parentadi*.[68]

During the twenty years of his absence from the Accademia Fiorentina, Grazzini acquired more notoriety for his editorial activities than acclaim for his comedies. He had long lamented the plight of poetry, which, he said, had succumbed to the pedantry of his age: "imitation of Petrarch and Bembo and excessive poetic refinement have half sated and bored the world because everything is almost replete with flowers, foliage, grass and shadows, caverns and billows and sweet breezes."[69] The popular, traditional poetry of the Florentine people had passed into oblivion (Verzone, p. 111, vv. 15–17) and simple verse had been replaced by the hermetic lines of the moderns:

> I remember when a canto was so beautifully written and so clear that everyone learned it by heart; but now the canti tell us nothing though the authors foolishly try to say a lot with few words; as always, whoever tries to embrace too much gets nothing and ends up a fool. [Verzone, p. 408, vv. 33–44]

To save Italian poetry from the hands of pedants, Grazzini began to collect and edit, not only the traditional poetry of Tuscany, but also the burlesque poetry of such writers as Burchiello and Francesco Berni. Like the triumphs (*trionfi*) and the carnival songs (*canti carnascialeschi*), the burlesque poetry of Berni represented for Grazzini a natural, spontaneous art which had been neglected for the more stylish and difficult poetry preferred by his contemporaries.

Grazzini's praise of Francesco Berni—a kindred spirit because of his wit and unstinting criticism of whatever displeased him—knew no bounds. In a poem entitled "In nome di Francesco Berni" ("In the name of Francesco Berni"), he recommends Berni's poetry as a panacea for the ills of the world:

> Whoever wants to flee melancholy, boredom, anxiety, vexation, and grief, or cast off the pangs of jealousy (the "hammer of love," as we call it), let him read this work of mine. Free of Bembo's cacklings and Petrarch's chirpings, it will fill him with delight. He will hear about those festering whimsies which come upon me and, in spite of myself, must

> be expressed lest I go mad. Let all those friars keep their silence and not try to interfere or excommunicate me! They would be in the wrong fifty thousand times, and, anyway, you don't do such things to the dead. And so what if I failed to observe Lent? I always went and confessed. But not to drag this thing out and waste time, let me say that whoever wants to live happily at every moment, without learning and all that rot, let him buy and read my rhymes. You shall hear me sing the praises of the most worthy heroes as I recall the plague (certainly more beneficial than old wine!) and then eels, cardoons, miller's-thumbs, and peaches, things more dear than gold! [Verzone, pp. 359–60]

Francesco Berni died in Florence on May 26, 1535, and as a memorial to a poet whose works were "manhandled, disfigured, and ruined through the fault of publishers," Grazzini collected, corrected, and published all the poems to which he had access.[70] The first of the two volumes in his edition was published by the Giunti press in 1548, and it was prefaced by a letter to Lorenzo Scala, which provides us with all the information that we have concerning the preparation of this edition. Grazzini states that he received assistance in preparing the edition. He felt that the care which was taken in editing was such that Berni, himself, could not have wished for more. According to Antonio Virgili, however, editing the poetry of Berni was not only difficult (for there were few original manuscripts with which to work), but it was also hazardous because of the danger of giving offense unless references to individuals in the ofttimes scurrilous verse were omitted. Both the editor, Grazzini, and the publisher, Giunti, were faced with insurmountable problems—to which Grazzini does not admit—and consequently the edition is less accurate than we are led to believe.[71] Virgili does not excuse Grazzini's inaccuracy, because the fault lay not only with the necessary precautions which he had to take, but also with the haste with which the edition was prepared. In a more recent study of Grazzini's edition, Ezio Chiòrboli states that Grazzini also made changes in the texts according to his own tastes and inclinations, a practice common to all editors of the sixteenth century.[72]

Many of the changes which Grazzini made in the text of Berni's poetry bear witness to the editor's concern for the purity of the Tuscan language. He often replaced a word of popular usage with a more literary term, corrected popular spellings, and changed Berni's style where it did not conform to his own preferences.[73] Grazzini also arranged the poems without any care for their chronology; and since, as Virgili points out, there is neither a biographical note in the edition nor annotations to the poems, an uninformed reader would be unable to discern any logical development in Berni's style or thought if he were dependent on the poetry itself.[74]

This edition, the first of two volumes, had three printings: 1548, 1550, and 1552. The second volume was published in 1555, again by Giunti; and although there is no certainty, it is likely that this volume, too, was edited by Grazzini.[75] In the second volume there are only a few poems of Berni; it is devoted to lesser-known burlesque poets. In fact, in the dedicatory letter to the first volume Grazzini had indicated his intent to publish some of his own poems in this volume:

> I hope . . . soon to pay my respects to you with my poetry and to send you the first part of my burlesque poetry, for whatever it may be worth. I have already gathered much of it together in order to publish it in the second volume of the burlesque works of various authors which is now being prepared. If no one interferes, it will soon be published.[76]

None of Grazzini's poems appeared, however—why, we do not know.[77]

Grazzini, who had hoped his edition of Berni's burlesque poetry would help keep alive a tradition of popular poetry, must have had a similar motive for undertaking an edition of the poetry of Domenico di Giovanni, familiarly called il Burchiello. Grazzini had even more in common with this fifteenth-century predecessor than he had with Berni. Berni, a man with a broad cultural background, had spent his life in the courts of Italy. Burchiello, like Grazzini after him, frequented the local shops of Florence (he was a barber by trade) and participated in the informal literary gatherings of acquaintances.[78] Burchiello and Grazzini were undoubtedly familiar with many of the same locales, and they probably spent a good part of each day conversing with friends and participating in the gossip about their neighbors. Burchiello's poetry, in large part a product of the city which Grazzini knew and loved so well, was especially attractive to him. Burchiello represented the true Florentine spirit, witty and capricious, and Grazzini wanted to keep this spirit alive by editing his works intelligently. He expressed his feelings in a sonetto caudato, written in the name of Burchiello, which prefaced his edition of 1552:

> Is it really possible? After having been cut, twisted, and stamped on by ignorant and villainous printers for so long, I am once again made whole and healthy. Some chopped off my feet, others my arms, and they mangled me within and without. Now, safe and sound and cleansed of errors, I have been reborn to my original state.[79]

Here, just as in his letter of preface to the 1548 edition of Berni's poetry, Grazzini defended the accuracy of his editorial work. Again, however, given the lack of original manuscripts, this edition fell short of Grazzini's intentions.[80]

Burchiello and Grazzini, both citizens of Florence, were well acquainted with the canto carnascialesco, a literary form indigenous to their native city and one of the most cultivated genres of popular poetry during the fifteenth century.[81] Florence, under the rule of Lorenzo il Magnifico, witnessed the full development of the canto carnascialesco: in a frenzy of exuberant celebration, the citizens lined the streets to watch magnificently arrayed processions and to applaud the often anonymous canti carnascialeschi. The festivity of such occasions was best described by Grazzini himself in a letter to Don Francesco de' Medici:

> Most magnanimous and kind prince: Among the various diversions, spectacles and celebrations which, according to the times and the seasons, are held publicly in Florence, the mascherate or canti carnascialeschi (or whatever we wish to call them) are, in every way, a wonderful and very beautiful festivity. Although both *calcio* [football] and jousting are also marvelous, they cannot be held at night and [in addition], they are of short duration. This is not true of the trionfi and canti carnascialeschi. If they are beautiful, well done, and organized with all the necessary appurtenances, one can never witness a more delightful thing, especially at night when they are accompanied by a procession of torches. But the invention must be, first of all, noble and accessible to all; the words must be clear and fitting; the music must have a sustained melody of cheerful tone, the voices lovely and in harmony. The costumes should be appropriate to the entire concept, ornate, richly worked, and gaily colored. The furnishings and instruments which are used must be well made and gaily painted; if horses are needed, they should be beautiful and well saddled.
>
> And . . . roaming about the whole city, during the day and late into the evening, they can be seen and heard by everyone; they can be sent to wherever one might wish some festivity, even to young girls at home who, peering through a jalousie or screen, can see and hear without being seen by anyone.
>
> Then, once the festival, which has given so much pleasure to everyone, is over, everyone can read the words [the canti are published] and, at night, throughout the city, they are sung. [The canti] are then sent, not only throughout Florence and to all the cities of Italy, but to Germany, Spain, and France as well; they are sent to relatives and to friends.[82]

In publishing an edition of the canti carnascialeschi, Grazzini again hoped to contribute to the preservation of a popular literary genre which expressed the witty and fun-loving spirit of the Florentine people and which, at the same time, documented the Tuscan language as used by the popular poets.[83]

Along with the changing political, social, and religious climes, the canto carnascialesco and its variations—the trionfo, the mascherata, the *carro*, etc.—had undergone changes. As Florence's wealth began to decline after the economic prosperity of the preceding century, the lack of financial backing so necessary to the organization of a spectacle caused a loss of interest in the composition of the canto carnascialesco.[84] Cosimo, after the political turmoil preceding his acquisition of the Florentine state, was sensitive to criticism of his government, and the Church, attempting to renew its power and to revitalize its position as the defender of public morality, was not tolerant of the critical comments of the public. Without the possibility of criticizing public institutions or satirizing the clergy, the canto carnascialesco lost its lifeblood.[85] Denied the possibility of social satire, the canto carnascialesco, which had always taken advantage of the double entendre to introduce the most lascivious themes, could now only exploit obscenities. Carnival songs became a mere exercise in puns and plays-on-words.[86]

By the middle of the sixteenth century, then, as the canto carnascialesco was being replaced by more complex forms of verse structure and was feeling the influence of the stylized and refined poetic techniques of the period, Grazzini became the champion of the old songs, criticizing the new.[87] He was, in turn, criticized for his attacks on contemporary poets who, he said, had contributed to the decadence of the traditional Florentine carnival song.[88]

One of Grazzini's main concerns, as I mentioned above, was to preserve the canti carnascialeschi, with their colloquialisms and local color, as documents of the living language of Renaissance Florence. Even in this instance, Grazzini's concern for linguistic purity cannot be divorced from his continuing argument with the Aramei and the many innovators who, according to him, were corrupting the pure language with new and unfamiliar terminology. By his decision to edit the canti carnascialeschi, Grazzini was taking a stand once again against the moderns who slighted their own Florentine heritage.

As he tells us in his letter to Francesco de' Medici, Grazzini set about collecting all the poems available to him:

> For the common good and for everyone's pleasure, I put myself to the task of finding all the poems, and collecting them for publication, as I did with the poems of Berni and the works of Burchiello; but the effort involved in accomplishing such an undertaking was greater than it had been before because I found so few volumes, and those which I did find were full of errors and written as if by tradesmen. Half the words were missing and there were the strangest abbreviations so that I was helped by my knowledge of verse and rhyme.
>
> I had at first thought it wise in editing the poems to pay close attention to when they were written and to arrange them chronologically, but I found this an impossible task since they were all mixed up and carelessly transcribed.
>
> In addition, I had hoped to give every author his due, but I couldn't do even that, for the canti and old trionfi, with the exception of Lorenzo de' Medici's, were without the author's name, and by asking the oldest men around, I found few who remembered; even among those who did, there were many disagreements and contradictions; so when I wasn't completely certain, I omitted the author's name and put the poem among those of dubious authorship.[89]

The editorial problems were clearly even greater than they had been for his editions of Berni and Burchiello. Furthermore, as thorough as he attempted to be, Grazzini overlooked many fifteenth-century carnival songs which have since been discovered.[90] His edition of 1559 has, however, been of invaluable service to modern research.

Before the edition was printed in February, 1559, Grazzini was set upon by a certain Paolo dell'Ottonaio, then canon of

San Lorenzo, who accused him of having included in his collection inaccurate texts of the poems of his deceased brother, Giovanni Battista dell'Ottonaio. Grazzini wrote to Luca Martini on February 22, 1558, stating that the canon was given the opportunity to correct the errors in the text, but that he did not do so. Grazzini asked Martini to plead his cause before the duke, for the canon, urged on by the Aramei, was in the process of seeking a sequestration of the edition.[91] Grazzini said that he could not understand why there was so much criticism of his edition—"And what in the devil are they, anyway, but carnival songs?" But, certainly, the Aramei felt they had found the opportune moment for harming his reputation.

The duke referred the decision to the consolo of the Accademia Fiorentina. On March 8, 1559, a ducal order suspended the sale of the edition, and the 495 extant copies were handed over to Roberto Pandolfini, the appointed *sequestratario.* After a year of disputes, Pandolfini was ordered, in January of 1560, to remove from all copies of the edition those pages containing the poetry of Ottonaio.[92] In the same year, Paolo dell'Ottonaio published an edition of his brother's poetry based on a manuscript in his possession. Only in the following year, 1561, was the censored edition of Grazzini allowed to be sold.[93]

It is somewhat surprising that, since most of Grazzini's problems with the 1559 edition were caused by his enemies in the Accademia Fiorentina, he decided to apply for reinstatement in the Academy only a few years later. He did so at the insistence of an old and good friend, Lionardo Salviati, who, in 1566, held the position of consolo. According to a ruling made by the Academy in 1549, Grazzini was required to submit a new literary composition, and Salviati urged him to submit some of his eclogues to the censor, G. B. Adriani.[94] The eclogues, in which one does not recognize the caustic Lasca, were approved, and Grazzini was reinstated on May 6.

Almost nothing is known of his activities from 1566 until

1582 when the Accademia della Crusca, whose exact date of origin is still unknown, was officially constituted.[95] Apparently, even after Grazzini became active again in the Accademia Fiorentina, his interest lay in the small, private gatherings of his friends with whom he felt at greater ease and liberty. The purpose of these gatherings was to make less academic those studies which, under the patronage of the Medici, had become pedantic. The gatherings were private in order to assure the members freedom to read or not, as their fancy dictated and to treat things in the Florentine manner—with laughter.[96] The Accademia della Crusca evolved from these informal gatherings; the participants, it seems, called themselves Crusconi and their meetings *cruscate;* but Lionardo Salviati, who in October, 1582, was received into their circle, later urged them to baptize the new group the Accademia della Crusca.[97] One member, Bernardo Zanchini, protested that they were too old to think of organizing an academy, but Grazzini supported Salviati's proposal in words recorded by Piero de' Bardi and quoted by Biscioni:

> Are we, then, going to be weak and lifeless and white-haired and admit to being unable to maintain an academy like so many others? Do we consider ourselves so bereft of authority that we cannot find enough friends to support us in such a just cause? And now that we can count the cavalier Salviati among our number, do you think, Zanchini, that we should be so timid and fall under the weight of such a glorious task? Ah, you are deceiving yourself if you think we are incapable, and no one else here agrees with you. But while you remain frozen in your old age, we, guided by the warmth of such a great light [Salviati], will enthusiastically found and maintain this new academy.[98]

Salviati's proposal was made on January 25, 1583, and soon thereafter he published a dialogue, entitled *Paradosso,* under the name of Ormannozzo Rigogoli in which he stated that history should be satisfied with verisimilitude, rather than seek absolute truth; it would thereby come closer to poetry.[99] Salviati's hopes that this first publication would draw attention to the Accademia della Crusca were fulfilled when, soon after, it became embroiled in the linguistic debates over Torquato Tasso.

Although Grazzini had favored Salviati's proposal to formalize the cruscate into an academy, it is doubtful that he would have approved of the activities in which the Accademia della Crusca was soon to become involved. The formal organization of the cruscate into an academy which was to become one of the most active in Italy and which was to enter into the literary debates that Grazzini had always satirized, would have reminded him of the time, forty years before, when the Umidi succumbed to a similar fate. Twice, the congenial, informal gatherings of his friends—the tornatelle and the cruscate—had become literary societies. But Grazzini died before he had the opportunity to realize what was to happen to the cruscate.

Grazzini died on February 18, 1584, and he was buried in the church of San Piero Maggiore.[100] During his last years he had hoped to publish more of his work. He was unsuccessful, but soon after his death the Accademia della Crusca considered publishing his poetry.[101] It is the irony of history that, later, his works were used as *testi di lingua* in the academies which he had always scorned.[102]

The Man and His Character

There is no doubt that Antonfrancesco Grazzini was a well-known personality to his contemporaries in sixteenth-century Florence. His activities in two of the most important academies of the period, his violent polemic against many of the most important Florentine literary figures and scholars, his association with the best-known courtesans, and his participation in the exchange of gossip within Florentine society are all responsible for a wide circle of friends, and, needless to say, of enemies. Included among his acquaintances were the notorious Pietro Aretino,[103] Agnolo Firenzuola, Benvenuto Cellini, the famous courtesan Tullia d'Aragona, Anton Francesco Doni, the brilliant Bernardo Davanzati, and Benedetto Varchi. However, his close friends were the numerous Florentine burghers—for the most part insignificant individuals—who pass through his poetry in a procession of Florentine life as it was during the sixteenth century.

Of those who were well acquainted with Grazzini, few have left any clues to the character of the man. Anton Francesco Doni, whose *Marmi* are, in their own way, a panorama of Florentine life as it passes the marble steps of Santa Maria del Fiore, portrayed Grazzini as the enemy of pedantry, an aspect of his personality with which we are already familiar. About the literature of the period and the prolificacy of men of letters, Doni has Grazzini say that "one would need an enlarged brain or great patience to be able to read all the terrible books which are written these days; everyone wants to be a poet and scholar, everyone does translations and many try to write, and with what results!"[104] Others—for example, Benvenuto Cellini—in the sonnets which they exchanged with Grazzini, also characterized him as a man with an argumentative nature. Cellini accused Grazzini of being one who, "without knowing, casts words to the wind" commenting on subjects—in this case, the lively polemic concerning the relative merits of sculpture and painting—for which he was not qualified.[105] Later writers, basing their judgment on poems such as those by Cellini and on Grazzini's own poetry, have usually concluded that his was a personality typical of his age and especially of his Tuscan environment. In describing Grazzini, the preferred epithets have been *strano* and *bizzarro*.[106] He possessed the Florentine penchant for the practical joke as well as all the ambiguities which have traditionally characterized the man of the Cinquecento. He exemplified what Giuseppe Fatini has called the dualistic personality of the sixteenth century, a combination of pagan sensuality and Platonic idealism, of both immoral and moral tendencies, so that side by side with his licentious capitoli we find religious poems, and beside an ideal portrait of feminine beauty, one of stark and ugly realism.[107]

Only recently, however, has some attempt been made to study Grazzini, not just as a typical sixteenth-century personality, but also as an individual. To do this it has been necessary to go to Grazzini's work and, in particular, to his poetry. Grazzini's poetry is a document of his relation to his environment during a span of at least sixty years, and in it we find the true spirit of the man.[108]

The difficulty of dating Grazzini's poetry limits us to a consideration of each poem as a statement of Grazzini's feelings and reactions at a particular moment. From these individual moments we must attempt to derive a general impression of his personality.

From the few existing portraits of Grazzini, there is little that we can deduce about his person, although van Bever and Sansot-Orland have asserted that his eyes betray the "vivacité et . . . l'originalité de son esprit."[109] Grazzini is always represented as balding but with an ample beard of which he was proud and which he considered the greatest gift "which God and nature give to man": "Without a beard I would feel uneasy. It gives me such pleasure that I am more indebted to it than to my tongue" (Verzone, p. 480, vv. 106–8). There was an increasing tendency in Florence to go clean-shaven, and this new fad, along with other innovations in dress and customs, provided Grazzini with an opportunity to criticize his own age by comparing it unfavorably with the past:

> At the time when man still slaked his thirst with water, not with wine, and money was of no concern, man's extremities grew to a size required for his well-being with no concern for beauteous proportion; he was completely nude and his

> defects were overlooked. The greatest pleasure was to see a full-bearded man. But then art, the root of all our displeasure, found a thousand ways to cause us grief. [Verzone, p. 477, vv. 10–24]

Magrini asserts, perhaps with the portraits in mind, that Grazzini had a good and robust complexion.[110] From his poetry it would seem that he suffered from the cold and from insomnia: "Every time I come to Mugnana, strange to tell, I just about die of the cold. Yesterday the sky was so heavy with clouds that I, a weak sort of fellow, stayed inside and near the fire" (Verzone, p. 375; see also p. 128).

Magrini, who would attribute to Grazzini the *onesti costumi* of a moral and religious man, overlooks the vices to which Grazzini, himself, admitted.[111] He was promiscuous, frequenting many of the courtesans and prostitutes of his day, and he remembers many of them in his poetry: Armenia, Patricella, Anna Raugea, Milla Capraia, and Nanina Zinzera. He was well acquainted with the notorious Via Mozza, and his attitude toward this street and the women who inhabited it alternated between praise—"Every lovely courtesan should buy . . . a house on Via Mozza: it is such a gay and open boulevard that Florence can boast of none finer" (Verzone, pp. 398–99)—and censure: "Leave this sinful life behind and . . . return to God's fold to become his faithful handmaidens, . . . repentant of your erroneous ways" (Verzone, p. 444, vv. 73–80). It is likely that Grazzini also practiced sodomy although in many of his poems he satirized this vice in others. He took great pleasure in masculine beauty, and apparently he was particularly attracted to Raffaello de' Medici, whom Giovanni Grazzini has called an "even too intimate friend."[112] He was often a guest at Raffaello's villa, Ligliano, and once, during a period when his relations with his friend were strained, he wrote of the emotions which Ligliano evoked:

> Are you all happy now that I have failed in love and that my handsome Narcissus has left? . . . never again shall I

> love, and then, no one will do me harm. But if I tremble at the sight of Ligliano, what would I do were I to see its master? I'd like to appear outwardly different than I feel, but one cannot deceive oneself. [Verzone, pp. 77–78]

Promiscuity was common enough in the sixteenth century not to incur social condemnation, but Grazzini paid the price for his conduct by suffering the torments of venereal disease, a topic which occurs frequently in his poetry.[113]

Enough has been said by the historians of the Cinquecento about the moral tenor of the period for us to understand that Grazzini was, as regards his amatory life, a man of his age, freely indulging in whatever gave him pleasure. It is clear that he was not excessively immoral; but we cannot attribute to him the degree of virtue which one of his earliest critics, Magrini, did.

Another of Grazzini's characteristics has particular importance in his poetry. He was a gourmand, and loved the companionship of the dinner table: "for I know of nothing else in this world of wonderful things which gives more pleasure; and only those who can eat and drink with friends are truly happy" (Verzone, p. 585, vv. 28–33). It would seem, as he wrote to Lorenzo Scala, that food was a consolation for him, when he was upset. And it was a stimulation to his fantasy:

> I've really become a gluttonous fellow, like those who always have a supply of wine and larded bread beside them. See, then, what my life has become, how, in my imagination, I conjure up such tasty dishes. I'm always in want of some new tidbit, and my sonnets are of little importance for my only pleasure is in food and drink. [Verzone, p. 59]

Thus, in his poetry, following both his inclinations and the tradition of Berni, he constantly speaks of food—sausages, melons, peas, spinach, chestnuts, etc.—praising and, at times, criticizing it. In a capitolo entitled "In lode della zuppa" ("In praise of soup"), Grazzini felt the need to remind his audience that he had written poems on subjects other than food. And, somewhat repentant—for this poem must have been written fairly late in life—he stated that what he did write was written in jest:

> As you know, in the past I have praised sausages, apples, peas and melons, fennel, chestnuts, and whatever satisfies the appetite. But I don't want you to think that my muse inspires me to nothing else. I sang of madness, games, sleep, the behind, . . . and, to tell the truth, I did it all in fun. [Verzone, p. 621, vv. 1–13]

Grazzini's sensual nature does not distinguish him from the majority of his contemporaries, who also exalted the hedonistic life. For him, pleasure and that which was useful in contributing to one's well-being were the motivating forces behind all activity, and he advised that man eschew whatever did not contribute to them: "As I see it, one should flee, as if from a horrible evil, whatever is of little use or pleasure" (Verzone, p. 549, vv. 25–27). If one can derive pleasure from something useful, such as a bath, the pleasure is increased: "Whatever is useful or delightful gives great pleasure; but if one can have them both together, that is peace and contentment!" (Verzone, p. 492, vv. 34–36). But we can, I think, justifiably distinguish Grazzini from those of his contemporaries who espoused a hedonistic philosophy as a means of rebelling against all moral strictures: in this sense he was not one of the scapigliati of the sixteenth century who defied tradition and who refused to acknowledge any moral standard.[114] Rather, Grazzini looked upon pleasure as a means of escape, a return to a golden age when life was not burdened by the complexities of civilization and the foolish concerns of modern societies, when man's rational nature was not such as to fill his mind with doubts and misgivings. He identified pleasure and sensual gratification with an idealized world of simple emotions:

> See how many ills come from thinking; without it and the threat of death, life would be a pleasure. In the golden age of yesteryear, the world was happy and all beasts lived together in sweet accord; everyone feasted on wild fruits, giving no thought to what was "mine" or "yours." Snakes fed not on snails, and, naked, men and women lived together innocently. Happy lovers took their pleasures freely, their bed a lovely flowered meadow. There was no need for arduous labor: without cultivation, the earth provided all man's needs. Death was no threat, as man slowly lived out his life. The climate was always temperate, never hot or cold. In such a state, man and animals lived in peace and enjoyed eternal spring. Then from Pandora's box issued forth all the ills which fill our lives with grief, and, in less than an hour, the world went to ruin. Pride, envy, and avarice, accompanied by an equal amount of lust, arose in human breasts. . . . [Women] were no longer attracted by manly virtue and valor; they were moved to compassion only by gold and silver. Oh, I could speak on, so dismayed am I by how much a traitor thought has been to man, who will never again be happy. [Verzone, pp. 582–84, vv. 55–136; see also p. 484, vv. 7–12, p. 490, vv. 31–33, p. 543, vv. 64–66]

In comparing the corruption of his own age with an ideal age of the past, Grazzini was employing a traditional theme of literature. It is, therefore, difficult to know how sincere he was in his criticism. But we must remember that he lived during a period when the Church began a zealous crusade against immorality and corruption in life and in art. Grazzini, like any individual who professed himself a Christian, must have condemned the vices of this world. At the same time, he longed for a world in which one could indulge his senses freely and without inhibition. He, too, must have questioned the meaning of life, and, unable to understand it and to reconcile his desires with his sense of morality, saw life as a dream from which man would awake to a better world: "Our life is a troubled dream, this world is naught but a pack of lies: those who were the living were just dreaming and we who are alive do but dream.

So, with little joy and boundless grief, those who will come will be dreaming" (Verzone, p. 439, vv. 115–20). If, then, Grazzini's conduct was immoral, he was not an amoral man. He did envision a world and life of complete liberty, one in which he could freely give himself over to pleasure. But he knew that in this life, at least, "wise men should do as the blessed: live temperately and virtuously, avoiding extremes and vice" (Verzone, p. 380, vv. 13–16).

Thus it is not insignificant that Grazzini admired an extravagant personality like Stradino. As one critic has pointed out, Stradino represented a type of ideal man: he combined a carefree nature, unencumbered by ambition and quick to seize the pleasure of the moment, but his life was tempered with a kindness and generosity which recommended him to all. His life was spent free of responsibility and he died happy.[115] Grazzini might well have been describing such a life when he said, "The true good and the happy life consist of taking one's pleasure honestly" (Verzone, p. 543, vv. 61–62). And continuing in a tradition which goes back to Jacopone da Todi, Grazzini in a capitolo entitled "In lode della pazzia" ("In praise of madness"), more fully expresses this antihumanistic attitude toward life:

> Cursed be the liberal arts, often the cause of infinite grief. My only wish would be for madness, the only happy state! . . . madness is a gift of heaven, never to be acquired through knowledge or gold. . . . the madman enjoys life and need fear no shame or harm. [Verzone, pp. 560–62, vv. 28–84]

There is, however, a contradiction between the carefree life which Grazzini fancied in his poetry and his own life, as he lived it. It is this contradiction which Fatini described as basic to the character of sixteenth-century man. And it is this which led Giovanni Gentile to say that with Grazzini "the poet did not correspond completely to the man."[116] In some ways Grazzini's life did conform to the ideals which he described in his poetry; for example, he was not ambitious for money and social prestige: "Don't think that I am simple-minded and, like Midas, crave silver and gold. To hell with them! Nor do I want others to bow before me. Hogwash, all of it! I'd choose any lowly state over that of a king or emperor" (Verzone, pp. 559–60, vv. 7–15). We might question the sincerity of such remarks. But Grazzini was quick to complain about his displeasures and discomforts, and had either his financial or social condition been the source of dissatisfaction, he would certainly have expressed it in his poetry.

Less sincere, however, are the comments which Grazzini made concerning the vanity of man's desire for personal glory.[117] He expressed scorn for those who thirsted for immortality: death carried with it all of man's aspirations and accomplishments. Rather than strive for what may be unattainable, man should instead live for the moment, "and since there is no way to ward off death, I think I'll remain young while alive and thus, with my thoughts, I'll become immortal" (Verzone, p. 578, vv. 64–66). And our aspirations, however absurd, can be realized only in our dreams. The glory of man lies in his ability to create for himself a fantasy world in which he can become whatever he wishes:

> Oh, most lovely imagination, you give me more pleasure than would a kingdom. You are man's only good, and misery, poverty, boredom, and grief flee before you. You make our life happy and permit us to desire with joy the death of those who expect much in exchange for little. . . . You are man's only good, too wonderful to be praised sufficiently in our lifetime. So, I'll stop, saying only that man, with his imagination, can have what he most desires. [Verzone, p. 580, vv. 121–42]

But this attitude, which in his poetry became an ideal of life, was not entirely consonant with Grazzini's character. We know from his protracted disputes with the Aramei that he did fear for his reputation; and in his later years, he hoped to establish the immortality of his name with the publication of more of his works. He was too conceited to dismiss criticism of his work or his person.[118] His conceit was accompanied by a need for approval.[119] Although he liked to consider himself the equal of his contemporaries, he was haunted by the knowledge that his learning suffered in comparison to that of many of his acquaintances. It is not just idle speculation to assume that much of his disagreement with the academicians stemmed, not from his disapproval of them, but from what we would now call feelings of inferiority. And we might even say that he took pleasure in suffering at the hands of his critics.

If, on the one hand, Grazzini was sensitive to criticism, especially if it detracted from his own image of himself as a poet and man of learning, on the other hand, because of his argumentative nature, he relished the lively exchange of insults with his contemporaries. Furthermore, he entered the arena of debate over subjects about which he could not have been very knowledgeable and consequently made himself vulnerable to criticism and scorn. Although he often praised the quiet, undisturbed life of the country, he was never really happy unless he was in Florence, actively participating in the spirited colloquies of his cronies. He enjoyed the relaxed atmosphere of the villas of friends where "naked morning, noon, and night, you can enjoy the fresh air—there is no better way to do it!" (Verzone, p. 542, vv. 46–48). But as all critics have observed, the cupola of Santa Maria del Fiore was always in his thoughts, if not in his sight (for an example, see Verzone, p. 369, vv. 81–88). The cupola and the campanile represented the only place in which he was really happy—at home, in Florence, among his friends:

> Oh saints in heaven, I'm home and once again alive and healthy. Let me hear no more about villas here and there. No more shall I wander among beasts and wild thickets. This is Florence, my beloved Florence! Here one mingles

> with people, not animals, and strolls about the piazzas with his friends. Here I can talk to and see my friends, sleep and eat and drink as I please. [Verzone, p. 500, vv. 1–15]

Ever gregarious, Grazzini even when in the country could not restrain himself from sending his friends invitations to come and join him: "You are eagerly awaited by all the plants and flowers, which are almost enamored of you" (Verzone, p. 105, vv. 12–14).

From what we have been able to discern of Grazzini, he did not differ from most of his Florentine contemporaries. He was aggressive and was aroused to an expression of his opinion without much provocation. He was, as Magrini has humorously and aptly described him, like "one of those medieval machines which, if touched, release a spring and let forth a shower of blows in all directions."[120] He was intolerant of criticism but always ready to criticize others. He was a gossip and felt no compunction in slandering even his best friends. He possessed a sense of morality but indulged himself when faced with temptations. He was quick to complain and slow to forgive the slightest mistreatment. He was, finally, sensitive and proud. He took pride, not only in himself and in his work, but also in his native city of Florence. It is, in many respects, Grazzini's love for Florence which often makes it difficult to describe the man. For all his work—poetry, comedies, and novelle—is a mirror which reflects the character and life of sixteenth-century Florence and of Grazzini, not as an individual, but as a Florentine citizen. Life, for Grazzini, *was* Florence of the Cinquecento, and it is this supremely important aspect of his work which should serve as an introduction to any study of his literature.

CHAPTER II

THE *VITA FIORENTINA* IN THE WORKS OF GRAZZINI

FRANCESCO DE SANCTIS, one of the earliest critics of Grazzini, saw in Grazzini's art a valuable document of Florentine life and language: it captured the spirit of the late Renaissance in Florence during years of political, social, and religious turmoil. At the same time, however, De Sanctis denied Grazzini the inspiration of a great artist: "What is Lasca lacking? A hand which trembles." Grazzini, said De Sanctis, lacked the seriousness of a true artist and scribbled down things as they came to him; he left things unfinished and was never more than superficial; he was always spirited and often careless, particularly in his plots and structure.[1] Critics since De Sanctis have both agreed and disagreed; none, however, has taken issue with his opinion that one of the most valuable facets of Grazzini's art is its popular inspiration. The poetry, the comedies, and the novelle all reflect the Florentine scene and the Florentine spirit of the late Renaissance. Opinion on how accurately and how effectively they do so varies with the critic. Nevertheless, De Sanctis' judgment served to lift Grazzini and many of his contemporaries from the disrepute in which they had long been held; rather than cast them aside as writers who wallowed in the moral degeneracy of their age and who filled the page with obscenities, subsequent criticism subjected many sixteenth-century authors to a reevaluation. We have come to realize the importance of much minor sixteenth-century literature as documents of an age. Even the obscenities and the emphasis placed on the instinctive nature of man reveal an important aspect of attitudes and social mores. The literary value of such writing depends, of course, on the individual author.

Of those writers who portrayed Florentine life in the sixteenth century, Grazzini is perhaps without equal.[2] It is for this reason that D. H. Lawrence chose to translate one of Grazzini's novelle. He considered his art to be the most perfect expression of the Florentine spirit and to be the most accurate reflection of Florentine society. Lawrence even valued Grazzini's art for its eternal qualities: it captured those elements of Florentine life which still exist.

> Here we are kept sharp to essentials, and yet we are given a complete and living atmosphere. Anyone who knows Florence today can picture the whole thing perfectly, the big complicated *palazzi* with far-off attics and hidden chambers, the inns of the country where men sit on benches outside, and drink and talk on into the night, the houses with the little courtyards at the back, where everybody looks out of the window and knows all about everybody's affairs.[3]

Not all literary critics share Lawrence's enthusiasm, fired, one must admit, by his love of Florence and of things Italian. If Lawrence was carried away by the descriptive nature of Grazzini's novelle—what De Sanctis called the "superficial aspects" —other commentators, in considering Grazzini's work in all its aspects, have found much to criticize. Many feel that Grazzini's art suffers from his lack of a profound moral sense. Some, while recognizing his ability to recreate an environment, deny him the necessary psychological insight for effective characterization. And there are those—and this is most important for the matter at hand—who state that Grazzini's art was limited by his provincialism, by his having been confined to a "small, enclosed historical world" which was almost delimited by the city gates.[4] If there are, as Lawrence would have it, eternal qualities to his art, there are lacking, several commentators have observed, the universal qualities which lift a true work of art out of its historical and geographical context and make it accessible, and more important, meaningful to all.

One can hardly quarrel with this last objection raised by the critics: we know that Grazzini rarely left Florence and that, when he did, he never went far and was always anxious to return. He seemed to lack all curiosity about anything which did not occur within the shadow of his beloved cupola. Necessarily, then, life for Grazzini was Florence; and his art was a diary in which he recorded life as he knew it. Grazzini's limited experiences are responsible then for what we most prize in his art: a panorama of daily life in bourgeois Florence.

As modern historians and critics have come to recognize the sociological importance of many works which had earlier been disregarded, they have been faced with the dilemma of deciding how extensively and how faithfully the writer portrayed life. What in the artist's work was a reproduction of reality and what a product of his prejudices and fantasy? Of even greater concern has been the difficulty of sifting out of the literature those elements which are simply traditional and classical and which had often become so much a part of the artist's cultural heritage that he incorporated them almost unconsciously into his work. The confusion caused by the blending of traditional characterizations, attitudes, and themes with the contemporary scene has given rise to innumerable studies, particularly of the classical elements in and sources of the sixteenth-century comedy and novella.[5] Such a concentration has meant that critics have seldom been concerned with just how the literature is original and to what extent it *does not* depend on literary borrowings.[6]

This positivistic approach to sixteenth-century literature sought to discover how much the Renaissance erudite comedy owed to the classical comedy. It also traced the influences on the novella back to the time of Boccaccio and before. It has shown how there was a mutual exchange of elements between the comedy and the novella—both ideal hybrid genres upon which to test the critic's ability to discern sources.[7] Poetry has been treated in much the same way. Volumes have been written both on Petrarch's influence on lyric poetry and on the traditional themes in jocose, burlesque poetry. If, in every field of literature, from the theatre to the love lyric, classical and traditional influences were so obvious, it is no wonder that many sixteenth-century writers have been criticized for their lack of inspiration and originality.

Such charges inevitably touch Grazzini, who tried his hand at every type of literature, and the charges are justified since in every genre he is guilty of imitation. His comedies, as Gentile and others have clearly shown, owe much to the classical comedy. In the *Cene*, his collection of novelle, he used the traditional, medieval framework as a pretext for the stories, and well-known plots and themes. In fact, he openly admitted his debt to Boccaccio. In his burlesque poetry, his dependence upon, not only Francesco Berni, but Domenico di Giovanni and the entire tradition of Florentine humorous verse, is obvious. Finally, in his lyric and pastoral poems, which have received almost no attention, his imitation of Petrarch and the Petrarchists is almost servile.

If we accept the thesis that Grazzini's art was significantly influenced by life in Florence (and his works are too full of references to his contemporaries, to private and public disputes, to Florentine streets and shops not to accept it), and, if we want to see how he represented Florence in his work, we must decide how much of the life which he depicted is truly Florentine and not the product of tradition.

It was Grazzini's opinion that contemporary literature—and the comedy in particular—should represent contemporary life. Although he accepted the Ciceronian definition of comedy ("comedies must be the image of truth, an example of customs and the mirror of life"[8]), he felt that the writer of comedy should studiously avoid the pitfall of borrowing from the classical comedy because

> [today] we have other customs, another religion and another way of life. Therefore, comedies should be written in another way. In Florence, we no longer live as they once did in Athens and in Rome: there are no slaves, adopted children are not common; scoundrels no longer come here to sell young girls, nor do soldiers, while sacking cities or castles, take children in swaddling clothes, raise them as their own and give them a dowry; rather, they are intent upon robbing as much as they can, and if, by chance, young maidens or married women fall into their hands, they would deprive them of their virginity and honor, provided that they had not decided to hold them for ransom.

But since the modern writer had not made the distinction between contemporary and ancient life, the comedies had become "a mixture of ancient and modern life, of the old and of the new."[9] Grazzini also scorned the use of comedy as a means of enlightening the public because "whoever wants to learn about the civic or Christian life, doesn't go to the comedies to learn it; he does so by reading well the thousands of good and holy books and by attending sermons, not only during Lent, but throughout the year."[10]

Such, in theory at least, was the purpose of the comedy: it was to mirror contemporary life and act as a source of amusement rather than as a means of teaching morality. That Grazzini did not consistently follow his theory has been made clear in several studies on his theatre.[11] In actuality, Grazzini did heavily imitate the classical comedy.

There is, then, a contradiction between what he proposed for the comedy and what he actually did when he wrote his own plays. The contradiction does not seem too difficult to understand when one considers that a primary preoccupation of Grazzini throughout his life was the polemic between the pedantic advocates of traditional literature and the proponents of a modern literature which would break away from the past. Among his enemies were a great many of those pedants who tenaciously upheld the authority of Aristotle and the Italian masters. Grazzini would understandably take the position of the moderns, if only to antagonize his enemies. It is not unlikely, therefore, that his criticism of those who imitated the classical comedy stemmed from his polemics with the traditionalists.[12] In his own work, however, he was incapable of completely disregarding the devices of traditional comedy writing.

Since my concern in this chapter is to discuss Grazzini's work as a literary document of sixteenth-century Medicean Florence, a thorough discussion of source material would not only lead away from the primary purpose, but it would also repeat many facts which have already been brought to light by the several studies of traditional and classical themes in the Renaissance comedy and novella. Here it will suffice to indicate briefly those elements of Grazzini's work which continue in the tradition of earlier literature.

It is for his characters that Grazzini owes his greatest debt to tradition. As I shall show, characters in the comedies and novelle acquired many attitudes and characteristics which Grazzini borrowed from his contemporaries in Florence, but the prototype of the character remains the traditional figure, either as it appeared in the classical comedy and then, repeatedly, throughout the erudite comedy of the Renaissance, or in the traditional novella and, again, in the *novellistica* of the sixteenth century.

Populating Grazzini's comedies are the familiar servants, the descendants of the slave in Plautine comedies, who continue to outwit members of an older generation, usually for the benefit of their young masters (*La Spiritata*, I, iii; *L'Arzigogolo*, I, i). These servants, together with the old men with whom they often match wits, usually sustain the interest of the play. An old man's stubbornness is often the cause of the play's action and provides the servant with an opportunity to display his ingenuity: a father may refuse to allow his daughter to marry the man of her choice, and the servant's shrewdness often helps to resolve the situation in favor of the young girl and her lover (*La Spiritata*); he may be miserly, and in the case of Ser Alesso (*L'Arzigogolo*), miserliness combined with a desire to be young again provides the basis for complexities of plot which make the old man see the error of his attempts at rejuvenation while it gives his servant, Valerio, an opportunity to make off with his money and to give it to the son, Dario. Faithful to tradition, the servant is witty, shrewd, and resourceful. He usually tests his abilities on old men who are tight-fisted, stubborn, and easily duped.

As in the classical comedy, the young people on whose behalf the servants act are insufficiently developed. The young men are stereotyped victims of a frustrated love, solely interested in their own pleasure and always ready to deceive their fathers. Like Federigo in *La Pinzochera*, they express themselves with trite phrases, trying to clothe their selfish interests with an aura of elevated sentiments:

> Let one who has experienced the pleasure of possessing what he most desires tell of the joy and sweetness of his great fortune. Alas, I could never tell of such pleasures, but I could speak very well about distress, unhappiness, and grief. Surely, one who has never felt the sorrows and passions which are endured for love doesn't really know what pain

> is. Poets, moved by the sorrow of love, tell of the gods who, unable to bear love's torments, often left their realm in the heavens, and of Jove, who took the form of many things: a bull, an eagle, a shower of gold. [I, v][13]

The young girls in Grazzini's comedies almost never come onto the scene. Here, too, Grazzini followed in the tradition of classical comedy.

Young people are important only when they possess some idiosyncrasy which gives them comic value. The most noteworthy example in Grazzini's plays is Taddeo Saliscendi in *La Strega* who, listed among the interlocutors as an *innamorato*, is, in truth, a Renaissance version of the classical *miles gloriosus*, the braggart soldier. Taddeo, boastful of feats which he has known only in his fantasy, is one of Grazzini's most colorful and successful characters, providing instances of witty dialogue with his servant, Farfanicchio, who describes him as *stravagantissimo*. He comes onto the scene with "a German-style cap, a French-style mantle, a Florentine sack coat, a Spanish-style collar, Gascony hose, and Roman slippers; he is sullen, odd-mannered, and plumed like a Spanish horse" (III, i). Having borrowed Taddeo from the roster of classical prototypes, Grazzini was able to use him for a satire on the modern dandy who considers himself a man of war until he learns what war is:

> In war one must endure both heat and cold, hunger, thirst, and sleeplessness; when one does sleep, it is usually on the ground with his weapons . . . and if, heaven forbid, one becomes ill, he can't get bread and water, much less medical attention. [IV, iii]

Taddeo Saliscendi is one of several characters in Grazzini's comedies who are based on stock comic types representing "professions," and derived either from the classical comedy (the miles gloriosus, the pedant, etc.), or the vast repertoire of Renaissance erudite comedies (clerics, procuresses, etc.).

Whatever its source, the prototype was familiar to the public; and just as the audiences attending the improvisations of the commedia dell'arte were to applaud and favor certain stock characters of that theatre, so the audiences of the erudite comedy came to favor certain comic types. At their best, such types were means of satirizing or depicting elements of sixteenth-century society.

Elements of contemporary life were easily assimilated into traditional characters. It appears, however, to have been much more difficult to initiate changes in the external structure of the comedy. Even Grazzini, the champion of innovation, defended the traditional division of the comedy into five acts.[14] He also retained the prologue, which was common to most Renaissance comedies and which owed its origin to the classical comedy, where it had served to summarize the plot. In the Renaissance comedy, it became a vehicle in which writers of comedy defended themselves against the accusations of their critics, recommended themselves to their audience, explained their purpose and the reason which led them to write the play and to use either prose or verse.[15] Grazzini's prologues incorporate both functions: in certain instances they give a plot summary (*I Parentadi*), but most often they provide a means for expressing the author's ideas about the purpose of the comedy, the way it should be written, etc.[16]

Grazzini's technique of plot structure is also traditional. Basically, he employed two devices which were, by the middle of the sixteenth century, standard tools for all writers of comedy. The first concerns the development of the plot: a seemingly insoluble problem is established in the early scenes of the play; then a *beffa*, or practical joke, is devised in order to resolve the problem; and finally, by a series of complexities involving misunderstandings, masquerades, and deceptions, a solution is brought about. Generally the solution provides the audience with two young lovers united, an old man (usually the father of one of the two youngsters) deceived and forced to withdraw his opposition to the match, and, finally, one or more servants remunerated. Such a skeletal plot may be superimposed upon and made to fit any of Grazzini's comedies, so little do the general developments of the plays differ. And the same general outline describes, of course, numerous comedies of the Italian Renaissance.

The second device concerns the solution of the plot: Grazzini employed the classical dramatists' technique of recognition scenes whereby the play's solution is brought about by the sudden appearance of a missing child or parent. What is so striking about Grazzini's use of recognition scenes is that they are in complete contradiction to his theories on the modern comedy. He had stated in the prologue to *La Gelosia* that there were no recognition scenes (*ritrovamenti*) because "in Tuscany nowadays, they never occur, just as one never encounters those scoundrels or merchants who purchase maidens and make sales of women."[17] And later, in the prologue to *La Spiritata*, he again admonished against this device: "Be assured that in this . . . play there shall be none of those long and boring recognition scenes, nor any of those recognitions which, today, are silly and impossible but with which other comedies are usually filled."[18]

Resolving this contradiction would not seem very important because there is no need to make Grazzini the artist entirely consonant with Grazzini the polemicist. I think that the contradiction points out clearly the fact that Grazzini straddled the fence between two periods: as an artist he carried on a tradition in literature which was fast coming to an end, but in his approach to literary problems, he showed signs of the critical spirit of the sixteenth-century scapigliati in rebellion against the old literary order. His comments in the two prologues cited above reiterate his concern for a literature which would express the spirit of a modern world attempting to break with the past. It should also be remembered that Grazzini, as daring as he was in his criticism of others, was very concerned about the reception which his own work would receive. In writing his plays it was not in his own interest to antagonize too much the men of letters whose censure could destroy one's hope for fame and recognition.[19]

Although Grazzini never theorized about the novella, I think we can assume that he considered its function identical to the comedy's. In many respects, as Pellizzaro has claimed, the differences between the two genres during the Renaissance were purely formal.[20] Many themes and character-types were common to both. Often the medium chosen by a writer seemed to depend on caprice rather than on the suitability of one genre over the other for the exposition of the subject. And, like Grazzini, many writers used both mediums. It has been pointed out, in fact, that the stylistic differences between Grazzini's comedies and novelle are very slight; his novelle are so suited to stage production in their extensive use of dialogue that they often give one the feeling that they are sixteenth-century comedies in narrative form.[21] In the novelle and comedies, the similarities are such as to suggest that when Grazzini chose to use the novella form, he did so only because he found the narrative most suitable to his artistic temperament.

Structurally the novelle are ordered within a framework: each of several young men and women recite stories which, unlike those of the *Decameron* which center upon a given theme, are arranged according to length.[22] Both the characters and themes of the *Cene* have their origin in the traditional novella as it developed from Boccaccio and Franco Sacchetti to Firenzuola and Giovanni Francesco Straparola. We find the pedant who is duped (*Cena* I, ii), clerics who are castigated for immoral conduct (*Cena* I, vi) and for ignorance and pride (*Cena*, I, viii), old men who are married to young wives and who are deceived by them (*Cena* I, x), simpletons and practical jokers who themselves become the victim of a beffa (*Cena* II, ii; *Cena* I, iii). And each of these characters retains much of his traditional makeup. The pedant, for example, is ignorant and overbearing, dirty and ill-mannered.[23] Grazzini describes one, the dread of his young pupil, as "the most tiring and contrary man who ever lived, and, in addition, he was ignorant and dull-witted." He not only bullies the boy, but he spies on him:

> The tutor had no other desire than to follow him around and keep after him; he watched him as if he were a young girl to be protected, letting his father know how necessary it was to keep an eye on him; . . . on his account, youths behaved more badly than ever and scorned all virtue. [*Cena* I, ii]

Similarly, clerics, often lascivious and ignorant, take advantage of their position to dupe the layman. Just as Frate Cipolla (*Decameron,* VI, x) had defrauded his congregation, a *fratel minore* is able to convince his people by lies that the punishment delivered upon him by the family of a young girl after whom he had lusted was the work of evil spirits:

> "Last night, while I prayed, three enemies of the Lord, ugly and frightening devils with a fist full of whips, came to me from I know not where or how; they gave me a great fright and then inflicted upon me a hundred lashes and so smashed my bones that I doubt whether St. Anthony, St. Nicolaio of Tolentino, or any other saints were ever so tanned by them. And then, naked, I was led to the cloister and they tied me as I was when you found me. They returned to my quarters and turned everything upside down; they tore open the mattress, poured flour, wine, and oil all about, and smashed my pots. But what is worse, they opened and broke all the coffers and chests and robbed me of a sack containing a good two hundred ducats which, after years of deprivation, I had saved from alms, offerings at mass, confessions, and the collection boxes. . . . And with that money I had intended to purchase a table for the main altar—the one with a painting of the Assumption—and a new pulpit. Now that I am poor, as you so well see, and, one might say, crippled (for I shall never be the same again), I recommend myself to

> your charity in the name of the Passion. And I remind you that devils never inflict harm on anyone but the good, as we hear tell in the sacred book of the Holy Fathers about so many Saints and good men." In this way, he said enough and entreated enough that men and women tried to outdo each other in giving him charity. [*Cena* II, viii]

We find the hand of tradition even in the details of the *Cene.* Like Boccaccio, whose novelle were "the most beautiful . . . delightful . . . and wise stories" that one could find (*La Introduzione al novellare*), Grazzini wished to stress the importance of the power of love. Although, in truth, the finer sentiments were of little interest to him, he had one of the narrators, Galatea, say at the close of a novella, "And so the cleverness of a young girl in love overcame the adversity of fortune and gained for her great happiness, joy, and delight; for her husband, pleasure, comfort, and honor; and for her place of birth, great usefulness, fame, and glory" (*Cena* II, iii). Similarly, interspersed in the narrative are comments on "envious fortune," whose whim controls the fate of men.[24]

It is clear, even from this cursory discussion, that Grazzini was heavily indebted to the comic tradition in his theatre and in his novelle. If we want to consider this a fault, a lack of originality, we must, of course, direct the same accusation against all writers of comedy, novellieri, and poets of the Renaissance, the great and the mediocre alike. The external forms in literature and the modes of expression were a common heritage, fully shared, to express the personal feelings of the author. As one critic has said, referring particularly to imitation in sixteenth-century verse, writers felt that "thoughts and feelings, or rather, the most delicate and subtle gradations of feeling, must be intimate and one's own, while the means with which we express them and the art of harmonizing them may well be common to many."[25] Usually, then, we must look beyond the timeworn techniques of the artist to see what of his own feelings and his own world is being expressed. This is what we must do in order to see how Grazzini portrays sixteenth-century Florence.

Earlier in this chapter I mentioned the fact that Grazzini's art portrayed what G. B. Salinari has termed on more than one occasion a "small, enclosed historical world,"[26] where concern is limited to the insignificant events of everyday life. Grazzini seldom touched upon the larger problems of society, which only indirectly influenced the lives of his characters. He spent most of his own life in a world which was limited to neighborhood gossip, social gatherings, and petty feuds. It was his affection for the city of Florence and this life which he knew so well that brings them so vividly to life in his art. In his works he extols the city until it becomes a place of almost mythical beauty; his characters pause in their activity to contemplate its wonders. Citizens never want to leave. Says Giudotto, in *I Parentadi:* "There is no other city on the face of the earth where I would more willingly remain. Even the fresh water which Florentines throw away in the summer is worth more than what there is to be found in any other city of Italy" (I, i). Newcomers are enchanted:

> *Diego.* Thank the Lord that we have arrived in Florence! . . .
>
> *Martiningo.* Master, this is a fine city.
>
> *Diego.* You can say that again! For beauty, it defies comparison with any other city in Italy.
>
> *Martiningo.* I'm sure it does. Can't you see the lovely streets and squares, the beautiful buildings, towers, and churches all about us? [*La Sibilla,* IV, i]

Grazzini portrayed Florence in great detail. His characters live on well-known streets—Via Camaldoli, Via Ghibellina, Via de' Servi, Via Chiara; they stroll past Santa Maria Novella, Santa Croce, Santa Maria del Fiore, Santa Reparata, and Santa

Trinita on their way to the Mercato Vecchio, the Mercato Nuovo, and the Ospedale degli Innocenti: "Guasparri, halfway across the bridge, saw the Guardia . . . which was coming from Borgo San Friano, and he went along the Fondaccio, . . . and almost running, he ended up near the Bargello" (*Cena* II, vi). The streets and piazzas of Florence are populated by personages whom Grazzini treated as if they were well known to his audiences. They are part of the Florentine heritage: "Amerigo Ubaldi, as you probably well know, was as handsome, clever, and pleasant as any Florentine youth to have ever lived"; "Not many years ago, there was a very skillful doctor in Florence and his name was Master Mingo"; "there was then in Florence, during Scheggia's day. . . ." Grazzini's constant references to people and to places leave no doubt in the reader's mind that he is always in Florence.

Grazzini chronicles life in Florence in all his works, and if we turn attention first to his burlesque poetry, we find that he does so with a journalistic technique. He records events which actually took place, and usually he does this without any attempt at writing true poetry. His style is too immediate and often the subject matter has documentary rather than literary importance. One example will serve to illustrate Grazzini's journalistic style.

> Bettin, bear with my long story and I'll tell you something which will make you disown the Lord. . . . You've certainly heard of the arrival in Florence of the magnificent Marchioness of Pescara. . . . the day after Easter, while several of us were in the church of Santa Reparata awaiting the wise and good preacher, a friend of mine brought forth some sonnets which I wrote ages and ages ago. And, when asked who had composed the verses, he said, quite casually, the Marchioness. When the news got around, everyone crowded about him. And the beauty of it is, my dear Bettino, that a man of great respect and learning who was there began to look at one sonnet and then another, commenting very pompously, "Oh, this is beautifully written!

> Oh, how well this is composed!" And after hearing the poetry, everyone stood about in wonder, their mouths shut tight and their eyebrows raised. And then they whispered among themselves, saying that it was divine in its display of erudition. [Verzone, pp. 60–61, vv. 1–41]

Like much of Grazzini's poetry, this sonetto caudato was written as one would write a letter; the author's only purpose was to comment to Bartolommeo Bettini on the affectation and hypocrisy of his contemporaries. Needless to say, there is no literary value to the poem, but it clearly demonstrates the importance which Grazzini's poetry has for biographers and historians of the period, especially for those interested in Florentine life.

In other poems Grazzini records Florentine characteristics and habits, modes of dress, theatrical events, and even weather conditions. His poetry actually serves as a reference work in which one can find all the traits of character, all the situations, the very psychology of the Florentines as they are later represented in the comedies and novelle.

Grazzini documents the social life of the Florentine burgher, centering upon the shop or the home of a friend where he would spend his free hours, drinking, gossiping, and gaming with his neighbors. It is probable that Grazzini himself, as a young man employed in a pharmacy, participated in these social gatherings. Later, as he became active in literary circles, he joined other groups which, although more pretentious, still served as the center of social activities. He was very familiar with these groups, known variously as *tafferugli* and tornatelle, and in one poem he described how they were to be organized.

> So that you may know just how a tafferuglio is organized and just what is most appropriate for it, I'll first say that a lovely and comfortable house must be found. The company should not exceed twelve in number, and they should be affable men of worth who intend to have a good time until

> they die. Preparations for the gatherings should not be too elaborate, nor should the table be laid too sumptuously. But a successful tafferuglio requires that great care be taken in selecting a good wine: there should be both a white and a full-bodied red. . . .
>
> The tafferuglio may be organized in many ways, provided that it not meet in a brothel or inn. And gaming, in particular, should be avoided because it is the sure enemy of every pleasant gathering. The primary purpose of the tafferuglio is lively conversation and discussions on knighthood and love. [Verzone, pp. 585–87, vv. 49–111]

According to Grazzini's description, the members of the tafferuglio were all of one mind. They enjoyed having a good time. As we can see from numerous other poems, the principal activity of these men was the quest for pleasure. They followed the advice of all Renaissance poets to enjoy the moment; for, as Grazzini himself warned, "beauty is like a flower which, fresh and bright in the morning hours, fades at vespers and dies by evening. Whoever fails to enjoy it will find himself betrayed by hope" (Verzone, p. 486, vv. 73–78).

Grazzini described his own activities, which must have approximated those of his companions. The daily routine included strolls through the streets of the city and pauses to chat with friends (Verzone, p. 500, vv. 10–15). Favorite pastimes included playing games of skill or attending athletic events. The popularity of such activities is documented by the variety of games which Grazzini records: *rovescina*, *ronfa*, *cricca*, *primiera*, *trionfini*, *noviera*, *tredusasso*, *germini*, *tarocchi* (Verzone, Capitolo XVIII); *la palla a maglio* (Verzone, Capitolo XXVI); *la palla al calcio* (Verzone, Capitolo XXIV), to name but a few.

Grazzini and his acquaintances associated with the well-known Florentine courtesans and exchanged comments with each other on their preferences (Verzone, pp. 399–400); they advised one friend and then another on the tactics to be used in amorous pursuits: "If you wish to enjoy her and extinguish the fires of passion, be liberal with her now that you have such a fine opportunity" (Verzone, p. 389).

Often, during the summer, this life of idleness was transferred to a country villa where they enjoyed themselves even more freely at the expense of the host. Here, the principal activities included eating, sleeping, hunting, and fishing:

> Ladies and gentlemen in a happy group find pleasure in all they do. Here we have all the amenities of a large city: shops and inns, churches and squares. And there is no shortage of good things to eat; just thinking of them makes my mouth water. [Verzone, pp. 487–88, vv. 7–21]

> For one who likes to hunt there are handsome hounds and many hares and country folk who will always lend a hand. I need say little about the fishing for, new moon or old, you can catch any variety in the ditches and streams. [Verzone, pp. 368–69, vv. 49–56]

Grazzini's poetry also attests to the limited interests of the Florentine bourgeoisie. Although Florence, during several decades of the sixteenth century, underwent severe political and economic crises as the house of Medici struggled for supremacy over the city, in Grazzini's poetry we find almost no allusions to such problems. For most of the Florentines, life went on as before, and their primary concern was the insignificant daily problems which made up the normal pattern of their lives. The burlesque poetry reads as a local newspaper in which problems of immediate interest to the majority are given priority. Consequently, we find references to a local bakery, or to a dog which has been killing the neighbors' chickens:

> This new shop which handles white bread really is a nuisance, for people just about kill each other to get some; just walking by the shop, one hears such a fracas that it would seem famine had returned. [Verzone, p. 420]

> Lutozzo, that's really some little dog you have there: she tears up everything from shoes to books and she killed

> another hen. She'll probably start in on sheep and oxen until she'll be more feared than voracious wolves. [Verzone, p. 359]

The weather, an important factor to the success of harvests, is also a recurrent item in Grazzini's journalistic poetry. On two important occasions, in 1529–30 and again in 1547, he wrote of the devotions paid to the image of the Virgin of the Impruneta for the cessation of flooding.[27] Contrasting these devotions to the Virgin with the popular belief in auguries, Grazzini also documented with a derisive tone a moment when the Florentines awaited a doomsday flood:

> Let it be known that doomsday is upon us and that you who have not done so should go and confess. The astrologers have all read the signs of disaster, but they haven't told us if we will be roasted or boiled. Oh Moon, you swine! Bestial Saturn! Cuckolded Jove and bedeviled Mars! Don't harm us so! I ask mercy for the world, but perhaps the astrologers miscalculated and are off a few hundred thousand years. [Verzone, pp. 125–26]

More than just documenting daily occurrences in sixteenth-century Florence, Grazzini's poetry represents the mentality of the Florentine bourgeoisie. The above sonetto caudato is one of many similar examples in which we find evidence that the Christian spirit of the people was accompanied by a continuing interest in unorthodox practices. Upon numerous occasions Grazzini ridicules the popular belief in auguries made by necromancers who victimized society and who led the credulous around like "unfortunate sheep" (Verzone, p. 412). The people persisted in their traditional prejudices against the clergy, lawyers, and men of medicine. Even Grazzini, although he continued in the tradition of Italian humorous verse, showed by his vehement attacks on these men that there still lingered among the people a deep mistrust of men of learning. Priests still personified greed and carnal vice—"they have large abbeys and incomes, and not knowing what to do with all the money, they happily feast on sumptuous meals" (Verzone, p. 397, vv. 29–31)—and the cure of one's ills was better left to home remedies than to the doctors, who were in need of care themselves (Verzone, pp. 374–75).

Undoubtedly, Grazzini shared in many popular superstitions and prejudices.[28] However, at times he championed the cause of modernity and seemed particularly interested in the problem of children in society and their relationship with their parents. On one particular occasion in his poetry, which is seldom bent on moralizing, Grazzini chides those parents who deprive their children of learning for the sake of bringing more money into the household:

> In their youth, rather than studying, they do the work of lackeys, and barely twelve years old, they are sweating in some shop like oxen. Oh mothers and fathers, how unjust your desires! Don't you see of what good your selfishness is depriving them? [Verzone, p. 495, vv. 10–18]

It would seem, at least as portrayed by Grazzini, that the Florentines possessed few virtues to recommend them. If they were religious, they were also superstitious. Living in the center of Europe's most renowned center of art and progress in the field of economy, they still retained age-old prejudices against progressive ideas. They were avaricious (Verzone, p. 495, vv. 8–9). They were fickle: "all evils come from the infirm and ever-changing Florentine minds which are constantly active and never quiet a moment" (Verzone, p. 380, vv. 30–32). And they were petty in their criticism of others, relishing every opportunity to spread gossip. In reading Grazzini's poetry we sense the maliciousness in the exchange of gossip.

> Messer Goro, it would be too vile to write of this person who is neither man nor beast but something born to spite and shame the good. What ever induced you to speak well of one who never had a good thing to say? [Verzone, pp. 46–47, vv. 1–6]

It is, of course, in the tradition of burlesque poetry to exaggerate faults and vices, and these are the aspects of the people which Grazzini portrayed. The documentary value of his poetry, and then of his comedies and novelle, lies in the evocation of the popular Florentine spirit, limited in its perspective by prejudice and faultfinding. But those aspects of the Florentine character which we find in Grazzini's portrayal —skepticism, humor, pride, and a strong critical nature—are all part of that genius which brought Florence to its inimitable position in Renaissance civilization.

The journalistic and documentary qualities of Grazzini's poetry must be taken into account when one is considering the representation of Florentine life in the comedies and novelle. In these works we find many of the elements of the burlesque poetry; but, in the language of Benedetto Croce, who denied any literary value to journalistic literature, mere fact has acquired poetic form.[29] Starting from the narration of pure fact in his poetry, Grazzini was able to infuse it with his own inspiration and create a literature which, since it has its basis in the people and events of the time, we might call popular. In his work there is a development from the journalistic nature of his burlesque poetry to the novelle. In the latter the real people and situations which were the material of his poetry acquire a less immediate quality and merge into the narrative until they become an expression of the Florentine spirit. The development is from the particulars of historical truth to an art form in which the sharp contours of the particulars are lost and we are left with the essence of the Florentine life which the artist wanted to evoke.

The Comedies

In reviewing a modern production of Grazzini's comedy, *La Strega,* Eligio Possenti described the opening scene as follows:

> The action begins at daybreak and lasts until sunset. When the play begins, a weak light, just barely splashed here and there on the roof and facades made golden by the rising sun, allows the spectator to perceive the set and the actors. A bell rings. The baker passes with his basket upon his head. A blacksmith slowly pulls his nag behind him. Everything is still heavy with sleep. The cobbler, humming a tune, drags his bench from his shop; the innkeeper brings out his barrel, some tables and stools. It is a dawn which yawns upon awakening.[30]

By means of a tableau, the producer tried to capture the spirit of Grazzini's comedy. The action takes place in the piazza, and it revolves around the life of the Florentine bourgeoisie. Though the action and dialogue are often spirited, the comedy mirrors the fundamental idleness of the people who pass from their home to the tavern and who spend their day gossiping, quarreling, and participating in petty intrigues. This same spirit pervades all of Grazzini's comedies. Implicit in them is an attitude toward life which scorns all cares and considerations. The characters live for the moment and share a philosophy which is often repeated in the dialogue: "in this life, true wealth lies in taking one's pleasure" (*La Spiritata,* V, iii).

As his characters scamper across the scene, intent on the pursuit of their own happiness, Grazzini keeps vividly before us the fact that we are in Florence and that these are the Florentines whom he knew.[31] Of considerable interest are his references to local shops and taverns, which place the action even more specifically in the neighborhoods of the city. There is the Campana inn, on Borgo San Lorenzo, and the Fico, "the most popular hostelry in Florence" (*La Strega*, V, x; *La Pinzochera*, I, vi).[32] Florentines spent much of their time at these and similar inns, and they even had a vocabulary pertaining to them. In *La Gelosia*, IV, iii, a servant is chided for the amount of time he spends at an inn: "Staverna, staverna, oramai!" ("De-tavern yourself, de-tavern yourself!"). And his master, Alfonso, tells us that he is at the fire, drinking and exchanging novelle. This pastime was not limited to the literary circles of the tornatelle![33]

References to local taverns and to the churches and streets of Florence are only one means by which Grazzini made his comedies unmistakably Florentine. He introduced the names of his personal friends, giving to the comedies some of the many autobiographical elements which characterize his poetry.[34] He introduced the camaraderie of the brigate who spent idle hours in town, dressing in costume for diversion (*La Sibilla*, II, v), or who spent summer days in the country "to kill a pig and make merry" (*La Pinzochera*, I, vi). The youths attend performances of recent comedies (*La Gelosia*, IV, iv), discuss the literary academies, and participate in games which were so numerous, says Taddeo Saliscendi, that they were "organized according to the season and the month" (*La Strega*, II, i). The characters comment on current modes of dress, on the preparation of meals (*La Sibilla*, III, vii; II, v), on the exorbitant fees of medical doctors (*La Pinzochera*, III, iv), on inheritance rights, and on current legal procedures (*La Strega*, I, ii; V, i).

We see Florence from various points of view. In the eyes of many of its citizens it has degenerated to the point that "money is held more dear . . . than life" (*La Spiritata*, V, i). It is "a paradise inhabited by devils" (*La Strega*, IV, v), and, consequently, its citizens no longer feel safe on the streets: "These are not times to go wandering about without good reason" (*La Gelosia*, I, ii). Masters mistreat their servants,[35] everyone is subject to the most vicious gossip (*La Pinzochera*,

I, vi; V, x), and lawyers, doctors, clerics, and even nuns are corrupt (*La Sibilla*, V, vii). For others, usually strangers in the city, Florence is a just and a "beautiful and hospitable city" (*La Strega*, IV, vi; V, ix).

I have indicated only a few of the many instances we can cite to demonstrate how consistently and consciously Grazzini introduced elements of the Florentine world into his comedies. The examples which I have chosen are the topological features of the plays. They serve as constant reminders that we are in Florence. But Grazzini's reputation as one of the most Florentine of all Renaissance comedy writers does not rest merely on his frequent mention of churches and taverns. Rather, it is due to his ability to capture many aspects of the Florentine spirit during the late Renaissance.

In the tradition of the classical comedy writers, Grazzini places the action of his plays in the streets and squares of the city. However, his concern remains with the domestic situation, the *vita privata*, which always, and often without dramatic logic, unfolds in public. As in all Renaissance comedies, action which has occurred within the home is narrated by one character to another or directly to the audience.[36] Taking his license from tradition, then, Grazzini brings family life into the streets. And it is here that we see mirrored the condition of the family. The comedies are concerned with the relationship between children and their parents, between masters and their servants. They reflect the attitude of a people torn between hedonism and religious piety, a people who indulge themselves with food and idle chatter at one moment and run off to hear mass at the next. In many instances we are made aware that the family, as an institution, was undergoing changes, particularly as women and children began to assert their independence.[37] To be noted particularly are the strained relationships between children and their parents. There is probably more significance to Damiano's statement in *La Pinzochera*—"whoever has children has many enemies" (IV, xiii)—than would generally be supposed considering that the theme of the miserly father and the deprived son had long been part of the comic tradition. In Grazzini's comedies we note that children are extremely selfish. Their only concern is their own gratification. In *La Sibilla,* Caterina excuses her son's conduct because he, like all young people, "thinks of nothing but his own pleasure; and, in truth, what else can he get from life?" (I, i). Her husband, Michelozzo, is not willing to accept this justification, and, however unreasonable he may seem, we might see in his opposition to his wife and to his son a defense of the decaying paternal authority.

That parental authority was weakening under the growing independence of children can be seen elsewhere in Grazzini's comedies, but perhaps nowhere is it brought more to the fore than when a son openly defies his mother and treats her with less respect than he would a servant. In fact, the scene in *La Pinzochera* to which I am referring has all the flavor of a lively exchange of repartee which, though common to all of Grazzini's comedies, is usually reserved for the servants.

Riccardo. Good day to you.
Albiera. Where are you going so early?
Riccardo. As if you didn't know what I am accustomed to doing.
Albiera. Be careful that you don't get moldy by staying at home for a day! And this is just the day that I need you here.
Riccardo. Why today?
Albiera. Because I must be gone all day.
Riccardo. Stay away all night for all it matters. [I, iii]

The defiance of parental authority and the growing independent spirit of children might well be seen in light of the uncertain and changing moral and social values of the late Renaissance. Children were now able to begin to assert themselves more effectively against their fathers. It is significant, therefore—as pointed out earlier in my discussion of the burlesque poetry—that Grazzini reflects ideas concerning the rights of children. The father is often made to represent an antiquated and unjust authority, imposed irrationally on his child. As Federigo, the love-smitten young man of *La Pinzochera*, says, "whoever has a father has no freedom" (I, vi). He is making reference to the fact that his father will not allow his marriage to a girl whose mother had a bad reputation when she was young. Ambrogio, his friend, ridicules a society which would make a child assume the guilt of his parent, and in a dialogue of pure social commentary, states the inherent right of every individual to be judged on his own merit.

> *Ambrogio.* It seems unfortunate that so much attention is given to idle chatter in this city; if the girl is good and sweet, isn't that enough without worrying about her family tree?
>
> *Federigo.* You know the proverb: the child of a hen can't help but know how to scratch. And so my father is afraid that she'll end up acting and speaking [like her mother].
>
> *Ambrogio.* If this rule holds true for animals, I assure you that it does not for men. I could mention any number of girls born to well-bred mothers who are shamefully disgraceful; and, on the other hand, there are many born of notorious hussies who seem the epitome of good manners and virtue. [I, vi]

In Grazzini's comedies not only do we find a weakening of the father's authority over his children, but also the weakening of his control over his wife. The mother becomes increasingly important as she defends her children against the authoritarianism of the father, and, in some instances, she actually controls the family.[38] Gerozzo, in *La Pinzochera*, laments his inability to control his wife:

> What can I do if my wife has put on the pants and expects to wear them? You know how impetuous she is: if she's the

> least bit vexed, she suddenly flares up, and she would use any opportunity to start an argument. [II, vi]

And in the first scene of *La Sibilla*, Caterina argues with her husband, Michelozzo, defending the need for a parental authority tempered by good judgment.

> *Michelozzo.* Can it really be, though, that he is so witless that, tossing aside any consideration for his social position, he would marry, not just a foreigner who has no background, but a girl with no more than five hundred ducats for a dowry? He could have three thousand without any trouble! . . .
>
> *Caterina.* Just what do money and nobility have to do with love? He is young and his only interest is in enjoying himself. . . .
>
> *Michelozzo.* All you offer are words.
>
> *Caterina.* But would it really have been too much to make him happy?
>
> *Michelozzo.* Talk! That girl is behind it all!
>
> *Caterina.* Sibilla is a lovely young girl, well brought up and virtuous. And besides, she loves him.
>
> *Michelozzo.* He'll also love the girl we'll find for him, and she will be most beautiful, virtuous, noble, and very wealthy.
>
> *Caterina.* God only knows! Then he'll rebel and refuse to marry; perhaps he will despair and even take up with women of the street; and then we will never be happy with the constant feuds. . . . And by his marrying her, we could all be happy and have peace in the house.

The scene continues in this manner with Caterina presenting rational arguments in favor of her son's marriage to la Sibilla. Michelozzo continues to reject them for fear of losing his control over the family. At the end of the scene, Caterina submits to Michelozzo's stubbornness, but we realize immediately that she will have her own way even if she must employ the deceit and trickery of which her husband accuses all mothers and their children.

It is not insignificant that a character like Caterina is portrayed as a rational and headstrong person, for, as the father's role weakened, the mother's grew more influential. She, perhaps alone, upheld the dignity of the family and traditional standards of morality. To attack the woman was to attack the last bastion of decency. Might not this be one reason why misogyny is seldom present in Grazzini's comedies?[39]

In Grazzini's comedies, the breakdown of the family structure is but one manifestation of a general laxity in the moral fiber of the Renaissance Florentines. When Grazzini's characters state repeatedly that life's one pleasure is self-gratification, they are denying any concern with moral, social, and political problems. They are confessing to their own apathy. Rather than voice disapproval or even concern, they accept their condition. The fact, for example, that Florence was crushed under the tyranny of Cosimo's government is not reflected in the dialogue of Grazzini's theatre. Perhaps, after the upheaval within the Medici house, Cosimo's control provided the Florentines with a revived sense of stability which they had not known since the glorious reign of Lorenzo. In this new prosperity, however superficial, they tried to recapture the carefree life of the past.

But the carefree life in Florence during the sixteenth century was an ephemeral one. The people no longer enjoyed the economic prosperity of an earlier day. Life in Laurentian Florence was but a nostalgic memory. The Church was preparing to reassert its strength and to bring back into its fold the wandering spirits who had fallen into a life of ease and turpitude. These impending changes could not have passed unnoticed by the Florentines. Their life, still reflecting the pleasure-seeking attitudes of the early Renaissance, was perforce disturbed by Savonarola's voice still echoing in their ears.

Although Grazzini was no moralist, his portrayal of Cinquecento Florentine society could not help but reflect the spiritual and moral weaknesses of a people who felt a need to justify its amorality. The moral apathy of Florentine society, attended by a conscious awareness of its spiritual decay, is a leitmotiv in Grazzini's comedies. We find reflected, for example, a way of life in which Petrarchism had become, not just a literary device, but a practice. There was an attempt to raise sensual gratification to a lofty sphere, to excuse an indulgence of the instincts as an expression of pure love. It is important that there was a need to justify sensuality when, at an earlier time, self-indulgence was accepted without questioning its moral legitimacy.[40] We find, too, in Grazzini's comedies, that which Salza has called the cynicism of the sixteenth century, the tendency to laugh at and to satirize its own vices and its own institutions.[41]

To capture the spirit of a people attempting to preserve the last vestiges of sanctioned amorality, Grazzini brings to his theatre a world completely devoid of refinement; gross habits are accompanied by gross language. It is a world of servants, prostitutes, pimps, and libertines. There is no place for ideal loves; characters are constantly struggling with one another in a grotesque and frenzied dance of animal instincts.[42] I have already mentioned that, in the classical tradition, the motivating force behind the comedies is the consuming passion of a lover. And, as we have also had occasion to see, his feelings are often expressed in coarse double entendres (see n. 40).

Appeasement of the sexual appetite is a major preoccupation of Grazzini's characters, but it is only one. Few commentators have noted, for example, the recurrent theme of gluttony in Grazzini's theatre.[43] The action of a comedy is often delayed while one of the participants complains at having missed a meal, and in other instances, the characters go into a state of ecstasy upon recalling a meal or anticipating one soon to be enjoyed. The servants in *La Pinzochera* (II, i), in a scene entirely extraneous to the development of the comedy, reminisce upon leaving an inn, while in the same comedy (II, iv), Ambrogio, to show that not only servants were gourmands, rhapsodizes over a meal which he has had prepared. And, finally, even a miser like Michelozzo in *La Sibilla* (II, v) cannot refrain from spending his money on the preparation of a meal as described to him by his servant, Vespa:

Michelozzo. I want you to go and order the meal. What are you thinking of getting?

Vespa. Well, it certainly wouldn't do not to have some squab and thrushes, together with a brace or two of partridges and capons.

Michelozzo. Good, good.

Vespa. And it wouldn't be bad if we could get a nice young veal or else a fat little kid.

Michelozzo. Wait! Wouldn't we be spending perhaps a little too much?

Vespa. No, not at all. And it would be a most fine and honorable meal.

Michelozzo. Are you sure?

Vespa. We are thinking of having some nice broths and then various dishes of innards, livers, and other delicacies to begin the meal; for the last courses we'll have some fritters, fruit, and cheese, all topped off with a beautiful salad.

Michelozzo. And how are you preparing the meat dishes? . . . I'd like something boiled; and, to tell the truth, I never really consider it a meal unless I have a nice, thick soup.

Vespa. Just as you wish: we'll boil the capons and thrushes together with a piece of dried meat and fresh sausage.

Michelozzo. Oh, it's all going to make the most sumptuous meal! . . . So appetizing and succulent and tasty.[44]

The Florentine appetite for money was apparently as large as it was for food. We might recall that Grazzini, in his poetry, chided the Florentines for their materialistic nature. And in *La*

Gelosia (I, ii) Filippo, bemoaning the avarice of Giovacchino who would allow the marriage of his daughter to an old man for financial gain, calls the vice an "insatiable thirst! . . . Just look at man's appetite for money! It would be better to drown or bury her. Poor child! And wretched are any other children born to such fathers." Filippo's lament implies that the hierarchy of human values had been upset. Accordingly, Michelozzo in *La Sibilla* (I, i), chides his wife for expecting him to allow his son's marriage to a girl just because she is virtuous. Don't you know, he asks, that money has replaced virtue in the esteem of all men? "You are mad! Money, money, money, and a little less attention to virtue and goodness. Nowadays, one who has money is good and beautiful and virtuous." Giovangualberto (*La Spiritata*, V, i) is even accused of placing more value on money than on human life.

Avarice is, then, one of the dominant themes of Grazzini's theatre. The love of money takes precedence over almost every other consideration so that, at times, even physical passion is weak beside it. Gerozzo (*La Pinzochera*, III, iv), lusting after Diamante and willing to sacrifice his family for his passion, hesitates when he discovers that he will have to spend money to satisfy his desires. Alesso (*L'Arzigogolo*, I, i), too, had been circumspect with his money. But growing old, he realizes the meaninglessness of a life spent in accumulating wealth, and he decides to try and recapture his lost youth by indulging in physical pleasures:

> In this life, those who are really fortunate are the ones born rich and who can, especially when they are young, have a good time by spending freely. What happens to those who are born poor cannot happen to them. Those few poor ones who manage to gain some wealth are old before they do and then it is too late for pleasure; and they become more and more avaricious. If we old ones possessed the whole world, we would still not be satisfied. As they say, we are like an animal who lives only a short time and eats nothing but soil; yet it is never sated for fear of there not being enough. . . .

> Although I am old, I don't want to be like this; rather, I want to live like a gentleman and have a good time. Like my son, I'll throw money away and let others scrimp and save. What else can we get out of life but a little bit of pleasure?

Alesso feels no moral compunction for having been a miser. His advanced age has not increased his wisdom but has only served to remind him that very little time remains to his pleasure. Time, as Pierfilippo says, "not only . . . flies, but vanishes more quickly than a lightning bolt or an arrow" (*La Sibilla,* I, ii). Alesso simply decides to follow the dictum of his age, to enjoy life by indulging himself in a different way than he had done before.

All the elements of Grazzini's theatre contribute to his portrayal of a society caught up in the excesses of animal instincts.[45] The comedies are populated with procuresses and prostitutes, pimps and tricksters. When a character is not actively seeking his own pleasure, he is assisting that of another, usually in anticipation of a reward. Pullini's description of this activity as a grotesque and frenzied dance is aptly stated. In keeping with the instinctive nature of their characters, the comedies are peppered with gross obscenities which contribute significantly to the general atmosphere of the plays.[46]

In our consideration of the *fiorentinità* of Grazzini's theatre we must acknowledge, finally, the important role played by the language of the comedies. I say acknowledge because perhaps no other aspect of Grazzini's literature has attracted more commentary. It would be useless, here, to repeat the many examples which commentators have cited to show Grazzini's use of Florentine idioms and popular expressions.[47] Suffice it to say that Grazzini's use of Florentine expressions served a dual purpose. First, it gave to his comedies the local color and flavor by which he strove to create a truly Florentine literature. And, second, and certainly not less important, it contributed to the efforts of many Florentine writers to prepare the terrain for a literary language and to raise the local idiom in the estimation of their contemporaries.[48]

The Novelle

In the novelle the role played by the "vita fiorentina" is even more significant than in the burlesque poetry and in the comedies because it becomes a more essential element of the narrative art. The burlesque poetry, as we have had occasion to see, is often no more than a chronicle of events, invaluable for the biographer and historian of the period, but limited in its value as literature. It is too immediate in its portrayal of current happenings and betrays the fact that Grazzini (no more, of course, than many) used verse to express his own complaints or as a harpoon in his polemics with his contemporaries. Too often the poetry never rises above the banality of its subject matter, even when it testifies to the author's great cleverness and facility with language. At best, Grazzini shows himself akin to Francesco Berni in his ability to transform by his fantasy the banal into a humorous interplay of grotesque images. What prevents him from rising to the heights of Berni is the absence of the moral sense which is always present in his predecessor's work. In the comedies, autobiographical fact and contemporary Florentine life are presented with less immediacy than in the poetry. Grazzini, the writer of plays, was checked, as it were, by tradition, and in writing plays which he hoped would find a receptive audience he could introduce elements of contemporary life only in a tangential way. These elements never dominate the comedies but are introduced into what are, basically, classical plots and characters. In other words, despite modification of classical characters and themes in an attempt to "modernize" the comedy, the fundamental nature of the comedy does not change. In the novelle, on the other hand, we find a much more complex relationship between Grazzini's art and life. Contemporary Florentine life is supremely important for it penetrates every fibre of the narrative, and, at the same time, it is only incidental in that the author transforms the realities of the moment into what Giovanni Grazzini has called a "symphonic metaphor of life."[49] Unlike the poetry, which chronicles life in Florence, the novelle are limited in their value as socio-historical documents, despite the fact that Grazzini attempted to give verisimilitude to his fiction.[50] The critic Bruno Porcelli went so far as to claim that "in the Florentine novelle, . . . the situations and characters are taken from contemporary life, so that they are transported to an ideal time where there is no longer any distinction between epochs."[51] I would hesitate to accept this: the specifically Renaissance Florentine flavor of Grazzini's *Cene* is one of its greatest assets, and the vita fiorentina is an integral part of his art. It is more accurate, then, to say that historical reality and fact become the basis for a mythical reality, an evocation of the Florentine spirit by a synthesis of all elements of life as the author knew them.

In this chapter I am less concerned with how Grazzini integrated Florentine life into his art than with those elements of sixteenth-century Florence actually portrayed in the novelle. The novella is a genre which permits greater latitude to the author's imagination; Grazzini was less shackled by tradition than in the plays and poetry, and the novelle incorporate a much wider range of Florentine customs and habits than do the comedies. The scene becomes even more thoroughly Florentine since, unlike in the comedies, it is not restricted to one type of locale.

We might select, by way of example, the sixth story of the second *Cena* which, if examined solely for its evocation of an environment, is among the most Florentine of the novelle. "There once lived in Florence a good man named Guasparri del Calandra," a middle-class artisan similar to the many other *bontemponi* we have encountered in Grazzini's work. He is a person "both kind and quite clever," who, after inheriting some money from his brother-in-law, gives up his trade, and, "having abandoned his shop, decided to give himself over to pleasure." He spends his evenings at the home of Pilucca, a Florentine sculptor and architect, "who lived in a house on Via della Scala, where there was a lovely garden in which to spend summer evenings eating under a thick, green arbor." Guasparri and Pilucca, together with their cronies Scheggia, Monaco, and Zoroastro, enjoy the companionship and mutual practical joking which characterized the many brigate populating Florence during the Renaissance. Eating and conversation were the major occupations: "chatting after supper, they always had the strangest conversations and often spent half the night speaking of witches and enchantments, of spirits and the dead." In this novella, Guasparri becomes the victim of a beffa, the success of which depends upon his fear of the dead. As the beffa develops Grazzini follows his characters through the streets of Florence. One night, alone and frightened at the prospect of encountering spirits, Guasparri makes his way home from Pilucca's house on Via della Scala to his own on Borgo Stella: his itinerary takes him from Santa Maria Novella along the Via de' Fossi and, finally, to the Ponte alla Carraia. Waiting for him at the bridge, his friends are prepared to carry out the first part of their beffa by frightening him with ghoulish stick figures. In the great detail with which Grazzini describes the preparation for the beffa and its effect on Guasparri we sense the pleasure that this most Florentine of authors took in narrating the activities with which he was so familiar:

> It was September and, fortunately, it happened to be as black as pitch outside; according to the plan devised by Zoroastro and Scheggia, the two companions had come to the first piles just beyond the Ponte alla Carraia. Each had a pike with a small piece of wood attached to the top to form a cross and these were draped with very long, white sheets.

> At the top of each cross had been placed a frightening mask which had lamps of artificial fire for eyes and one for a mouth. They all burned brightly and shot forth a terrifying greenish flame; each mask had long and sparsely set teeth, a deformed nose, a pointed chin, and the most awful disheveled hair which would have frightened, not only Caius and Bevilacqua, but Rodomonte and the Count Orlando as well. Resting on those empty piles which run along the banks of the Arno, they seemed to lie in wait and, at the time, such monsters were called "cuccubeoni" by the Florentines. Guasparri, whose thoughts were on such unearthly things, approached with extreme caution until he came to the bridge. As soon as Scheggia saw him, he whistled softly as a signal that they were to raise the cuccubeoni very slowly. As he began to cross the bridge, Guasparri cautiously turned his eyes and saw one of those horrible things rise very slowly. He was so overcome by fright that he summoned up only enough strength to shout, "Christ, help me!" And then he remained transfixed to the spot. And the cuccubeoni rose higher and higher so that, with one on one side of the bridge and another on the other side, both seeming to rise from the river, they appeared to be growing taller than the campanile. So stunned and frightened was Guasparri that he thought he had thirty thousand pairs of devils before him. He thought they were slowly approaching him, and fearing he would be swallowed alive, he again shouted, "Christ, help me," and, turning heels, he fled back from whence he came, never once turning back until he reached Pilucca's house.

This does not mark the end of Guasparri's torment. Once again he is victimized by his prankster friends, but, finally, he sells his house on Borgo Stella, buys another near San Piero Maggiore and, upon the advice of a relative, stops associating with his companions.

In this novella, just as in many others, Florence, the city, becomes more than just a setting for the narrative; it is a protagonist, an integral part of the action which, at times, seems to depend upon the city for its stimulus. Not only does Grazzini map Florence, but he makes it come alive with his own enthusiasm and with the peculiarly Florentine quality of the beffa. Florence becomes associated with the carefree life of men like Pilucca and Scheggia so that the epithet "il Fiorentino" becomes synonymous with a man who is "shrewd, mischievous, and bizarre" (*Cena* I, vii). The passage cited above gives some indication of the importance which the bizarre nature of the Florentine and his *gusto conviviale* has for Grazzini's novelle.[52]

The atmosphere of the novelle is permeated with the camaraderie of the brigata, the significance of which to the *Cene* cannot be understated. We recall that Grazzini's fondest memories were those of the carefree hours spent among his friends in the Florentine shops, eating and discussing the most varied topics. For Grazzini, a man without a family, life with the cronies of the brigate must have been the Florentine milieu he knew best. The members of the brigate exemplified the jocose spirit, the biting wit, which had traditionally been associated with the Florentines. Their activities, even when they included the coarse pranks we find documented in the *Cene,* were a way of life which grew out of their somewhat grotesque sense of humor.

As I mentioned earlier, the brigate vary in type according to their membership. Some are of a more aristocratic nature than that of Pilucca and Scheggia, but their activities remain constant—eating, drinking, and devising beffe.[53] In the novelle, just as we have seen reflected in the burlesque poetry, the organized brigata is the center of social activity, and as Bruno Porcelli has observed, the very pretext for the telling of the stories—young men and women exchange novelle before a fire on a cold winter's night—reflects the atmosphere of the brigata as much as it does the need to employ the traditional framework.[54]

The vicissitudes of Guasparri del Calandra may serve to introduce another aspect of Florentine life in the *Cene.* Guasparri's superstitious nature was shared by many of his contemporaries. In many of his works, Grazzini vividly portrays the extent to which pagan superstitions and practices had continued to survive among the Italians during the Renaissance and how they had become intricately involved with the rites of the Church.[55] Often, in his poetry, Grazzini chided the heathen practices of necromancers and astrologers who took advantage of the gullible. In several poems addressed to a necromancer, Don Nasorre (the familiar name of Piero Cardi), Grazzini testifies to the following which false prophets had and to the material gain which it brought them (see Verzone, Ottave LXIX–LXXIII). Don Nasorre and others like him were familiar figures to the Florentines and were the basis of Grazzini's well-known portrait of Zoroastro, a beffatore who practices exorcism. Grazzini gives a detailed description of a professional trickster who was considered "a great philosopher and necromancer."

> He was a man of about thirty-six to forty years of age, large and well built. He had a ruddy complexion and a serious and fierce mien. His black hair, falling almost to his chest, was quite bizarre. He had practiced alchemy and witchcraft: he had seals and certain magic signs, strings, amulets, bells, various containers and burners with which to distill potions from herbs, earth, metals, stones and wood; in addition, he had unborn paper, lynx eyes, drivel from rabid dogs, the bones of fish and dead men, ropes used for hangings, daggers and swords which had inflicted mortal wounds, the clavicle and knife of Solomon, herbs and seeds which had been gathered during various lunar phases and under various constellations, and a thousand other gadgets, tales, and mumbo jumbo with which to frighten the foolish. He practiced astrology, physiognomy, palmistry, and a hundred other fantastic things. He believed in witches, but was particularly taken with spirits. And yet, for all this, he had never been able to perform any supernatural feats, although he devised a thousand outrageous lies and tales to make people believe that he had. And having neither a father nor a mother, and being fairly well off, he had to

> spend most of his time alone in the house, unable to find any domestics willing to stay with him. [*Cena* II, iv]

The occult sciences, employing trappings like those of Zoroastro, were widely practiced. The wife of a former goldsmith who had given himself over to alchemy curses the ruin which has been brought down upon her family by his dealings in magic. He, once esteemed an intelligent man, is mocked by his fellow townsmen, thinking that he, like many, "had gone mad because of that curse called alchemy" (*Cena* I, v). In *Cena* I, x, we see how the practices of medicine, magic, and religion had become so confused that a medical doctor, to cure a woman, employs drugs, mumbo jumbo, and prayer:

> The doctor told the servants to bring oil and flour for a poultice as he wanted to perform an enchantment, seeing no other way of keeping the girl alive. Turning to them, he ordered them to also bring him a glass of wine and one of water and they quickly obeyed. Then he took a glass in each hand and appearing to say certain words over each glass, he gave them to Fiammetta, handing her the wine with his right hand, the water with his left. He told her to take four sips from each glass and then told the servants that if they wanted to be sure that their mistress lived, they must immediately go, one to the highest and one to the lowest part of the house, and recite four rosaries, each one in devotion to the four Evangelists. And he told them to be sure that they recite the rosaries completely and slowly and not to leave until they had finished.

The superstitious nature of the Florentines lends itself well to Grazzini's novelle because it becomes the basis, not only of beffe such as the one concerning Guasparri, but also for macabre stories (e.g., *Cene* I, vii and ix) in which the author shows himself a master of the grotesque and the lugubrious, a precursor of manneristic prose such as we find fully developed, for example, with the *Sueños* of Quevedo.

Elsewhere in the *Cene* we find many of those elements of

the Florentine character which we have already discussed at length while treating the comedy. Here, too, there is present the Florentine taste for money and food. Monna Laudomine degli Uberti, like so many of her counterparts in the comedies, represents the avaricious parent who is willing to sacrifice her daughter's happiness for financial gain (*Cena* II, iii). Master Manente, the beffato in Grazzini's best known novella, is famous for his gluttony and his mannerisms while eating and is the near prototype of the many gourmands in Grazzini's works (*Cena* III, x). As Bruno Porcelli has indicated, Grazzini also portrays the Florentine's pride in his cultural heritage.[56] In *Cena* I, viii, a young man called Tasso reduces a haughty abbot to ridicule for having minimized the value of Michelangelo's work in the sacristy of San Lorenzo.

Much of the Florentine milieu in the comedies is more conspicuous than it is in the novelle, for it remains something almost extraneous to the action of the plays. Often it is the material of scenes which lend little to the swift development of the action but which are introduced for their flavor. The result is often less than successful, for the action remains in part divorced from the spirit of Florentine life. But in the novelle, the action arises out of the milieu and the pace of the narrative is consistent throughout. We sense more readily the spirit of the brigata and the Florentine conviviality. Often the entire action is built upon one aspect of life in Florence or one trait of the Florentine people, and, consequently, there is a marriage of the narrative with the spirit of the age.

CHAPTER III

THE POETRY

The Burlesque Poetry

GRAZZINI'S reputation now rests on his seven comedies and on his collection of novelle, one of the most noteworthy of the sixteenth century. During his own lifetime, however, Grazzini's comedies enjoyed a rather limited success. And probably only a few of his acquaintances ever read his novelle.[1] To his contemporaries, Grazzini was known primarily as a poet. The name il Lasca was associated with humorous verse, be it that which continued in the tradition of the Florentine carnival song or that which, in the tradition of Berni and the Berneschi, satirized and ridiculed individuals and institutions alike. He apparently became recognized, too, for his Petrarchan sonnets since several of them were included in collections published during the sixteenth century.[2] But his reputation as a lyric poet was undoubtedly confined to the literary circles which, under the influence of Tullia d'Aragona and other well-known courtesans, sought to express lofty sentiments in imitation of the Petrarchists. In this chapter, therefore, I will necessarily be concerned with compositions which were quite familiar to the author's contemporaries and by which he gained his notoriety, but which have received only the most cursory attention from modern critics and students of sixteenth-century literature.

It was probably to Grazzini's disadvantage that he attempted his hand at almost every type of poetic composition then in vogue. His prolificacy, to which he readily admitted, prevented his concentrated labors on one style of poetry or, more significantly, on his comedies and novelle, which, even in their unfinished state, attest to what might have developed into one of the most polished collections of short stories of the Italian Renaissance. But this is speculation and, in truth, Grazzini, in his many statements of self-criticism, revealed a character which was little adapted to the personal and artistic discipline requisite for such an undertaking. Twice, he tells us, he began a collection of verse romances entitled *Ruggier da Risa*, but failed to complete the work (no part of which has been found) because he could not resist the call of the comic muse to continue with his occasional poems. As if in a dream, Ruggiero came to him, just as Mercury had come to the misguided Aeneas, and reproached him for his lack of perseverance:

> Where have you lost your spunk and intelligence? What kind of feeble subject have you chosen? After all, what does Ligliano really mean to you? You're going to reap a bad harvest if you continue with such vile business. What has become of your style? What have you done with your genius by composing madrigalesse? You must have had your fill of all those fanciful and burlesque writings, which would be enough to amaze the most uncivilized!

But for Grazzini, the pleasures of Raffaello de' Medici's villa, Ligliano, were too much of a distraction for him to heed Ruggiero's words. Even when Apollo appears to assure him that he possesses "so much of my strength and divine poetic genius that, when mixed with love, they make such poetry, or rather madness, that the impossible often becomes possible," and reinforces Ruggiero's reprimand ("You should *do* something and not babble on so much"), he smiles and says that he will begin work seriously again "when I have nothing else to do" (Verzone, Madrigalessa XXXVII, pp. 301–5).

When Grazzini describes his poetic genius as a sort of madness which makes possible the impossible, we might understand him to mean the ability of his comic nature to find humor in the most commonplace situation. Perhaps he did feel some compunction at not having been more serious, at not having followed the advice of those inner voices, Ruggiero and the god Apollo, but undoubtedly he realized that his inspiration was for comedy and the burlesque genres. His expressed desire to attain wider renown for epic, lyric, or heroic poetry might well be attributed to the envy he felt in the presence of his enemies, the pedants. But the madrigalessa from which I have quoted is, in fact, no apology. He intended to continue writing in his customary way but wanted to let it be known that he was nowise inferior to his more erudite contemporaries. The many Petrarchan and pastoral sonnets which we can read today are evidence of Grazzini's attempt to demonstrate his abilities at competing with the more serious versifiers of his day. Apollo reassures him of this: "And remember to have no fear of those who think that they know too much" (Verzone, p. 304, vv. 47–49).

Just these few comments are enough to make us realize that, as a poet, Grazzini was a complex personality, torn between his true calling to follow in the footsteps of Berni and his need to prove his worth as a Petrarchist. The two, of course, were irreconcilable. Berni, and Grazzini after him, avowed their enmity toward Petrarchism. But Grazzini also had moments when he could not ignore its influence and did, on one occasion, write to Benedetto Varchi, calling him his second master, "having already, upon your advice, chosen Petrarch for my first."[3] On the one hand, then, we have Grazzini the critic, the scapigliato who scorned the empty, effeminate, soulless poetry of the Bembists; on the other hand we find him repeating the same prosaic verses which he criticized for having "half-sated and bored the world." The implications of the contradiction are significant. They do not involve Grazzini alone, but his entire age. The timeworn devices of traditional Italian poetry began to come under the scrutiny of severe critics. The elevated, Platonic sentiments which had been taking their toll on poetry were slowly being replaced by a more realistic, down-to-earth consideration of human passions. Grazzini and many poets like him pointed the way to the poetry of the seventeenth-century Marinisti.

This study of Grazzini's poetry will consider both his humorous verse—which Verzone chose to edit under the all-inclusive title of "poesia burlesca"—and his serious verse. Within these two general categories there are various verse forms, e.g., the sonnet, the ottava, and the madrigal, which are not always determined by the subject of the poem. For example, the capitolo was traditionally used in burlesque poetry for treating subjects of the most trite nature in a mock-heroic way. But Grazzini often let the forms overlap and was as likely to sing the praises of a mule in a madrigal as in a capitolo.

As I have said, Grazzini was best known to his contemporaries for his burlesque poetry, and it is this which is considered first. How well known he became for his comic or satiric verse is attested to by his own statement that he had composed "so many simple and clear poems that everyone, ladies and lovers alike, enjoyed them" (Verzone, p. 408, vv. 26–28). His renown, in fact, gave him cause for complaint. Repeatedly he struck out against those who profited by using his name to sign their own work, and he was eventually forced to declare:

> Anyone who publicly parades his work anonymously is a fool. . . . Despicable is a man who would write under my

> name . . . and from now on, no work should be attributed to me unless it is accompanied by my signature. [Verzone, Madrigalessa XXXVIII, pp. 305–7]

Yet we can hardly believe that he seriously intended to carry out his plan to protect his name, for he himself was not above writing in the name of another.

Undoubtedly, the fact that others wrote in his name provided Grazzini with a sense of his own importance. He enjoyed his notoriety and claimed that it was due to the fear which his pen instilled in the hearts of his enemies. He used it like a sword to wage war on pedants and on those who belittled his talents. In attacking Vincenzio Buonanni he served notice to all that he was always victorious in contests of infamy and maliciousness:

> May everyone learn to leave Lasca alone. I have never been the instigator of a squabble, but if anyone challenges me to a contest of verse, as learned as he may be, he'll surely get the worst of it. [Verzone, pp. 403–4, vv. 41–48]

That Grazzini was as successful as any of his contemporaries in the art of insulting we can readily believe; that he was never the instigator of an argument, as his lines to Buonanni would have us believe, is very doubtful.

It should be kept in mind, I think, that Grazzini's pride in the fear which he boasted of instilling in his contemporaries was not too well founded. He was certainly not a Florentine Pietro Aretino or a Paolo Giovio. Little had to be feared from a man whose influence was as limited as his. At most, as the incident with the Aramei demonstrates, he was capable of causing great annoyance with the persistence with which he continued to lampoon his enemies. His braggadocio was intended, rather, to preserve his reputation among his cronies who enjoyed testing each other's wit in burlesque verse. In fact, as we see in the following lines written to Bernardo Ulivi,

Grazzini was often annoyed by those who took him too seriously. He praised Ulivi who, unlike most, did not resent "every little word":

> I always enjoy writing to you, my dear Bernardo, for you are both a gentleman and a good companion. . . . One can take you into his confidence, and with you he can laugh and joke and chat away, . . . write and exchange clever words. . . . And you don't fly into a rage, screaming and shouting, cursing and raving as if you were Orlando or Mandricardo. [Verzone, p. 292, vv. 1–24]

Although in many instances Grazzini's venemous lines were sincerely motivated, usually his poetry was patterned after a tradition which sought out scandal and licentiousness, making them the subject of poetry solely for their shock value. He himself confessed to a certain Master Macario how much his poetry continued in the tradition of his Florentine predecessors, "I regret having written that poem. I was following a poetic tradition and certainly meant no harm" (Verzone, p. 429).

In continuing the tradition of popular Florentine poetry and as the immediate successor to the burlesque style of Francesco Berni, Grazzini inevitably became heir to the anti-literary sentiments of his illustrious predecessor. We shall have occasion later to discuss more fully his verse polemics against the academicians and the theorists of style. But Grazzini could not divorce himself completely from the academic environment in which he wrote. He was quite familiar with the many tracts which mushroomed in the academic circles, and so it does not surprise us that, however formal and nebulous it may be, a theory of his own poetry did develop. To be more explicit, Grazzini attempted to describe how his poetic genius found its inspiration. Considering his affection for Berni, it is even less surprising that he finds close parallels between his own method of writing and what he assumed to be Berni's. Berni—or rather, Grazzini speaking in his name—describes his moment of inspiration as "festering whimsies which come upon me and which must be expressed lest I go mad" (Verzone, p. 360, vv. 9–12). Elsewhere, Berni is described as possessing "an instinct for hitting the bull's-eye" (Verzone, p. 512, vv. 4–6). As Grazzini would have it, Berni was suddenly assailed by an idea which his *naturale,* or bent for the humorous, would urge into verse before he was overcome by the madness of frustration. In effect, this also describes the process by which Grazzini himself claimed to have composed. We can describe it in more detail by a piecemeal procedure, drawing from many of his poems.

His ability to write poetry is due to what he calls a "fury, or, rather, a vice, or even a sweet malaise." It is useless to seek it out, for, "no matter how learned, rich, or handsome one may be, he cannot versify without having received a call from heaven" (Verzone, pp. 441, 405). Those in possession of this gift must experience a degree of madness, "because poetry and madness are born simultaneously and spring from the same source" (Verzone, p. 482, vv. 47–48). Once the gift of creativity is visited upon a man, he continuously feels the compulsion to write (Verzone, Dedication of Capitolo III, p. 467; p. 544, vv. 1–3).

One cannot be much concerned with these statements as a theory since Grazzini is not himself serious, but they should be considered in connection with the polemical aspect of his poetry. Grazzini is taking a stand against the literati and the entire humanist tradition which championed imitation and perfection of style, placing inspiration and original creativity in a subordinate position where they languished and disappeared. He is giving impetus to the call for a renewed spirit in poetry and urging the fantasy of the individual, unfettered from the bonds of humanist pretentiousness, to express itself.

In this context, and to conclude my introductory remarks to the burlesque poetry, I wish to call to the reader's attention three of what I consider to be the most significant capitoli of Grazzini: "In lode della pazzia" ("In praise of madness"), "In lode del pensiero" ("In praise of thought"), and its counterpart, "Contro al pensiero" ("Against thought") (Verzone, pp. 559–64, 576–80, 580–84). In each of these long poems Grazzini concerns himself with the necessity of the free play of one's imagination in the creative process and vehemently condemns pedantry as a deterrent to all creativity.

To date, the only authoritative edition of Grazzini's burlesque poetry is Carlo Verzone's *Le Rime burlesche edite e inedite* (Florence: G. C. Sansoni, 1882). Verzone collected Grazzini's poems from the numerous anthologies in which they had appeared during the preceding three centuries, and in his edition he tried to separate the spurious from the genuine. This edition has, since its publication, been the most complete and valuable guide to a reading of Grazzini's jocose poetry.[4] Verzone's edition contains 178 sonnets which, with few exceptions, are sonetti caudati. In his use of the coda—a stanza of varying length attached to the sonnet form—Grazzini followed in the tradition of the jocose poets, Burchiello, Berni, and others who had derived its use from the Florentine and Pisan popular poets of the late thirteenth and early fourteenth centuries.[5] The coda, as it was employed by Grazzini, can vary from a simple three-verse stanza consisting of a seven-syllabled line and two hendecasyllables, rhyming DFF (the first line rhyming with the last line of the sonnet form thus: ABBA ABBA CDC DCD DFF), to several tercets, continuing the pattern DFF FGG GHH etc.

Besides the sonnets there are 136 ottave, 56 madrigals, 61 madrigalesse and 4 madrigaloni, 55 capitoli, 40 canti carnascialeschi, 3 canzoni a ballo and 7 canzoni, and 30 epitaphs. Except for the madrigalesse and madrigaloni, all of these forms, like the sonetto caudato, are familiar to anyone acquainted with popular Italian poetry. However, Grazzini is credited with having originated the madrigalessa and madrigalone. Crescimbeni made the observation that they differ from the madrigal only in their extended length and humorously added that the madrigalessa received its feminine name because, like women, it is long-winded.[6]

As I have already noted, in matter of content the difference between one form and another is almost negligible. The capitolo, of course, retains its function as the form by which the most banal subjects—the "unpoetic material of life"[7]—are treated in a mock-heroic way. The canto carnascialesco and the canzone a ballo, in the tradition of those genres, concern, by and large, various professions which are praised only for the obvious sexual allusions and obscenities that come from the use of double entendres. But Grazzini probably chose any of the other forms by mere caprice. Consequently, one must be concerned with theme and not form.

If one were to seek a unifying principle in the burlesque poetry, he would inevitably conclude that it lies in the polemical nature of the poems. Grazzini took a position on almost every subject which lent itself to argument and, we might add, on several which did so only in his own fantasy. The polemical nature of his poetry owes its existence to many factors, the primary one being the argumentative predisposition of the man. This side of Grazzini's character is clear from the discussion of his life in the first chapter. Also, by its very nature, burlesque poetry invited the poet to express his points of view since individual poems were exchanged in a verse parley or *tenzone*. Moreover, the sixteenth century was the age of scathing criticism on the part of the scapigliati who—if Grazzini cannot be counted among the members—certainly shared many feelings with him.

The scapigliati, whether we consider those of the sixteenth century or their better-known counterparts of the nineteenth century, professed dissatisfaction with tradition and attempted to deny its validity by open disrespect for the past and for those who revered it. In the sixteenth century, this meant, of course, that the classical authors were objects of scorn and that slavish imitation, especially of Petrarch, was ridiculed and satirized. During the Renaissance, the irreverence of Berni, Nicolò Franco, and Grazzini toward humanistic culture contributed to hastening its disappearance, and their insistence on realism and the expression of the individual personality in poetry foreshadowed the literature of the next century.[8] But these attitudes of the scapigliati only indicate a general dissatisfaction with the status quo, and it is difficult to find a complete denial of traditional humanist ideals in any one author. In his polemics with his contemporaries, therefore, Grazzini is often contradictory, taking first one side and then the other, sometimes denying all value to the past and then evoking the glories of his predecessors.[9]

This is particularly true of Grazzini's attitude toward poetry, both as it had been written and was being written in his own day. As is clear from the discussion of his edition of the canti carnascialeschi, he bemoaned the fact that contemporary poetry had succumbed to the obscurities of the moderns: "Poets who write canti are intentionally obscure so that they can then write a commentary on their own verses. Imagine what pleasure people get from such stuff!" (Verzone, p. 407, vv. 1–6). The hermeticism of modern poetry relegated it to the academic circles and the common people for whom it was intended were incapable of understanding it. Of course, Grazzini is referring specifically to the canti carnascialeschi or popular carnival songs which had also felt the effect of literary technique. He ironically described the corruption of the canti carnascialeschi in a sonetto caudato written on the occasion of the presentation of the *Mascherata dell'ore:*

> This was certainly a wonderful canto and it was not tainted with pedantry. Ladies, a new god of love is now before you: his words are so weighty with wisdom that twelve lines seem a hundred. They are verses classically inspired and filled with knowledge culled from astrology. This is how

> canti should be written! Good riddance to the songs of chimney sweeps and cobblers! We prefer hermetic conceits full of obscure meanings, songs which are subtle and abstruse! [Verzone, pp. 110–11, i]

For Grazzini, Florence's past was reflected in her old carnival songs; they recorded the *joie de vivre* and the festive air which supposedly characterized the city under Laurentian rule. But Florence had since changed and so had her popular poetry. Utilizing the Renaissance *ubi sunt* theme, he expressed his nostalgia for Florence of the past and the poetry which it had inspired:

> Florence, what has become of those festivals and games which once delighted the lovely ladies? The youths of today have foresaken noble deeds and go about serenading in the dark. The god-like deeds of yesteryear are gone, and Florence, your money-hungry children have abandoned the carnival songs for serenades. [Verzone, Ottava XCIII, p. 423]

Grazzini attributes the corruption of poetry to the pedants and classicists who, in truth, can hardly be blamed for the inevitable decline and eventual disappearance of the carnival songs once the economic, social, and political environment in Florence no longer contributed to their sustenance. But he does so because of the particular affection in which he held popular poetry, not because he was unaware that the real fault of the pedants lay in their harmful influence on *poesia d'arte*. This, too, he criticized, but before we pass on to this subject, let us see how Grazzini contradicted his own statements regarding the canti carnascialeschi.

Grazzini, as I have observed, participated fully in the spirited activities of his contemporaries, and though he lived during the last years of Florentine prosperity, he witnessed many of the elegant and costly celebrations of the Medici. He numbered among his friends those who were responsible for their organization. It is not surprising, then, that he was taken with the pomp and lavishness of late Medicean pageantry, in which he could imagine a revival of tradition and, at times, a surpassing of all previous festivals. Consequently, he could praise the *Mascherata de' sogni* as "the gayest and most beautiful yet. I can hardly find words to praise the magnificence of the *carro* [the decorated float used for the parades]" (Verzone, p. 227, vv. 1–7).[10]

As indicated above, Grazzini polemicized against the corruptive influence exercised by the classicists and pedants on lyric poetry. In so doing he contributed to the tide of criticism that had been sweeping over the Petrarchists or Bembists. In his burlesque poetry he eulogized Berni, Ariosto (Verzone, pp. 366–67, 395–96), and Pulci (Verzone, pp. 440–41), with all of whom he felt an affinity of spirit—and cursed Petrarch's devastating influence on Italian letters:

> How ridiculous are your high-flown verses which imitate Petrarch's and make anyone who reads them burst with laughter! Even Petrarch's help cannot enrich what is essentially empty, so why don't you forget about your pretensions and get to work learning something? If you don't, you'll pay for it. [Verzone, p. 91, vv. 15–29]

This criticism is repeated throughout his poetry, if not openly, by the much more effective method of making a joke of the Petrarchists' style. He uses their prosaic lines and images to express the most banal sentiments. In almost any poem one can find an example of the use of this technique. (It is interesting, however, that Grazzini was particularly fond of repeating the Petrarchan line, "spero trovar pietà, non che perdono," ["I hope to be shown compassion and granted pardon"] for I find at least four versions of it in just a cursory glance at a few poems.[11]) Not only are verses and images taken from the Petrarchists, but their laments as well. But in the burlesque poetry they are laments over having become impotent or syphilitic or laments expressed upon the occasion of a prostitute's departure. And, as we find in Berni and the poetry of the following century, there are a few poems which enumerate the qualities of a woman with Laura's golden tresses and white teeth displaced by a disheveled head of hair and no teeth at all. Finally, the whole repertoire of the Petrarchists is reduced to ridicule in a poem such as the sixth capitolo. Borrowing from Petrarch's canzone "Standomi un giorno solo a la fenestra," ("Standing alone one day before my window") Grazzini substitutes for the symbolic vision of the poet, his own; it is the very unpoetic figure of Stradino who has come to revile the Aramei:

> Yesterday morning, I fell asleep while daydreaming in bed. In my sleep I saw the skies open wide and a light pour forth. The light enveloped a blessed soul whom I recognized and addressed: "Welcome, Consagrata [Stradino]." Rejoicing that I recognized him, he turned to me and with the voice of a lovely swan he said, "Continue doing me honor and pay no heed to malicious tongues." [Verzone, p. 481, vv. 1–18]

In several poems of this nature (in which, however, the game of absurdities is not carried to such lengths) Grazzini places ridiculous figures in a vision and satirizes the very basis of Petrarchist sentiment which would equate a woman with angelic beings.

Grazzini's attitude toward the Petrarchists is part of the anti-academic position which he assumed throughout his burlesque poetry. For him, Petrarchism was just one manifestation of the stagnancy which characterized the thinking of literary men who convened in academic circles to display their learning. The discussion in Chapter I of Grazzini's vehement polemics with members of the Accademia Fiorentina suffices to show how scornfully he looked upon organizations which propagated erudition for its own sake. This does not mean, however, that Grazzini was not interested in much of what went on within academic circles. He himself contributed to the discussions which raged, for example, over problems of language reform and showed himself to be acquainted with the positions taken by illustrious men in the debates over the superiority of the Florentine dialect:

> Trissino, a good and scholarly man, justly called it Italian, taking his authority from Dante. Sannazzaro called it Tuscan and Bembo, that man of profound learning, was the first to call it the Florentine language. [Verzone, p. 361, vv. 25–32]

It is not surprising that Grazzini favored the dialect of his own city. Although he alternately calls it Tuscan and Florentine, he makes it clear that he does not consider the speech of neighboring cities any more pleasant than the barking of dogs (Verzone, p. 362, vv. 49–56). To illustrate further the polemical quality of Grazzini's poetry, we should note that the following lines in praise of the Florentine dialect are from a canto carnascialesco, a genre which was normally reserved for less important considerations.

> We all write in that most sweet and lovely language, Tuscan —or better yet, Florentine—a language which, because of your three great men [Dante, Boccaccio, and Petrarch], is known and respected in both Rome and Greece. [Verzone, pp. 178–79, vv. 4–11]

Personal resentment significantly influenced Grazzini's attitude toward the academicians. He not only held them responsible for the demise of the Umidi, but he also felt that he had long been persecuted by men more learned than he. Undoubtedly his distaste was tinged with envy and a feeling of persecution. In his burlesque poetry the *pedante* and the *pedagogo* become more than representatives of the academic circles; they often lose all association with erudition and become a force which stands in opposition to Grazzini. The times, for example, that Grazzini blames them for stealing a friend are too numerous to cite. One poem in particular, addressed to Donatello's statue of St. George, reveals the extent of his bitterness against the pedants.

> Come, my verses, and help me sing the praises of St. George's beautiful limbs. No one can compare to him and I ask God to bless Donatello for having created such a beautiful lad who will never change. And I shall not have to search constantly for new god-like creatures and suffer because of them; the Aramei will not deprive me of St. George as they did of those other two lights of my eyes. [Verzone, pp. 528–29, vv. 88–105]

In the burlesque poetry, polemic is not confined to the academies and their members, but extends to a variety of subjects, including one which is of particular interest to us: the writing and performance of the comedy. Grazzini documents the lively competition which existed among his contemporaries in their attempt to gain renown for their work (Verzone, Ottave CII, pp. 430–31 and XCV, pp. 424–26), but more important for the history of the Renaissance comedy, he describes the state of comedy during the period in which the commedia dell'arte was gaining popularity. He bemoans the fact that the modern comedy had weakened to the point where the intermezzi became of more interest to the public than the comedy itself (Verzone, Madrigal XX, p. 229), and that they were plagued by "long-winded things that . . . provide little pleasure and less laughter" (Verzone, p. 207).[12] At the same time that he laments the failures of modern writers of comedy, he praises the Zanni, those early performers of the commedia dell'arte, whose performances had begun to replace in the affection of the populace the stale plots of the *commedia erudita*.[13]

> Poets have really done themselves in this time: the Zanni have been so successful that the scholarly comedy writers

> might as well go hang themselves. All our Florentine comedy writers are crying bitter tears: Buonanni, the Cini, Cecchi, and all the rest of the literati, so long admired, are now just scorned and Lasca winks his eye and grins. [Verzone, p. 430]

Grazzini's affection for the Zanni is evident in his own plays in which, by the attention given to the quick dialogue between servants and the use of jargon, we can see that he incorporated many elements of the commedia dell'arte.

Grazzini polemicizes against too many aspects of his society and culture for me to be able to include them all in this discussion. Many have already been mentioned in the consideration of the vita fiorentina in his works (doctors, courtesans, priests, and moral corruption), and others which I have not mentioned (soldiers and social niceties among them) follow in the tradition of Berni and do not shed any new light on the subject under study.

I have spent considerable time on the polemical nature of the burlesque poetry because it is the very essence of Grazzini's inspiration. When he is not polemicizing, one can feel an absence of purpose and the poems fall either into nostalgic reminiscences (which are certainly not alien to his polemics, either) or into exercises in technique which demonstrate his facility with language and flights of fancy but which show, as well, a lack of poetic substance.

One example of the former is a madrigalessa addressed to Piero Cellini, a particularly lyrical poem in which Grazzini laments the destruction of the Ponte Santa Trinita by flood waters, doubly tragic because of the memories of the happy evenings it held.

> Pierone, I write to you with tears in my eyes. You probably know that the calm and clear Arno became a treacherous fury and overflowed its banks, flooding the surrounding countryside. It had no mercy, taking farms and houses, beasts and men alike. Little was left which did not feel the

> effects of its fury. But all this ruin would have been little had the Arno spared the bridge of Santa Trinita. It was there that all our friends, you and I, gathered: we'd stand and watch the stars till morning while Betto Arrighi pointed out the constellations. With other friends, too, I'd spend my days at the bridge and seldom did a day pass that I wouldn't walk by it and around it six times or more. Looking at it now, I weep and curse and feel such grief that I can hardly contain myself. The only hope which sustains me is that one day it will rise again, more beautiful than ever. [Verzone, Madrigalessa XL, pp. 307–9]

A poem such as this makes all the more clear how much of Grazzini's own life and experiences went into novelle like the one about Guasparri del Calandra.

In a letter to Lionardo della Fonte, Grazzini stated that the primary function of his verse was to entertain and to provoke laughter. For this reason it was necessary that he give particular attention to the effect of his language and his "conceits." By "conceits" we might understand him to mean the poetic absurdities which he created by juxtaposing inappropriate subjects and styles. The conceits came from a fantasy which was able to combine nonpoetic subjects with traditional poetic devices for a surrealistic and grotesque effect. Hence the importance of sleep to Grazzini's creative process: the irrational and illogical products of the dream world are often the basis of his inspiration for he tries (or he purports to try) to recapture them in his verse: "to laugh because of the delight of the conceits, over the way in which they are arranged and stated, thinking of how, while sleeping, one can chance upon words and rhymes so fitting to the material and so observant of the requisites of poetry" (Verzone, Dedication of Canzone III, p. 143). For Grazzini, the humor of his verse depends upon a distortion of reality into irrational relationships and upon the flagrant abuse of classical and humanist concepts of poetry and poetic material. In short, much of the humor depends upon the unexpected. Of course, Grazzini's unconventionality is derived primarily from two things: first, his novel subject matter is a free imitation of Francesco Berni's, and, second, his rejection of poetic theories in favor of a more personal style was meant to antagonize the classicists. But now, several centuries later, we recognize in Grazzini's style more than just a means of ridiculing his enemies and of causing laughter; in it we find the embryo of later poetics and poetry. In his taste for the trivial, the grotesque, and the word for its own sake we see what Riccardo Scrivano, in his essay on Vasari, called the manneristic or prebaroque elements of Cinquecento style and a foreshadowing of the poetry which would, in the seventeenth century, be categorized as Marinista.[14] We see, too, in the intrusion of the personality of the poet into his poetry and in the importance given to fantasy, elements of a primitive romanticism. None of these elements which can be found in Grazzini's poetry was exclusive to him, of course, but their combined presence points up the fact that in his work we also find the tendency of the later sixteenth century away from Renaissance literary ideals toward new, but not necessarily superior, concepts of style which would align literature more closely with reality.

The major source of humor in Grazzini's poetry—just as in Berni's—lies in the contrast between the nonpoetic subject and the dignity of the style with which it is treated.[15] Two contending teams in a game of calcio take on the characteristics of two opposing armies in battle and the style becomes epic or mock-heroic:

> Come talor che fuor di muro, o tenda,
>   l'un esercito incontro all'altro è posto,
>   ch'ognuno aspetta ch'il nimico offenda,
> e sol gridi e minacce di discosto
>   s'odono allor; ma come il primo muove
>   gli altri di poi gli seguon dietro tosto:
> così costoro accinti all'alte prove,
>   sospesi stan mirando ognuno attento
>   come al nimico nuoca ed a sè giove.
>
> [Verzone, p. 532, vv. 118–26]

> (As two armies, outside the city walls and beyond their camps, face to face, prepare to do battle and the one waits upon the other to attack, in such a way are they [the players] prepared for wondrous deeds, looking fixedly at the enemy to weaken his strength and increase their own.)

An owl, certainly one of the most unpoetic birds imaginable, is the object of the poet's love in a four-part madrigal which mixes Petrarchan and Dantesque lines for one of Grazzini's most flagrant abuses of the Renaissance lyric:

Quanta dolcezza, Amore,
  sentir mi festi allor che dormendo io
  tener mi parea in braccio il gufo mio!
  Ma mentre ch'io 'l mirava intento e fiso
  e ch'io voleva al delicato viso
  ed a' begli occhi suoi chiari e vivaci
  dar mille e mille baci,
  il sonno e 'l gufo sparvero in un tratto;
  ond'io forte gridando come matto
  dissi: o fortuna porca, o destin ladro,
  deh! chi m'ha tolto il mio gufo leggiadro?
  Oh sonno traditore,
  che per dar qualche requie al mio dolore
  potevi, e per ristoro de' miei danni,
  farmi dormire almeno otto, o dieci anni!
Nel mezzo del cammin della sua vita
  il mio bel gufo pien d'amore e fede
  renduto ha l'alma a chi quaggiù la diede;
  e senza più girare
  or quinci, or quindi le sue luci chiare,
  senza più dimostrarne
  gli atti suoi vaghi e darne
  alto piacer colle sue divin'opre,
  poca terra lo cuopre;
  ma io, della sua dolce vista privo,
  morto non son, nè son restato vivo;
  e però con ragione,
  lontan dalle persone,
  senz'aver giamai più pace, o conforto

Pl. 1. Antonfrancesco Grazzini, "il Lasca." From Carlo Verzone, ed., *Rime Burlesche*.

Pl. 2. Device of Accademia Fiorentina, from Salvino Salvini, *I Fasti consolari dell'Accademia Fiorentina* (1717).

Pl. 3. An idealized version of a Renaissance banquet, from the first edition of Cristoforo di Messisbugo's *Banchetti*.

Pl. 4. An idealized sixteenth-century kitchen, from Cristoforo di Messisbugo's *Banchetti*.

TVTTI I TRIONFI,
CARRI, MASCHERATE
ò canti Carnaſcialeſchi
andati per Firenze,
Dal tẽpo del Magnifico Lorenzo vecchio
de Medici; quãdo egli hebbero prima cominciamẽto, per infino à
queſto anno preſente 1559.
Con due tauole, vna dinanzi, e vna
dietro, da trouare agieuolmen
te, e toſto ogni Canto, ò
Maſcherata.

INCLITA PROLES

IN·FIORENZA
MDLVIIII.

Pl. 5. Title page of the 1559 edition of the *Canti carnascialeschi*.

ne vo piangendo il mio bel gufo morto;
e quasi ad ogni passo,
tenendo il capo basso,
a Giove chieggio, sospirando forte,
il mio gufo, o la morte.
[Verzone, pp. 239–40]

(Love, with how much sweetness you filled me as I slept and seemed to hold my owl in my arms. But as I stared at it, longing to cover it with kisses, it disappeared with sleep and I awoke shouting, "Cursed fortune! Who took my lovely owl?" Oh traitorous sleep, you who could give peace to my grief by keeping me under your spell for eight to ten years! Midway in its life, my loving owl rendered up its soul; no longer casting his loving glances nor blessing me with his divine movements, he is covered with earth. But I am neither dead nor alive, and I shun human contact to weep over my poor dead owl. With head held low and with measured steps, I, sighing plaintively, ask Jove for my owl or death.)

In the same way, Grazzini sings in praise of a pig, "sweet and gentle pig, the best of all animals, most desired by diners" (Verzone, p. 460, vv. 40–42).

From the point of view of language—or more particularly, vocabulary—Grazzini selected words for their auditory value. And since he wrote burlesque poetry, their value was directly proportionate to their comic effect. Consequently, the word "salsiccia" (sausage), both for its sibilant qualities and then for the phallic image which it suggests, is what Grazzini would call "a word to be enjoyed" (Verzone, p. 461, v. 60). But his interest in words is often disastrous to his poetry, for it lures him into entire stanzas of rhymes ("Ma buon per voi, che sete dotto ed atto/ a ogni cosa, e che dite e che fate/ e promettete e date/ e portate e donate/ e correte e saltate,/ pescate ed uccellate,/ ponete e trapiantate") and into testing his virtuosity with repetitions ("non è lungo lungo, o corto corto,/ nè dura troppo troppo, o poco poco"), suffixes ("cani, cagnacci, canuzzi e canini"), and puns ("Or dunque, Doni, che pro vi faccia,/ ricevete il capitol ch'io vi dono,/ ed accettatel con allegra faccia;/ perchè far non vi posso maggior dono") to the point of monotony. With such importance given to the value of the word, it does not surprise us that Grazzini, in his evaluation of the *Orlando Furioso*, gave more credit to the imaginative quality of Ariosto's names than to the poetic material:

> It is because the invention is more charming and lovely [than that of other romances of chivalry], that it is read and heard with such delight by all people. But greater strength and power lie in its peerless names; Ariosto's names will assure him everlasting glory. Agricane, Mandricardo, Agramante, Gradasso, Sacripante, and Rodomonte; Doralice, Marfisa, and Bradamante; the houses of Mongrana and Chiaramonte—names which surpass all others! Carlo, Ruggiero, Rinaldo, and the Count Orlando are names of such grace and joy that they would make even an old hag seem lovely and beautiful. [Verzone, p. 366]

In a consideration of Grazzini's facility with language, we must again speak of the extensive use which he made of the double entendre. To a devotee of popular poetry, this device came easily: Berni and the lesser known burlesque poets were masters of its use and, as Singleton has observed, it was the basis of the Florentine carnival song. It was a literary device, to continue with Singleton's observations, which perhaps owed its major stimulus to Boccaccio and consequently infiltrated all literary forms, the novelle no more than others.[16] As monotonous as this aspect of Renaissance literature can become and as valueless as it usually is, one must acknowledge the ingenuity of an author like Grazzini who was able to take the most uninteresting of items and find in them the source of obscene allusions. Many critics have found in this preoccupation with obscenity a reflection of the moral degeneracy of the period. Although there is a large element of truth in their observations, we must realize, too, that particularly by the sixteenth century, obscenities in literature were no more than ends in themselves, their shock value having been lost through overuse. The double entendre became a means by which one writer tested his wit against another's and, especially in the case of burlesque poets, was perhaps no more significant than was the Petrarchan phrase to the lyricist. Even a casual reading of the capitoli and the canti carnascialeschi will show that Grazzini was as adept at the art as any of his contemporaries.

To conclude these observations on the burlesque poetry, I must again emphasize its importance to an understanding of Grazzini as a writer who, in his conflicting sympathies with the popular literature of the past and the growing dissatisfaction with all tradition, represents the confused state of literary ideals in the later sixteenth century. When, in his burlesque poetry, Grazzini employs the Renaissance themes of carpe diem or expresses the humanist desire for the peace and tranquillity of a rustic life, we see him still under the influence of a tradition which, in other moments, he reviles. Grazzini, like others of his contemporaries, expresses the inevitable contradictions of sentiment and attitudes in all aspects of life when a deeply ingrained culture, such as humanism then was, is shaken by doubts and dissension without having yet been replaced by equally strong cultural forces.

The Petrarchan Lyrics and the Eclogues

As was stated at the beginning of this chapter, Grazzini was no more able than the rest of his contemporaries to avoid completely Petrarch's overwhelming influence, strengthened by the adulation of Pietro Bembo, upon the poetry of the sixteenth century. Like many followers of Berni—who, Giovanni Laini says, had entered the arena of poetry as Petrarchists—

Grazzini contributed his share to the plethora of poems which bore the stamp of the master of the Italian lyric.[17]

To date, no one has given Grazzini's serious verse more than cursory consideration. His most interested critic and editor, Giovanni Grazzini, dismisses it for its lack of inspiration and for the total absence of those personal qualities which enliven the burlesque poetry.[18] In a study such as the present the serious poetry must be taken into account because, although it is apparently contrary to the genuine literary interests of Grazzini, it attests to his academic experiences. Grazzini was much more familiar with the classical traditions of Italian poetry than is generally assumed. The poetry also documents the close relationship which must have existed between him and one of the most significant academic and literary figures of his day, Benedetto Varchi, whom Grazzini called his second master (Petrarch being his first). Luigi Baldacci has, in fact, commented on the obvious influence of Varchi's pastoral poetry on Grazzini's sonnets, and other critics of the period have noted that Grazzini's ambivalent attitude toward the Bembists might well have been conditioned by his changing relationship with Varchi, who represented for him both the insularity of the academic mind and the truly inspired poet.[19]

The only edition of Grazzini's Petrarchan poetry is that which Domenico Poggiali compiled at the end of the eighteenth century, at a time when the author's work was being unearthed from the Florentine archives for publication.[20] This edition, which could be supplemented by other poems since discovered, contains the eight eclogues which, at the insistence of Lionardo Salviati, Grazzini had submitted to the censors of the Accademia Fiorentina in 1566 to seek readmission. It also contains several sonnets, madrigals, and ottave, most of which are akin to the poems found in the many Petrarchan canzonieri of the sixteenth century. In addition, Poggiali included several of the burlesque poems which, of course, are to be found in Verzone's critical edition of the following century.

Of the poems which are included in Poggiali's edition, the most striking are the eclogues, because of all Grazzini's poems, they are the least suggestive of the author's literary experiences and of what we know of his personality. As a literary genre, the eclogue would normally reflect the refined literary tastes of the courts or, at least, of a man steeped in classical tradition. But Grazzini was alien to an environment (and, as far as we know, a training) which would be conducive to the pastoral genres, and we cannot help but feel that in writing the eclogues he was again testing his abilities to compete with the academicians and trying to still those voices which doubted his competence as a serious poet.

Of the eight eclogues, the first two are occasional pieces written to commemorate the marriage of Cosimo de' Medici and to mourn the death of a Florentine woman who remains nameless. The first is a dialogue in hendecasyllables between two shepherds, Mosso and Titiro, who, in the prosaic style of the Renaissance pastoral epithalamium, intone a prayer to the gods, asking that the marriage be blessed with offspring worthy of carrying on the illustrious name of the family. In a rare (for him) instance of commentary on the political turmoil of sixteenth-century Florence, Grazzini expresses his hopes that Cosimo's marriage will bring new possibilities for a future of lasting peace, so that Florence "will unburden herself of grief and woe . . . and . . . will soon become more rich and beautiful than ever" (Poggiali, p. 9). The second of the occasional eclogues is a dialogue in unrhymed hendecasyllables between Tirsi and Silvano, whose joy over the coming of spring is overshadowed by the memory of Amaranta, who recently died in childbirth. The elegiac subject is treated entirely according to the tradition of the Petrarchan lament over the passing of Laura from this world:

> Quante volte vid'io dai suoi begli occhi
> Scender lume cotal, ch'a mezzo il giorno

Scurava il Sole, e la pallida notte
Tornar via più che 'l dì lucida e chiara!
. . . .
Deh come al muover dei suoi dolci passi
Verde la terra farsi, e fiorir l'erba
Vidd'io più volte, e l'acqua viata e torba
Limpida divenir, placida e queta!
[Poggiali, p. 17]

(How often have I seen from her eyes come a light which, at midday, made pale the sun and which made dark night more brilliant than the clearest day! . . . Oh, how often have I seen her sweet steps make green the earth upon which she walked, and, as she passed, [make] flowers bloom and [make] water, once swirling and turbid, clear and calm!)

The remaining six eclogues do not bear any dedicatory inscription, and, as far as one can tell, were written in the tradition of the classical eclogue to express the universal suffering of the lover who is rejected by the object of his love:[21] in Eclogue III, Melibeo bemoans his fate at the hands of Amarilli who flees from him "more quickly than a gentle lamb from a ferocious wolf"; in Eclogue VI, Siringa makes a sacrifice to Venus so that Ghiacinto, "having become less haughty, hateful, and angry, will return to me as sweet, generous, courteous, and humble as before"; and in Eclogue VIII, Tirsi's desperation over his unrequited love for Lidia compels him to drown himself in the Arno whose waters, as he sinks in their depths, continue to murmur the name of his beloved.

The only possible attraction which poetry of this type could have had for Grazzini was the facility with which it lent itself to the bravura of poetic technique. If we look carefully at an extended simile (Eclogue V), we can see not only a reflection of those poetic images which were drawn from Petrarch's verse, but also an early example of that virtuosity which was to characterize later poetry and which was to bring such damning judgment down upon it. Tirsi sings of the beauties of Lidia in a song whose opening strophe is one long, hyperbolic, unbalanced simile. In the following four strophes, the poet continues to elaborate upon the attributes of the lady and then, in the sixth and final strophe, he refuses to acknowledge the beauties of nature upon which he has drawn for his comparison. They all suffer by comparison with Lidia.[22]

In the more than eighty sonnets and assorted madrigals and canzoni which follow in Poggiali's edition, we again find the themes of the eclogues (lamentations over unrequited love and the swift passing of beauty and pleasures) expressed in the same stylized manner of the sixteenth-century Petrarchists.

> Take pleasure, dear shepherd, in the longed-for fruits of your love, worthy rewards of the third heaven, so that when you are old you will not be filled with grief over that which can never be recaptured. [Poggiali, Sonnet XXIV, p. 88]

We also find the poet exhibiting his bravura in the manner of his successors, the Marinisti, who would have especially appreciated the following canzone (addressed to Bernardo da Diacceto) in which the poet compares his subject to the sun:

> Ardeano insieme a prova
> L'un dell'altro bel Sole innamorato,
> E quello avea la nuova
> Aurora, e questo Amore innanellato
> Crin vago almo dorato, e questo e quello
> Oro sì dolce ardea,
> Che l'un l'altro parea:
> Mai non viddi io sì bello
> Il ciel, nè spero ancor di rivedello.
>
> Erasi al Sole il mio bel Sole assiso
> Che pari altri non truova,
> E l'un ver l'altro a pruova,
> Sciolto il biondo oro suo di paradiso,
> Si specchiava nel viso del suo Sole,
> E'n questo specchio, e'n quello
> Si rivedea sì bello,
> Ch'al mio Sole parea d'essere il Sole,
> Ed al Sole il mio Sole.
> . . . .
> [Poggiali, pp. 129–30]

> (They competed with each other in brilliance, the one Sun enamored of the other. And that one [the sun] was encircled by the dawn and the other [the lady], with golden tresses, was crowned by Love. And the golden ring of both burned so sweetly that one seemed like the other. Never did I see the sky so beautiful, nor can I hope to see it so again. My Sun, who has no equal, her heavenly golden tresses falling loose about her shoulders, was seated in the Sun and they vied with each other. Each was reflected in its Sun and appeared so lovely that my Sun seemed to be the Sun and the Sun to be my Sun.)

Grazzini's pastoral-Petrarchan lyrics, in no way inferior to many which were written in the sixteenth century and often more capably handled than most,[23] are not only indicative of the poet's academic experiences and the strong influence of the literary circles of the period, but they are, too, as is so much of Grazzini's work, a reflection of a change which was occurring within literature itself. The pastoral settings, for example, lose much of the tranquillity which is found in the classical bucolic and foreshadow the sensual, naturalistic pastorals of Tasso and later poets. The style reflects the growing taste for pure linguistic virtuosity which, when it was used by less capable poets than Tasso, disintegrated into mere bravado.

CHAPTER IV

THE COMEDIES

ACCORDING to the *Tavola delle opere* which he compiled in 1566, Grazzini had already written six of the seven comedies which we now possess. *L'Arzigogolo* was probably written at a later date and it remained unpublished until the eighteenth century. Included in the 1566 catalogue are several dramatic works which were never published and have since been lost. Among them are four *commedie spirituali—La Croce, o santa Helena; Santa Appollonia; Santa Caterina; Santa Orsola*—which, Grazzini informs us, were written in prose. These spiritual dramas probably employed popular Florentine proverbs and metaphors and undoubtedly had much in common with the moral comedies of Grazzini's contemporary, Giovan Maria Cecchi.[1] Of the three farces listed in the catalogue, only *Il Frate* has survived in its entirety. All that remains of *La Monica* is its prologue; and, according to Gentile's theory, later discussed, *La Giostra* formed the basis of Grazzini's last comedy, *L'Arzigogolo*. Finally, Grazzini lists a *commedia regolare* entitled *Il Pedante* which, for a reason he does not disclose, he destroyed.[2] In this chapter I shall consider each of the six comedies which were first published together in the

Giunti edition of 1582 (see Appendix II), also *L'Arzigogolo*, which remained in manuscript until the eighteenth century, and, finally, the farce, *Il Frate*.

Structurally, each of the seven comedies has the traditional five acts of the commedia erudita and is preceded by one or more prologues. The prologues are often polemical in nature and serve to present the author's opinions on how the modern comedy should be written. In some instances the prologue recalls the *proemio* to a collection of novelle because it invites the complicity of the ladies and attempts to establish an immediate rapport between the author and his audience.[3] However, unlike the prologues of Plautine tradition, those which introduce Grazzini's comedies seldom describe the foregoing action of the play, a function reserved for the opening scenes of the first act. In the first and second acts, the playwright introduces his characters and prepares the audience for the central episode of the comedy—usually a beffa played on a gullible old man. The beffa is dramatized in the third act and since, as we shall see, the beffa was of greater interest to the author than were any of his characters or complex plots, once the beffatori succeed in their scheme the remaining acts—or the denouement—have little dramatic interest.

Even while relying on the traditional structure of the erudite comedy, Grazzini showed that he was little adept at dramatic technique. He gave little consideration to the overall effect of the comedy, to the possibilities of dramatic contrasts and to the interplay of motifs. The comedies often seem to have been constructed scene by scene so that the merit of any one comedy is attributable to particular dialogues or episodes and seldom to the play as a whole.[4] This weakness of structure or lack of dramatic unity is particularly noticeable, for example, in *L'Arzigogolo*, where there are two main lines of action, each so divorced from the other that the one is concluded before the other begins.

Only in exceptional cases is Grazzini any more successful in developing his characters than he is in handling the dramatic architecture. The characters, usually stereotypes taken from the classical or Renaissance comedy, fail to gain any dimension as personalities for they always remain subordinate to the action of the play. They function to create the bourgeois milieu of the play but they lack the individuality which a great playwright such as Molière managed to give to his characters even when borrowing from classical sources.

Despite this fundamental weakness, common to most of the learned comedies of the Italian Renaissance, Grazzini's comedies have a particular significance. First of all, they reflect a tendency in the Florentine theatre of the sixteenth century to combine the classical elements of the erudite comedy with the farcical elements of the popular theatre and, by the addition of the customs and attitudes of the contemporary bourgeois society, to create an art form which would capture the spirit of modern life.[5] In this respect Florentine comedy shows a particular indebtedness to the tradition of the novella, from which it borrowed its attempt to represent the tempo of contemporary life, tastes, and activities. Just as Boccaccio had woven into the fabric of his *Decameron* the very essence of Florentine society as it emerged from the Middle Ages into the new mercantilism of the early Renaissance, so the Florentine theatre of the sixteenth century strove to capture the life of the burgher in his own society.[6] Such an attempt, however, was fated to produce only limited success in a theatre which so slavishly imitated traditional themes and character-types. The Italian theatre had to await the genius of Goldoni to become an effective means by which to portray contemporary mores. Even during the late Renaissance the novella remained the genre best suited to such a task, and for this reason Grazzini reaches the height of his artistry in the *Cene*. As one critic has stated, Grazzini's comedies are in many ways preparatory to the prose of his novelle.[7]

In the glorification of the culture and the language of the

Florentine people in Grazzini's comedies, one can again discern his polemical spirit. His theatre has, in fact, been criticized for being intolerably Florentine.[8] Yet the spirit which manifests itself when characters marvel at the beauties of the city, for example, or when they use local expressions and criticize neighboring dialects, is important. For it places these comedies among the most interesting examples of that literature which actively tried to keep alive Florentine particularist traditions and spirit at a time of social decline and cultural suffocation.[9]

La Gelosia

The merit of Grazzini's earliest play, *La Gelosia*, rests in a few particularly humorous scenes and in the depiction of Lazzero, a disgruntled old man who becomes the victim of a plot to prevent his marriage to the young Cassandra. The comedy suffers from a lack of unity: there are numerous scenes which contribute nothing to the development of the main action which, I must add, differs so markedly from the first to the second half of the play that it is only in the final scenes that the threads of the action are somewhat haphazardly tied together.[10]

The complex plot concerns a young man, Pierantonio, who is in love with Cassandra but who is unable to marry her since the girl's father, Giovacchino, has promised her to Lazzero in exchange for the cancellation of some debts. Cassandra's brother, Alfonso, together with a servant, Ciullo, plot against Lazzero in favor of Pierantonio. Alfonso is motivated by his hopes of marrying Camilla, the niece of Lazzero. The plot involves disguising Orsola, a servant girl, as Cassandra and having her keep a tryst with Pierantonio—a meeting witnessed by Lazzero, disguised as the brother of Ciullo. Lazzero denounces Cassandra and all women for their infidelity. As a consequence of his having remained in the open air, scantily dressed, Lazzero is overcome by chills and is shown into Giovacchino's house where he is locked in a courtyard to suffer the cold some more. In the meanwhile, Alfonso gains entrance into the bedroom of Camilla and pledges his troth. The resolution of the plot is in keeping with tradition: Camilla and Alfonso must stay married and Cassandra, no longer able to bring honor to Lazzero's house, is given to Pierantonio.

The major weakness of this comedy—not readily noticeable from the sketchy summary above—is its structure. In the traditional manner, the opening scene of the play puts us immediately into the action: Alfonso is instructing the disguised Orsola to remain hidden until she has been signalled that the masquerade is to begin. In the second scene, by means of an extremely detailed conversation between Alfonso and Filippo (who, incidentally, never appears again), the audience is provided with the information necessary to understand the action as it develops. Until the end of the third act, with the exception of a few digressions, the action proceeds in a logical and rectilinear way: Lazzero sees Cassandra (Orsola) and Pierantonio together, inveighs against them, and then takes refuge in Giovacchino's house. The last two acts, which concern Alfonso's entry into Lazzero's house, are marred by confusion and a complete lack of dramatic unity. The confusion arises from Grazzini's having failed to clarify Alfonso's plans beforehand. In I, ii, Alfonso barely alludes to the action of the last two acts: "Much more will be done for me, being in love as I am with Lazzero's niece, Camilla; Ciullo tells me he's thought up I-don't-know-what trick so that this night will be a happy one for me." What Grazzini perhaps intended as dramatic surprise by saving all explanations until the final scenes leaves one, rather, with the unsatisfying feeling that the author was not clear as to how he could best resolve the action. The unity of the entire play is disturbed, first, by not having what amounts to the plot and subplot well integrated and, second, by having the plot carefully explained at the beginning of the play and the subplot only carelessly explained at the end.

The imbalance caused by the relatively well-constructed first three acts and the poorly constructed final acts is aggravated by the introduction of scenes and dialogues which detract from the development of the action. Yet this extraneous material does have a function in the play. On the one hand, it is meant to explain further the action. In many instances, however, it is a repetition of what had been explained before or what is self-evident. For example, the comic scene between Orsola, in disguise, and her mistress, Zanobia, who has discovered her (II, ii) is described to Alfonso by his servant Muciatto (II, iv) in a scene which is three times as long as the one which it is describing. On the other hand, many of the incidental scenes serve to stimulate the interest of the audience, whose attention might have lagged while attempting to follow the labyrinthine plot. These are often the most successful scenes in Grazzini's plays, since their humor depends on a rapid exchange of clever dialogue and not on situations and mistaken identities which were already tiresomely familiar to everyone. These scenes will later be discussed in more detail.

The central figure of *La Gelosia* is Lazzero, a reinterpretation of the old man of the classical comedy, the cynic drained of all human passion, whose only concern is to maintain the honor of his name. For this reason, the title of Grazzini's play is most inappropriate. Nowhere in the dialogue does Lazzero show any sign of jealousy at the unfaithfulness of Cassandra. Upon witnessing the meeting of Cassandra (Orsola) and Pierantonio, his reaction is one of surprise and relief that he had been fortunate enough to save the honor of his house: "Now I've really seen and discovered something which I would have preferred not to have seen or found out; yet I'm happy on the one hand, having lifted such infamy from my house" (III, x).

And he immediately begins to compare the precautions which he has taken to protect his niece, Camilla, with the careless manner with which Giovacchino has raised his daughter. If Lazzero's reactions are not in keeping with the title of the comedy, he himself is entirely consonant with the prototype upon which his character is based.

The humor of the scenes in which Lazzero appears is of a type common to the Renaissance comedy. It is provided by the incongruity of the man's character with the role which he must assume. Lazzero is stern, sententious, and fond of complaining, but, in order to verify the accusations made against Cassandra, he must assume the role of a conspirator in her meetings with Pierantonio. Having disguised himself as Ciullo's brother and being unaware that his identity is known, he must submit to ridicule as his fellow conspirators take the opportunity of joking about his virility. To protect his disguise, he cannot defend himself and must endure increasingly humiliating punishment which is climaxed by a night in the cold and the final irony of having his well-protected niece marry without his consent. This final humiliation concludes the comedy with justice, as conceived by the Renaissance writer of comedy, triumphant: youth and its passions are always in the right.

In *La Gelosia* an attempt at dramatic unity is made through the use of disguises, with Lazzero in his disguise as the brother of Ciullo being the central figure. He is complemented by two additional disguised figures: Orsola, of course, masquerading as Cassandra and, in the final acts, Alfonso disguising himself as Lazzero in order to gain access into the old man's house. Not only does the development of the action depend upon these masqueraders, but each contributes to heighten the irony of the play's resolution. First, Lazzero is deceived by Orsola at his own game. He is convinced that she is Cassandra but *everyone* is aware who *he* really is. Then, having left his own clothing at Alfonso's disposal, Lazzero falls victim to a trick for which he has unwittingly provided the materials. Unfortunately, this interplay of ironies loses much of its potential dramatic effect by the play's loose construction.

Needless to say, *La Gelosia* is heavily indebted to tradition. Its characters are derived from the stock of young lovers (Alfonso and Pierantonio), clever servants (Ciullo and Mucciatto) and foolish old men (Lazzero and Giovacchino) who are present in most comedies of the period. Its plot can be traced to several sources, among them earlier comedies and the *Orlando Furioso*.[11] Consequently, Grazzini's originality and inspiration are most apparent in those few scenes which are not an integral part of the comedy but which provide a diversion from the complexities of the plot and the prosaic dialogue. These scenes are usually given over to the servants or to a servant and his master. Their humor is either of a slapstick variety approaching the technique of the commedia dell'arte or else it is provided by witty dialogue and plays on words. Among the most effective in *La Gelosia* is the brief scene between Zanobia and Orsola (II, ii) when, to deceive her mistress, who has discovered her in Cassandra's clothes, the frightened Orsola pretends to be sleepwalking:

Zanobia. Oh, dear Lord! What's this? Orsola? Orsola?

Orsola. Uum, muum, uuum.

Zanobia. Orsola, can't you hear me? Are you asleep? Are you dreaming? Are you delirious? You little fool! You seem to have lost control of yourself! Oh, dear me! She's wearing my daughter's very best dress! Now Orsola, just what are you up to? Have you gone mad? Why, tell me, just why and who it was who dressed you in Cassandra's clothes? She's not answering just to spite me. Orsola, I warn you!

Orsola. Uum . . . what is it? I'm sleeping . . . sleeping . . .

Zanobia. Just what do you mean "sleeping," you little beast? Tell me how you happen to be dressed like this! What are you up to?

Orsola. Of all times! I was sleeping so well and now you have awakened me!

Another example is the scene between the two servants of Lazzero, Agnesa and Riccio, who bicker over whether Riccio should leave the house and Camilla unprotected (III, i). When Agnesa calls Riccio "una frittella, frittellina, frittelluzza" ("a fritter, a little fritter, a cute little fritter") we are reminded of the burlesque poetry and the pleasure which Grazzini must have taken from such scenes of pure linguistic virtuosity.

La Spiritata

We already know that Grazzini's early comedies were first performed upon the occasion of a banquet given in honor of some illustrious person. As the author himself tells us in a prologue to *La Strega*, *La Spiritata* was first played at the house of Bernardetto de' Medici, who was honoring the prince of Florence and Siena, Don Francesco (1560). It was particularly suited to such an occasion: it is comparatively short and both the dialogue and the action are swift, while the plot is relieved of unnecessary complications.[12]

The title of the comedy refers to the young Maddalena, who has secretly married Giulio with the intention of later making the marriage public. Before the marriage has been made known, however, the young couple inform their fathers of their desire to marry. Niccodemo approves of his prospective son-in-law, but Giovangualberto, a wealthy but miserly old man, will not allow the marriage of his son to Maddalena without a dowry of 3,000 scudi. Unable to comply with Giovangualberto's demand, Niccodemo decides to give his daughter to Pietropagolo da Casa Nuova, who will marry her with a smaller dowry. Giulio and Maddalena must devise a scheme to force Giovangualberto's approval. Maddalena pretends to be possessed by an aerial spirit called Tintinnago, who refuses to leave unless she is allowed to marry the man of her choice. Simultaneously, Giulio, with the help of friends and servants, makes Giovangualberto believe that his own house is inhabited by evil spirits. Disguised as devils, they frighten the old man by making ghoulish sounds at night while he tries to sleep. A necromancer, Albizo, is called upon to exorcise these several spirits and, since he is sympathetic with Giulio's cause, declares that Tintinnago will not leave Maddalena until its demands are fulfilled, and that when the evil spirits, or cuccubeoni, leave Giovangualberto's house they will take with them his dearest possession. To Giovangualberto's dismay, this turns out to be three purses containing 3,300 scudi. In possession of his father's money, Giulio gives it to Daniello, Maddalena's uncle, so that he may loan it to Niccodemo for the dowry. Giovangualberto is only too happy to receive the money and declares that the marriage can take place.

This brief summary of the plot will suffice to show that *La Spiritata* borrows even more heavily from the traditional comedy than does *La Gelosia.* In addition to a pair of young lovers set upon outwitting their fathers, we find a necromancer and the fully developed character of a miser. No less, too, than its predecessor, *La Spiritata* relies on standard situations: a marriage opposed by a father, a secret ceremony, a possessed girl, and a house filled with spirits.

In some respects, however, *La Spiritata* is superior to the earlier play. Lacking the number of dramatic devices required of a more complex plot (*La Gelosia,* we recall, has three characters in disguise), the comedy is more compact and moves easily to its conclusion without the interruption of monotonous explanations. Grazzini's dramatic economy eliminates an extraneous character like Filippo in *La Gelosia* by working the necessary explanations into the plot: Trafela, a servant, relates the foregoing action to the necromancer, whose knowledge of the facts is vital to the development of the action. Also, in *La Spiritata* there is more character development. Giovangualberto is consistently in keeping with the role of a miser and reacts to any situation accordingly. The corruption of his character is particularly evident in V, i, when Niccodemo pleads with him to save his daughter by permitting the marriage:

Niccodemo. I ask you to consider both me and my daughter.

Giovangualberto. If you'll give me three thousand ducats as a dowry, everything will be as you wish; if not, neither you nor that spirit had better try anything!

Albizo. I'll leave all this up to you. . . .

Niccodemo. Did you hear that?

Giovangualberto. Idle chatter, master. I wouldn't be surprised if you are in on this with Niccodemo and the spirit! I don't want your advice. But if this spirit loves her so much, why doesn't *it* find the money? Go ahead, ask him that and let's be done with it.

Albizo. He's not the kind of spirit that can do such things. Otherwise, he certainly would.

Niccodemo. In other words, you're stubborn and you refuse to do this good for her and this pleasure for me.

Giovangualberto. Come on, give up the money. You know what's in your best interests.

Niccodemo. Oh, you wretched miser! You care more for money than for people. . . . If it weren't for her good and for the possibility of a cure, I wouldn't let you see her for anything.

Giovangualberto. As if there were any shortage of lovely young girls in this city!

On the other hand, Lazzero of *La Gelosia* is a weaker role, not so well characterized. Lazzero has the dramatic disadvantage of not possessing any vice except the cynicism of an old man, and the humor of his role depends heavily upon an exaggeration of his physical disabilities.

More significant, however, than *La Spiritata*'s greater unity and fuller development of the central character is its lack of dependence upon the plot to sustain interest. The situation in which Giulio and Maddalena find themselves is, as Gentile has shown, not very original. But for this comedy, the situation serves only as a pretext, and once he dispenses with the explanations in the early scenes, Grazzini gives himself over to more inspired comedy. The plot which we have outlined above is, in truth, a scenario of a type not completely unrelated to that of the improvised commedia dell'arte. Just as the arte consisted of improvisations built upon a previously established situation, so do the scenes of this play spring from a situation which, in the quick and witty dialogue, becomes of secondary importance. Grazzini's art, like the commedia dell'arte, depends heavily upon clever dialogue, often spoken in a colorful language based on Florentine idiom and dialect. The best scenes show the influence of the commedia dell'arte slapstick—a natural outcome of Grazzini's interest in the Zanni and the developing new comedy form, and in the effective use of language, and his disapproval of current comedy.[13]

La Spiritata abounds with examples of Grazzini's great command of a dialogue reminiscent of the commedia dell'arte. Often, as in the scene when Niccodemo and Giovangualberto are deciding who is to go first to investigate the spirits which are in the latter's house, the dialogue seems incomplete without the appropriate gestures of actors adept at mime:

Trafela. Go on up, you two. . . .
Niccodemo. I certainly think we should. . . .
Giovangualberto. Do you want to come?
Niccodemo. Certainly, if you'll come too, and together we'll see these miracles.
Giovangualberto. Fine! But you go on ahead.

Niccodemo.	No, no. You, the master of the house, should go first.
Giovangualberto.	In this instance, I'll let you have that honor.
Niccodemo.	You're afraid! That's all I need to see!
Giovangualberto.	You're the one who's afraid!
Niccodemo.	Come on! Let's go up together.
Giovangualberto.	Give me your hand. . . .
Trafela.	Just listen to that!
Giovangualberto.	Christ, let me out of here!
Niccodemo.	Dear Lord, help me!
Trafela.	What did I tell you!
Giovangualberto.	I'm dead!
Niccodemo.	And I'm certainly not alive! [IV, iii]

We find, as before, the gusto for words that is present in the burlesque poetry, and the same relish in manipulating language. Giovangualberto's dialogue is particularly colorful, with its malapropisms and nonsensical rhymes. In a crescendo of mistakes which arise from his mispronunciation of "cuccubeoni," he calls them first "cruscabeccni," and then "cacamusoni" and "cornamusoni" (V, iv). Upon hearing that he has been robbed, he exclaims: "Alas! Suddenly I was overcome by spasms, miasmas, phantasmas" (V, i). Albizo, too, is addicted to linguistic virtuosity:

> E a fine che voi intendiate meglio, gli spiriti sono di piú varie e diverse spezie, come ignei, aerei, acquatici, terrei, aurei, argentei, folletti, foraboschi, e forasiepi, amabili, dilettevoli, sociali, e vattene lá. . . . questi son quelli solamente della luce: ci restano gli spiriti delle tenebre, che sono demoni, diavoli, archi, streghe, tregende, setanassi, versiere, arpie, ermafroditi, lestrigoni e infiniti altri. [III, iii]

> (And so that you may better understand, there are many and diverse spirits such as igneous spirits, aerial spirits, aquatic spirits, earth spirits, argentous spirits, goblins, *foraboschi, forasiepi* [i.e., wrens and tiny beings capable of easily getting about], loving spirits, spritely spirits, social spirits,

> and it goes on and on. . . . these are only the spirits of light: there remain the spirits of the dark such as demons, devils, *archi*, witches, *tregende* [hordes of witches], devils, she-devils, harpies, hermaphrodites, Laestrygonians, and innumerable others.)

Close attention to Grazzini's dialogue reveals other examples of linguistic skill—intentional rhymes, for instance, as in Giovangualberto's words, quoted above ("asima . . . spasima . . . fantasima").

Grazzini's use of popular expressions and colloquialisms has been referred to earlier. In the following scene between two servants speaking in the idiom of the lower classes, we have one of *La Spiritata*'s most brilliant scenes. It employs a popular language together with the double entendres and quick wit of the type which was soon to supplant the erudite comedy.

Guagniele. Oh, oh! ecco appunto di qua questa rubacuori. . . . Ben ne venga il mio amore! Buon dí e buon anno, speranzina bella.

Lucia. Noi siam tutti rifatti! che vai tu facendo, Guagniele?

Guagniele. Torno d'un servizio pel padrone: ombé, hai tu diliberato però di farmi morire affatto affatto?

Lucia. Eh, eh; in mal'ora; tu faresti meglio a badare ai casi tuoi.

Guagniele. Questi sono i casi miei, traditoraccia; m'innamori, e poi te ne vai; anzi, mi hai ammaliato, e or fai le vista di non mi vedere.

Lucia. Io arei fatto una faccenda a pormi con un tuo pari! Che vuoi tu ch'io faccia di te, che sei povero e brutto?

Guagniele. Or hai tu ben mille torti: vottelo provare per via di ragione. E prima, in quanto al povero, tu non puoi rammaricarti di me, non mi avendo tu mai richiesto di nulla. In quanto al bello, egli è vero che io ho un po' mala incarnazione, ma il resto della persona non può esser me' fatto.

Lucia. Sì, per fantoccio da ceri.

Guagniele.	Guarda, braccia svelte! Vedi, mano dilicata! Pon mente, gamba schietta! Guarda, cosce membrute! Considera, petto largo! Dirò ch'io son tre braccia nelle spalle. Ma la importanza è come io son fornito bene a masserizia in panni lini, e come io son morbido sopra il giubbone: tasta un po', Lucia; da' qua la mano.
Lucia.	Doh, sciagurato! che non ti vergogni? Levamiti dinanzi in mal'ora.
Guagniele.	Se io fussi so ben io chi, tu non faresti cosí, Monnaschifalpoco.
Lucia.	Va' via, dico; non mi dar piú impaccio, bestia balorda.
Guagniele.	Ahi, anima del cuor mio, non ti adirar per questo.
Lucia.	Non odi tu ch'i'ho faccenda e fretta?
Guagniele.	Faccenda e fretta ho io, che sono aspettato.
Lucia.	Orsú, ognun vada a farla.
Guagniele.	Io son disposto di venir teco un pezzo.
Lucia.	Meco non verrai tu: non vedi che io son giá a casa? Uh, uh! questa sportona mi ha quasi tirato giú un braccio.
Guagniele.	Che v'hai tu dentro?
Lucia.	Che ne vuoi tu sapere?
Guagniele.	Se tu hai cosí grandi l'altre cose come tu hai la sporta, i paperi possono menar a notar l'oche, non che a bere.
Lucia.	Tu non ne berrai giá tu, briccone. [II, v]

(*G*. Oh! Here comes that heart-breaker. Greetings, my love! Good day and a prosperous new year, my sweet hope. *L*. Here we are again! What are you doing about, Guagniele? *G*. I'm just coming back from doing an errand for my master. By the way, have you really decided to let me die of love? *L*. You'd do better to mind your own business! *G*. This *is* my business, you little traitor! First you beguile me, then you run off; rather, you bewitched me and now you act as if I'm not around. *L*. I would really have done a fine deed if I had bothered with the likes of you! What do you expect me to see in you, you're so poor and ugly! *G*. That's where you're wrong, and I'll prove it. First of all, you can't complain about my financial state since you've never asked me for anything. As for my looks, well, my complexion is not the best, but otherwise I'm well made. *L.* Yes, considering how bad you look. *G.* Look how well my arms are made! Just look at my fine hands and robust legs! What fine thighs and such a broad chest. I must be three arms' length across the shoulders. But the important thing is how well I look in these fine clothes and how pleasant it is to feel through my jacket: give me your hand, Lucia; squeeze a little here. *L.* Shame on you! Get out of my sight, you cursed fool! *G.* If I were you-know-who, you wouldn't act like this, Miss Uppity. *L.* Get away from me and let me alone, you beast! *G.* Oh, soul of my very own heart, don't get so angry. *L.* Can't you tell that I have things to do and that I'm in a hurry? *G.* I, too, must run; they're expecting me. *L.* Fine, we'll both go about our business. *G.* But I can accompany you a short way. *L.* You certainly cannot! See, I'm already home. Oh! This basket has just about broken my arm! *G.* What's inside? *L.* What do you care? *G.* If your other things are as large as your basket, ganders could get the geese to swim, not just drink! *L.* You'll certainly never drink any of it, you rascal.)

La Strega

Of Grazzini's seven comedies, *La Strega* has enjoyed the most popularity. Undoubtedly, it owes its reputation to Taddeo Saliscendi, one of the most fully developed and humorous characters in the comedies, and to its very Florentine milieu. In none of the other comedies does the city of Florence become such a significant part of the action and the dialogue. But even more than the two earlier comedies, *La Strega* suffers from all the complexities—kidnappings and recognition scenes, coincidental encounters of old friends—which Grazzini himself had reviled for contributing to the corruption of the genre.

Fabrizio has succeeded in establishing his mistress, Bia, in the house of Madonna Sabatina, reputed for her practice of witchcraft, and they live together in great secrecy. Here, too, his friend Orazio, the son of Luc'Antonio, is living with a Genoese girl, Violante, whom he had saved from kidnappers. Orazio wears a disguise because everyone, including his father, thinks that he has died at the hands of Turkish corsairs. The two couples live happily together until they run out of money. Orazio must make his presence known to his father, but it is decided that Fabrizio should go and announce to Luc'Antonio that Madonna Sabatina has, by means of her powers, prophesied the imminent arrival of Orazio. Skeptical but hopeful, the old man promises money to Fabrizio once his son has returned.

At this point another plot is introduced. Taddeo Saliscendi, a rich and fatherless fool, falls in love with Geva, the widowed sister of Orazio. Luc'Antonio will not permit their marriage for Taddeo comes from a family of tradesmen. In desperation, Taddeo threatens to go off to war. His mother, Bartolomea, and his uncle, Bonifazio, are anxious because if he were to be killed without an heir, his money would go to the church of Santa Maria Nuova and they would remain destitute. They are in favor of his marriage to Geva and appeal to Madonna Sabatina, through Fabrizio, to use her powers to help them. Fabrizio uses the opportunity to obtain more money.

To complicate the situation, Violante's mother, Oretta, arrives in Florence in search of her daughter. She finds her on the street in the company of Madonna Sabatina. Violante, unwilling to give up Orazio, feigns not to know her mother and tells Oretta that she has made a mistake. Madonna Sabatina aids Violante by claiming that she is the girl's mother. Grieved, Oretta encounters Luc'Antonio who, after a moment's conversation, recognizes her as the wife of an old Genoese friend to whom he owes a great debt of hospitality. He promises to help her by presenting her case to the authorities. Realizing, too, how rich Oretta is, he hopes that Orazio, upon his return, can marry her daughter. Unfortunately, however, he is reminded that Violante has by now lost her virginity.

When Orazio makes his presence in Florence known to his father, Luc'Antonio is overjoyed to discover that his son is already wed to Violante. And, in his joy, Luc'Antonio consents to the marriage of Geva and Taddeo.

The essentials of this complex plot are relegated to a few expository scenes. The substance of the comedy is given over to the comic routines of Taddeo Saliscendi and his servant, Farfanicchio. Taddeo, as we have had occasion to mention before, is based on the classical miles gloriosus who, in Plautus' comedy of that name was called Pyrgopolinices. Taddeo, like his prototype in the Roman comedy, is a fool and a coward who deceives himself into thinking that he is a man of courage with the potential of becoming a great soldier and of winning for himself the admiration of the world. Traditionally, in classical comedy, the character of the braggart soldier was intended to satirize the military. When introduced into the Italian comedy, its function became more extensive. Daniel C. Boughner, in his study of this character, states:

> On the Renaissance stage the intensive cultivation of the role was not confined to the military swashbuckler. In Italian drama, as in English, it furnished a ready means of satirizing other living types condemned by the commentators. The upstart courtier who like the soldier aped the graces of the gentleman was a victim of this pillory. . . . A far more significant type is the upstart risen from the ranks of trade.[14]

As Boughner goes on to say, Taddeo is one of the best examples of this latter type. His foolish ways are a light satire on the affectations of an individual (or a class) trying to elevate himself in the social hierarchy. The satire is accomplished by showing the incongruities between the man's character—that of a simpleton whose only interests are sensual pleasures and games—and the roles which he tries to assume. Farfanicchio's function, of course, is to point up the absurdities of Taddeo's pretensions. When Taddeo finally realizes that he is unfit for the military life, he decides to seek his fame in a civil position. Farfanicchio knows that he is only fit for the menial labors carried on by his father and grandfather.

Taddeo.	But wait, I want to run for office, become a banker or a magistrate or a mayor . . .
Farfanicchio.	Of crabs.
Taddeo.	Or a vicar . . .
Farfanicchio.	Of mice.
Taddeo.	Or a captain . . .
Farfanicchio.	Of bedbugs.
Taddeo.	Or maybe a commissioner . . .
Farfanicchio.	Of crab lice.
Taddeo.	What resolute pronouncements I'll make!
Farfanicchio.	Dissolute would be a better word.
Taddeo.	What wise judgments!
Farfanicchio.	I just bet!
Taddeo.	Then before long I'll be sent as ambassador to the king . . .
Farfanicchio.	Of the beggars.
Taddeo.	And to the emperor . . .
Farfanicchio.	Of Prato.
Taddeo.	And then, Farfanicchio, how will the title of Signore look on me?
Farfanicchio.	As if it were painted on! [V, viii]

The satirical nature of Taddeo's character is only one aspect of his role in the comedy. If we were to exaggerate this aspect, we would, I think, be giving Grazzini too much credit as a moralist. He seldom moralized, and when he was critical, it was much more in his nature to be direct. From what we know of Grazzini's character, we can be sure that he was most attracted by the opportunities which Taddeo provided for laughter, and, consequently, from the traditional figure of the braggart, he drew the most salient characteristics—the strange habit of dress, the stupidity, the verbal idiosyncrasies, the gross sensual appetite—then placed him in the bourgeois atmosphere of the comedy. Almost unavoidably, he added a bit of satire for good measure.

Since so much of the comic effect of Taddeo's role depends upon his costume, his ineptness, and his ridiculous dialogue with Farfanicchio, he bears a relationship to the stock characters of the commedia dell'arte and, specifically, to the braggart of that art form. The actors of the commedia dell'arte specialized in a humor which depended upon the exaggeration or distortion of a fault inherent in the character which they were portraying. Costume, language, and attitudes were all instrumental in heightening the comic effect. In almost every scene in which Taddeo appears, he is in a different costume. The costumes, of course, represent the man he would like to be; but, inevitably, he reveals how ill-suited they are to him. In full military regalia, he struggles with the helmet, screaming for the sadistic Farfanicchio to free him from his metal prison (IV, ii). In V, viii, he appears dressed as a romantic serenader, instrument in hand, but when he opens his mouth to sing of his love for Geva, Farfanicchio's remarks indicate that the actor portraying Taddeo must sing with a less than pleasing voice. Other scenes, too, depend upon visual effects: in III, i, his bravery is tested, and then fails when, accidentally struck in the face by an orange, he screams in pain, certain that he has been shot by an harquebus.

Few other characters in *La Strega* warrant attention with the exception, perhaps, of Madonna Sabatina and Bartolomea's servant, Verdiana. Madonna Sabatina is a descendant of the infamous Celestina, a woman too old to enjoy sensual pleasures and, therefore, envious of the youth to whom she shows maternal affection: "it is said that old age is an evil desired by all and that youth is a good unknown by one who possesses it" (IV, i). Verdiana, a minor character, possesses the wit and the perception of her counterpart, Farfanicchio, and, in her dialogue with her mistress, points again to the importance of the servant to the humor of the Renaissance comedy.

La Pinzochera

Of all Grazzini's comedies, *La Pinzochera* best illustrates how influential the novella was on Grazzini's theatre.[15] This comedy, except for its dialogue, closely resembles any one of the *Cene* which narrates the preparation and the successful completion of a beffa. In fact, the beffa which is perpetrated on Gerozzo is the same one used to fool Calandrino in Boccaccio's famous story of the heliotrope. Here, too, the bourgeois world of most Renaissance comedies is complemented by the presence of prostitutes, pimps, and procuresses who provide a variety of social milieu more often found in the narrative.

The beffa to which Gerozzo falls victim is, though the central action of the comedy, only one element in a plot which surpasses in complexity any of its predecessors. Gerozzo, an old man dominated by his wife, Albiera, is in love with Diamante, the wife of his neighbor, Alberto Catalani, though he has never seen her except from a distance. Gerozzo and Albiera have a daughter, Fiammetta, who is in love with Federigo. The boy's parents will not allow him to marry the girl for her mother had, as a young lady, a somewhat questionable reputation. Gerozzo and Albiera, who would ordinarily approve the marriage, are equally against it once they hear of the allusions to Albiera's past. Ambrogio, a friend of Federigo, is anxious to meet with Bita, a prostitute, but cannot find an appropriate place: he is disliked by her mistress, Antonia, and Bita herself refuses to go near a public tavern for fear of her reputation.

To accommodate his friend, Federigo allows Ambrogio to meet with Bita in his own house while his family is in the country. Also in the country are Alberto Catalani and his family, but Federigo and a servant, in possession of the key to Alberto's house, make Gerozzo think that Diamante is there and ready to receive him—thus clearing the way for Federigo to see Fiammetta, whose mother is also absent, on a visit to a monastery. Federigo then hires Sandra, a prostitute, and her mistress, Antonia, to pretend to be Diamante and her mother, neither of whom Gerozzo has seen close enough to recognize. To avoid the surveillance of the mother, Gerozzo is provided with two wax balls which a magician has supposedly endowed with powers to make both him and Diamante invisible.

The three meetings proceed as follows: Sandra flees into the street, unable to stand Gerozzo's breath, and while he is trying to induce her to place the magic ball in her mouth, they are discovered by Albiera, who has returned unexpectedly. After she upbraids him, she returns home. Fearful that she will discover Federigo in the bed of her daughter, the servants tell Albiera that they have caught the two lovers together and that they have bound Federigo. For their own honor, both families are then forced to consent to the marriage. Ambrogio and Bita suffer no setback because when Federigo's father comes to his own door, he is met by a servant disguised as a necromancer and is frightened away.

The titular character of *La Pinzochera* is of relatively minor importance to the action as we have outlined it above. Nevertheless, hers is one of the most fully developed roles in the comedy. Madonna Antonia is a *pinzochera,* or bawd, who attempts to give an air of dignity to her profession. In the Renaissance comedy, the pinzochera is generally a hypocrite who professes religious devotion while practicing witchcraft or acting as an intermediary for illicit lovers. It is her hypocrisy which distinguishes her from the bawd of the classical comedy and which makes her one of the few truly original creations of Renaissance comedy.[16] Antonia first appears reciting a monologue in defense of her profession.

> Oh Lord! How many and great are the struggles and torments of this life. Dear God, help us all and me, particularly. I am a poor widow, alone and abandoned by all. By my faith, I don't know whether I should ever have been

> born. And yet, my faith in the Lord, my many fastings and prayers give me reason to hope for rest, if not here, at least in the beyond. But having no choice but to live until God calls me and being without any means of support, I am forced to get along as best I'm able. I work and help one person or another who needs my services just to make ends meet. That's why today I dealt with Giannino; he promised me enough money to get along for a few days and I'll have to manage like this until the end of my days. [III, i]

Despite her claims, however, she soon proves herself a very capable and cunning woman for whom, as Giannino says, money is the only value (III, ii).

Antonia and her world of fraud and prostitution dominate the atmosphere of the comedy. Rather than portraying Florentine bourgeois society, *La Pinzochera* moves from the traditional path and focuses upon an element of society in which we find a freer indulgence of the instincts. Even Antonia's hypocrisy disappears after the early scenes and she unashamedly practices her trade for its greatest financial advantage. Seldom do we find in the erudite comedy such attention given to prostitution and to young girls like Sandra and Bita who ply their trade openly and belie the tradition of the virtuous maiden. In the world of *La Pinzochera* virtue is understood in the Boccaccesque or Machiavellian sense (and understandably so considering the influence of both on sixteenth-century writers of comedy). Each character seeks his own gain by the use of his ingenuity (Federigo declares, "let follow whatever may, provided that I realize my intent"), and even the virtuous maiden, Fiammetta, exercises her cleverness to deceive her parents.

Gerozzo, the central figure of the comedy, is a burgher who falls victim to the fraudulent machinations of this Florentine underworld. We are spared from feeling any sympathy for him, however, because he typifies the traditional fool of the comic genre: he is bullied by a headstrong wife who, he says, "has put on the pants," and to assert his masculinity and to show that he is still the master of his house he decides to initiate an affair with his neighbor's wife. Like his counterpart Giovacchino in *La Strega*, he is gullible, and like Giovangualberto in *La Spiritata*, he is a miser. He possesses, in fact, all the weaknesses and unpleasant traits which make him a perfect victim for a beffa.

It is to be remarked, however, that when the beffa originally planned by Federigo and Giannino backfires, the consequences are so grotesque and the humiliation which Gerozzo must suffer so severe that the comedy takes on serious overtones which are subdued only by the improbability of the situation. Gerozzo was to have been fooled into thinking that Sandra, the prostitute, was Diamante Catalani, and, except for his having to pay dearly for the time he spent with her, the beffa involved no other complications. But as we know, Sandra flees from Gerozzo into the street and the ensuing scene with the old man, convinced that he is invisible, attempting to stuff a ball of wax into the girl's mouth while his wife looks on, is more grotesque than humorous, especially when we realize that Albiera will recognize him, that he will be disillusioned and will suffer the humiliation of being caught with a prostitute in such an absurd activity.

Sandra. I'm going to leave if you don't stop that!
Gerozzo. You little traitor! . . .
Albiera. Tell me, Veronica, what were they doing at home?
Veronica. They were preparing things for supper.
Sandra. Stop it! People are coming.
Gerozzo. That makes no difference. Take this and put it in your mouth.
Albiera. What's going on there near our neighbor's house?
Veronica. I don't know.
Sandra. Oh! You're acting like a madman! Let's get inside immediately!

Gerozzo. Put it in your mouth! Quickly!
Albiera. Look, Veronica, isn't that Gerozzo?
Veronica. I'm afraid it is.
Sandra. Go inside before they get here! Hurry up, damn you!
Gerozzo. Stand still and keep it in your mouth! Then you'll see something marvelous happen.
Albiera. It certainly is he!
Veronica. Sir, what is going on?
Sandra. Let's get inside! They're almost upon us.
Gerozzo. Go ahead and close your mouth. Stop talking and wonders will happen.
Albiera. That shameless rascal! Look at that hussy; and they are just standing there! . . .
Sandra. My good lady, it is all his fault. He kept me here against my will.
Albiera. I'm quite sure! Get moving, speak, you swine!
Gerozzo. Stay away, you traitorous she-devil!
Albiera. Just listen to the way he talks to me!
Gerozzo. You dare to speak to me like this? A hussy?
Albiera. And he even pretends to be unjustly accused!
Gerozzo. You dare to address me in this way?
Albiera. Oh, I know he's bewitched or else he's completely mad!
Gerozzo. Now I see why you went to the monastery so often, you little spy! Oh, miraculous little ball! Don't you consider me worth anything?
Albiera. I've always treated you better than you deserved!
Gerozzo. You've completely ruined me! Never again will I be able to show my face in public! [IV, ix]

The delight which Grazzini took in the beffa is clearly evident in this scene. Its length (I have only quoted a portion of it) can only be explained if we consider how important grotesque humor of this sort was to him.

Finally, we might note, as Gentile did, that the minor plot of Ambrogio and Bita seems to have been introduced for no other reason than to necessitate the presence of Carletto who, disguised as a necromancer, keeps Damiano from his own door.[17]

The scene in which Damiano encounters Carletto serves no other purpose than to allow for the necromancer's gibberish ("Astiocche, malecche, tripocch . . .") and the humorous frustration of Damiano who begs that he speak Italian so that he might understand (IV, xiii).

La Sibilla

In *La Sibilla* we again find that Grazzini has patterned himself after the erudite comedy, and, just as in *La Gelosia,* has employed the dramatic devices which he considered ill-suited to the modern theatre. After the birth of his daughter and the death of his wife, Don Diego leaves for Spain in the company of Charles V. He provides his child (called la Sibilla) with a dowry of 500 ducats and one half of a medal by which he will be able to recognize her if he ever returns. La Sibilla is raised by Tommaso Pegolotti and then, upon his death, by his brother, Michelozzo. Michelozzo's son, Alessandro, falls in love with the girl, but his father, intent upon finding him a rich wife, hastens to marry her to an old doctor of law, Giansimone. To prevent the marriage, Alessandro and his servant, Vespa, hire the services of a trickster (*barro*), Ciuffagna, who, disguised as Don Diego, claims la Sibilla as his daughter and makes haste to leave with her. Michelozzo, unhappy that he will lose the money which her marriage to Giansimone would bring, does not doubt the impostor and lets la Sibilla go.

Meanwhile, however, the real Don Diego arrives to claim his daughter and convinces Michelozzo that he is not an impostor when he presents his half of the medal. Officials are summoned to the scene and find Ciuffagna and the girl who, frightened, runs away. The servants convince Giansimone to defend Ciuffagna in court should the need arise, and while he is away interviewing his prospective client, they introduce the young

Ottaviano into his house to meet Ermellina, Giansimone's niece, who is kept in seclusion.

The resolution of this complex plot produces more than the usual amount of festivities. La Sibilla is found and Michelozzo consents to her marrying Alessandro once Don Diego promises them great wealth. Giansimone discovers Ottaviano with his niece but is persuaded to allow them to marry. And finally, even Giansimone, unable now to wed the young Sibilla, happily agrees to marry Ottaviano's widowed mother, Margherita.

Aware of how commonplace a plot such as this was to the comedy of his age, Grazzini tries to give verisimilitude to the improbable circumstances by first placing the action in an historical context:

> At the time when the Emperor Charles V, coming from Naples and Rome, passed through Florence, where he stayed for I don't know how many days, and when, by chance, one of his men, who came from Valencia and was a rich and noble inhabitant of that city, lodged in our house. . . . this gentleman had a beautiful young Neapolitan for his woman and wanted to bring her home with him; as fortune wanted it, on the first evening, she, being with child, gave birth to a baby girl and died. [I, ii]

Pierfilippo is then made to comment on the possibility of truth being as strange as fiction: "Well, look at the things which happen to men! If this doesn't seem like a story—and yet it is the truth!" (I, ii). Throughout the comedy references are made to contemporary occurrences and customs to maintain the illusion of veracity. Giansimone, for example, assures Diego that his daughter cannot leave the city "because just this morning at tierce they locked the city gates because a miller had been killed in Piazza San Giovanni" (IV, iv). It becomes quite obvious that Grazzini is attempting to make the erudite comedy conform to his idea that the modern theatre should represent life as it is and, he must, therefore, justify any of the improbabilities which he borrows from tradition.

Perhaps less obvious than the influence of the classical comedy upon *La Sibilla* is that of the novella, manifested particularly in the extent to which chance ("fortuna") becomes a force in the resolution of the action. Much has been said about the role of chance in Boccaccio's novelle. Characters who are frustrated in their plans blame Dame Fortune's indiscriminate exercise of power. She becomes a hidden antagonist against whom men must test their cleverness. Her importance is less noticeable, however, in Grazzini's *Cene*, and, often, her power is acknowledged solely as a token of respect for the tradition of the genre. It is then somewhat surprising that the wiles of the infamous lady are blamed for all the reversals in this comedy. Alessandro and Ottaviano are the two pawns of chance, and, like two weights on the poles of a scale, the temporary success of one brings about the momentary misfortune of the other:

> I know that this time, too, fortune has acted both in my behalf and to my disadvantage, having first let Ciuffagna so easily steal away the girl from my father's house and then, so unexpectedly, causing him to lose her. And then, just at the point of getting the money, it caused Sibilla's father to suddenly appear. . . . Just look at the strange way in which Ottaviano will realize his intentions after having despaired. And I, who seemed to be constantly in the saddle, ended up going on foot. [V, ii]

La Sibilla, however, is a comedy and as such it must have a happy ending. Dame Fortune cannot continue to hold back her favors from young lovers. As in the novella, where love becomes the one force against which she is almost powerless, here, too, Pierfilippo exclaims that nothing could have prevented the eventual marriage of Alessandro and Sibilla (V, x).

Pierfilippo, the brother-in-law of Michelozzo, is a most antithetic figure in this comedy, populated as it is with so many comic types. He is, first of all, wise. In I, ii, his good sense contrasts markedly with the avariciousness of his brother-in-law, Michelozzo.

Pierfilippo.	In heaven's name, it's really a shame that a bumpkin and a fool should enjoy such a lovely, well-brought-up lass!
Michelozzo.	That's how it must be! He's rich and that's all that is important. Every other consideration is hogwash! But you make him out to be such a fool. How could he be if he's a doctor?
Pierfilippo.	. . . he surely strikes me as a fool. If I had been you, I would certainly have done otherwise. . . . I would have made Alessandro happy.
Michelozzo.	By God, I've really found someone who has my interests at heart!
Pierfilippo.	Wait! Just listen to me! Why do you need more than you already have? At your age, you're not about to have more sons, and the one you have is already too rich.

Later, Pierfilippo unselfishly provides refuge for the terrified Sibilla. And in the last scene of the play, his sense of justice and his rational solution for satisfying the disappointed Giansimone, make us wonder about Grazzini's purpose in creating such a character:

> Messer Giansimone, listen to me. By now you are . . . well, not really old, but, let's say, aging. You're not about to have more children even if you were to take a young wife. So, I want you to remember that Ottaviano, your son-in-law, is also your son; you should consider marrying Madonna Margherita and you'll all have a happy life. . . . You'll be joining two families into one without losing any dowry money; everything will belong to your children and, eventually, to your grandchildren. Your pleasure will be doubled. [V, xiii]

Since Pierfilippo's presence emphasizes Michelozzo's miserliness and Giansimone's foolishness, while his control over the final scene brings about a resolution to a seemingly insoluble situation, it is possible to consider him in the light of Grazzini's polemics against the excesses of the Florentine bourgeoisie. In particular, he points up the complete lack of reason in a man like Giansimone, who boasts of his learning. The fact that Pierfilippo had been absent from Florence and from such an environment for nearly thirty years makes this explanation more likely.

The central figure of *La Sibilla* is Giansimone. For the first time in Grazzini's comedies we encounter a man of learning, a doctor of law. He, in the comic tradition of his character, is senile, unduly concerned about his honor ("I have always set more store by honor than possessions") and fond of showing off his learning before servants by quoting Latin. Also in keeping with tradition, he is made more foolish by his attempts to marry a young girl. Considering Grazzini's dislike for such types, it is surprising that he provides Giansimone with a wife at the play's end.

I Parentadi

I Parentadi is undoubtedly the weakest of Grazzini's seven comedies. Not only does it borrow more heavily from the classical comedy, but it also lacks interesting characters and the milieu which in *La Sibilla* and *La Gelosia*, for example, compensate for the hackneyed plot. Although we do not know the date of its composition (since it is listed in Grazzini's catalogue, we do know that it was written by 1566), we might justly assume that it was one of the author's earliest plays, written at a time before he had taken a stand against the traditional erudite comedy in favor of a theatre more consonant with contemporary life and mores. Though it is difficult to perceive any development in Grazzini's style and manner of composition in the comedies, we may still note that in *I Parentadi* he presents the argument in the first and in the fifth acts, a method which he abandons in his other plays, presumably because it was unsatisfactory. He tells us in the prologue that he had adopted the method from Ariosto's *Il Negromante* in order to keep the audience's attention and to make the comedy as little boring as possible. By his own statement we realize that Grazzini was already aware that the erudite comedy needed to employ every conceivable device to sustain the audience's interest, and the fact that he never again used this particular device would seem to indicate that he preferred the comic scenes and clever dialogue between servants to the further complication of already complex plots. But *I Parentadi* shows that, particularly in his early plays, Grazzini closely imitated the commedia erudita. *I Parentadi* has all the weaknesses of the traditional *commedia d'intreccio:* it is completely unbelievable and so complex that it taxes the patience of the most attentive reader.

Lattanzio Marcassini, a Florentine, had gone to live in Sicily with a friend, Lucantonio Fiorinelli and, later, had married the latter's daughter. Returning to Florence in the company of his wife, her sister, Eugenia, and his son, Fabio, he was attacked by corsairs and separated from his family. Shortly thereafter, his wife gave birth to twins Cornelio and Porzia, and died. As the comedy begins, the family is living in Florence, each unaware of the others: Fabio, the heir to a rich man who had raised him; Porzia, who lives with her aunt, Eugenia; and Cornelio, disguised as a girl (Cornelia), who lives with the family of Giammatteo Lotteringhi and who is particularly fond of Lisabetta, Giammatteo's daughter.

Fabio has fallen in love with Cornelia, but aware that as a stranger in the city he cannot hope to have her, he hires the services of Spinello, Giammatteo's servant, to help him try.

Frosino, a parasite, who had been offended by Giammatteo at one time, plans revenge; he persuades Giammatteo that his wife has a lover and also convinces Cangenova, the wife, that Giammatteo is unfaithful. To prove his accusations, he tells Giammatteo to dress as a woman so that he might easily surprise his wife and her lover together; he tells Cangenova to dress as a man so that she will be admitted to the brothel frequented by her husband. Frosino intends by his trick also to satisfy two friends, Ruberto, Giammatteo's son, and Mario, a man who is in love with Cangenova. Ruberto had robbed his father of 500 ducats and is now hiding at the home of Porzia, whom he loves. Frosino plans to lead Giammatteo there so that he will meet his son and, out of paternal affection, forgive him. Frosino will then reveal the fact that his accusation of Cangenova was untrue but made to satisfy his thirst for vengeance. On the other hand, Cangenova will be led to Frosino's house where, if possible, Mario can take his pleasure of her.

To further complicate matters, Giammatteo finally discovers the true sex of Cornelio, finding him in the bedroom of his daughter, Lisabetta. He runs to Eugenia's house where peace is made with Ruberto. Cangenova, meanwhile, escapes the treacheries of Mario.

Cornelio, now bound with ropes, is sought by Fabio who still thinks that he is a woman. At this point Lattanzio arrives and recognizes by various means his three children. Ruberto then reveals the fact that he is married to Porzia; Cornelio marries Lisabetta and Giammatteo's rich niece is given in marriage to Fabio.

With such a complex plot, little time can be spared from the development of the action, and the characters of the comedy must therefore remain completely one-dimensional. They are like marionettes put through their paces for the sole purpose of resolving the several improbable situations which confront them. The only character who provides the comedy with any interest is the one who controls the action and who, one might say, pulls the strings of the wooden marionettes. This is Frosino, a character based on the parasite of the erudite comedy.

Consistent with his prototype, Frosino's malicious deeds in *I Parentadi* are motivated by his desire to remain the intimate friend of Florence's most prosperous citizens so that he might derive benefits from them. His desire to take revenge on Giammatteo stems from an incident in which the old man was responsible for his having lost a patron. He complains that Giammatteo had spoken to him

> about wanting to marry off his daughter and he gave me the job of seeing to it all. And when I had finished all the business and we were about to sign the contract, he said that he had been speaking of Cornelia, not of Lisabetta. And he feels no shame in wanting to give a servant girl to the son of Guglielmo Frangipani. So, since he wouldn't change his mind, he left me and Guglielmo looking like fools and the story got all around Florence. . . . This wouldn't have bothered me too much but then Guglielmo took it out on me, and I've lost out on going to dine at his house three and four times a week. Does this seem like something I can forget about so easily? And you know what those meals were like!

Frosino's plans for revenge include benefits to compensate for the loss of Guglielmo's friendship: making peace between Ruberto and his father will leave the son in his debt, and satisfying Mario's desire to seduce Cangenova will assure him a place at this man's table, since "I seek nothing more than to live well at the expense of others" (II, vi).

Although Frosino is derived from the parasite of the erudite comedy, there is much in his character which reflects the spirit of the bontemponi who participated in the activities of the Florentine brigate. He leads a carefree life which Fabio envies: "You never do anything more than chatter away and joke with your friends" (III, ii). His activities are those which Grazzini himself preferred: "he tells those funny stories . . . drinks and . . . eats a lot" (IV, ix). He takes particular pleasure in the way a story is related: "I don't laugh to be laughing at you

. . . but I laugh at the clever and lovely words with which you have told this entertaining story, and I shall have a good laugh every time I think about it; and even if it had happened to me, I would laugh" (IV, iii). And finally, even the beffa which he plans is much in keeping with the beffe of the brigate. Its purpose is not to resolve a situation but to take revenge in a way that will provide the beffatore with a good laugh.

L'Arzigogolo

There is little certainty that *L'Arzigogolo* was written by Grazzini; however, both Giovanni Gentile and the most recent editor of Grazzini's plays, Giovanni Grazzini, have chosen to consider it among his later works.[18] It was first published by Frighetti in the *Teatro comico fiorentino* (1750) from a manuscript in the Biblioteca Nazionale in Florence (Magliabechiano cl. VII, n. 178) which contains a flyleaf stating that it is in Grazzini's own handwriting. Critics at first doubted the authenticity of the manuscript since there was little similarity between the calligraphy which we know to be Grazzini's and that of the manuscript. Giovanni Grazzini, however, attributes the differences to the fact that the manuscript is in fact a transcription and does not, therefore, reveal all the peculiarities of Grazzini's own hand.[19] The major problem concerning the play's authorship stems from two facts: first, it is not listed in Grazzini's catalogue of 1566, and, second, it does not appear in the letter preceding *La Strega,* which mentions all of Grazzini's other comedies. Gentile's explanation is that *L'Arzigogolo* is a revised adaptation of the farce, *La Giostra,* which does appear in Grazzini's catalogue; Giovanni Grazzini believes that it was not mentioned in the earlier letter because the author, doubting the worth of a comedy which perhaps still contained many farcical elements and which was not consistent with the principles of good comedy writing as put forth in the prologue of *La Strega*, preferred to abandon it completely.[20] As a result of Gentile's authoritative study and Giovanni Grazzini's confirmation of his opinions by further textual and critical investigations, *L'Arzigogolo* has come to be accepted as one of Grazzini's last comedies. It is certainly one of the most interesting, both for its characters and the variety of its subject matter.

Basically, of course, the plot is not original. The author himself states in the prologue that "although it is not new, we hope that you will find it in part, if not completely, enjoyable, since it is entertaining, farcical, and ridiculous." Besides the debt which *L'Arzigogolo* owes to the novella and to the erudite comedy, one of its episodes—whose immediate source we do not know—is particularly reminiscent of the fifteenth-century French farce, *Maître Pathelin*.[21] The central episode of the comedy concerns the attempts of Marcello to obtain enough money so that he can win the hand of his beloved Cammilla, a foundling who had been raised by a widow, Monna Papera. The money is promised to him by his friend, Dario, who enlists the aid of his servant, Valerio. Valerio conceives a plot to obtain the money from Dario's father, the old procurator, Ser Alesso. It happens that Ser Alesso is in love with Monna Papera and thinks that she would return his affection if he were younger. Valerio tells him of a friend who possesses a rejuvenating potion and assures him that 100 scudi would buy enough to return him to his physical state at the age of twenty-five without, however, his losing the wisdom of old age. Overjoyed, Alesso takes the potion. Both his son and Monna Papera had been forewarned of the beffa and so his son pretends to mistake him for a thief when he tries to enter his own house, while Monna Papera will have nothing to do with him because he is a "youngster." Disillusioned over the failure of his attempts to please her, Ser Alesso, in a parody of the Renaissance lament over lost youth, bemoans his lost old age:

> Oh, old age of mine, where art thou now? All those years that I have thrown away, how gladly would I buy them back! Let me quickly go and look for him to see if there is a way for me to become old once again. And if I can become myself again, let whomever wishes have youth and its caprices, for I have seen by my own experience that it is not youth alone which pleases the ladies. [III, v]

Valerio assures Alesso that he can counteract the effects of the potion by vomiting before it is digested. The old man consents even though he is advised that the magic can never again be repeated.

Meanwhile, Monna Papera notifies Valerio that she needs Ser Alesso's help in a legal matter. A farmer whom she employs unwittingly sold a pair of oxen to a man she knows will never pay. Alesso and Valerio decide to bring the farmer, Arzigogolo, before a judge, and, by proving that he is crazy, make the sale invalid. Arzigogolo is advised to feign idiocy by responding to the judge's questions with the sound *sff*. As in the farce, *Maître Pathelin,* the farmer not only outwits the judge, but his legal adviser as well by continuing the ruse when asked to pay Alesso's fee. The comedy ends in a traditional manner when it is discovered that the judge is Cammilla's father. He consents to her marrying Marcello and Monna Papera agrees to marry Alesso.

The most outstanding fault of *L'Arzigogolo* is its weak construction. Gentile's theory that the comedy is derived from a farce is supported by the fact that the episode concerning Arzigogolo is appended to the first three acts after the beffa played on Alesso is completed. In no way, except for the presence of the same characters, is there any relationship between the two episodes. Nor does the story of Cammilla have any function in the play: the meeting of father and daughter after many years does not resolve any situation. (Marcello, we remember, was already in a position to claim Cammilla as his wife.) It is likely that the author added the recognition scene in order to claim *L'Arzigogolo* as a comedy; without this traditional element, the play would, despite its five acts, retain the characteristics of a farce. One need only consider Grazzini's three-act farce, *Il Frate*, to see how closely it resembles the episode of Alesso's rejuvenation in its dramatic simplicity.

Considered separately, however, the beffa perpetrated on Alesso and then the cunning trick of Arzigogolo to escape payment of the fee provide for some of the most successful comic scenes in Grazzini's theatre. The humor derives from Alesso's constant frustration, first when he is not recognized by his son and Monna Papera and then when Arzigogolo uses the same strategy to trick him that he had devised to deceive the judge.

Alesso and Arzigogolo are the most interesting characters of the comedy. Arzigogolo, whose appearance on the scene is very brief, is an unusual combination of the man of native Florentine wit and the stereotyped country bumpkin whose language reflects his lack of culture:

> Non so io che siete certi ser arrabbiati che pricolate il mondo quando volete? e ben lo sa la mia Bartola, ch'è stata pegnorata dal messere dieci volte con vostri ceteroni. [IV, vii]
>
> (Don't I know that you're all a bunch of madmen who turn the world topsy-turvy whenever you want? My Bartola certainly knows it, for she has been distrained ten times by you, sir, with a lot of garbled legal talk.)

Alesso, essentially derived from the traditional character of the old learned fool, is psychologically more developed in this than are similar characters in the earlier plays. In II, v, for example, he ponders at length over the advantages and disadvantages of Valerio's offer to rejuvenate him:

> Who knows? It may well be that he has the secret of youth. Everyday, new discoveries are made. There's a Latin proverb which says that in herbs and stones there are words of

great power. But if I do become young again, I'll no longer like Monna Papera because I'll only be attracted to young things; and if I don't like her, when now I want to like her, I'll despair. I'd rather be old than young and not enjoy what I like now. I know how young men are: they like silly young things. And were I to become young again, I'd be as foolish as they. And what is worse is that he has no potion to make me old again. I certainly won't let them fool me, for I want to be as I am. But then, if I become young, won't she like me more? Won't I please her more? Couldn't I gad about more and go out at night? I could sport a feathered cap, ride a lovely steed, and really please the ladies. And who'll keep her from loving me when I'm young? It might be a consideration for my age which will hold her back. She might say, "He's not right for me since I'm so old and he is only twenty-five." Oh, I'm so confused. Curses! What shall I do? I'd better think about it for awhile before I become infantile—I mean, young—again.

Il Frate

Of Grazzini's other dramatic compositions, the only one to survive was the farce, *Il Frate*, which, as we know, was for several centuries ascribed to Machiavelli.[22] Before its true authorship was determined, it was known as the *Commedia in tre atti senza titolo*, and as a consequence of the belief that it was written by one of Florence's most illustrious men, it enjoyed great notoriety, and received much critical attention.[23] It was compared both favorably and unfavorably to the *Mandragola*, and the most obvious points of comparison between the two plays were in the characters of Frate Alberigo and Fra Timoteo.

Except for the fact that there are few complications in *Il Frate* (appurtenances which, in the prologue, Grazzini relegates to the erudite comedy, where "we find things which are impossible and completely unrealistic"), there are few differences between this farce and the author's five-act comedies. In fact, as Marvin T. Herrick has noted, by the sixteenth century, the term *farsa* was indiscriminately used for any dramatic composition which did not fit the conventional categories of erudite comedy, tragedy, pastoral, etc.[24] Accordingly, having only three acts and none of the recognition scenes of the commedia erudita, *Il Frate* was classified as a farce.

The source of *Il Frate* is undoubtedly Boccaccio's novella about the illicit love of Ricciardo Minutolo for Catella, the wife of Filippo Sighinolfo (*Decameron,* III, vi). In Grazzini's play, Amerigo, the elderly husband of the young Caterina, is in love with Alfonso's wife and enlists the services of his servant, Margherita, to help arrange a meeting. Caterina, aware of her husband's intentions, succeeds in getting Margherita to betray Amerigo and to help her teach the old man a lesson. Margherita is a confidante to Frate Alberigo, who lusts after Caterina; together they propose a scheme to Caterina for punishing Amerigo. Amerigo is to be told that his beloved is waiting in bed for him, but Caterina will be there in her stead. (Alfonso and his wife have left their house and have given the key to Frate Alberigo.) Frate Alberigo takes his pleasure of Caterina while Margherita stalls off the old man who, when he does arrive, is reprimanded by his wife for his infidelity. Frate Alberigo makes peace between the couple, becomes their confessor and, needless to say, the lover of Caterina.

The influence of the novella upon *Il Frate* is particularly evident in the fact that most of the action is not developed throughout the three acts but is narrated to the audience by Margherita in a monologue which could well be a page from the *Cene:*

> Oh, in this way, huh? Who would have ever thought so! Friars! They're more vice-ridden than the devil! Just look by what horrendous means he has led her to do his pleasure. He told us in the house how he had found a means by which to free my mistress and to make the master forget about his

> neighbor. To do this, he told us to go to Alfonso's house; he gave us the key which, he said, had been given to him for one thing or another. He said that Madonna Caterina should get into the bed where her neighbor usually slept. I was to tell Amerigo that today was the day and that our neighbor wanted to make him happy because her husband had left and wouldn't be back until nightfall. We were sure that the old man would believe me and go without a second thought and that his own wife, under cover of the dark, would receive him. Then, once he had taken his pleasure of her, we knew that she would reveal who she was, reprimand him and shout him out of the house. The friar told us to leave the rest to him. Well, the mistress and I started out, got to Alfonso's door and went inside. We went into the salon and then into the bedroom. No one was in sight. My mistress quickly undressed and got into bed without a moment's hesitation. She asked me to leave the shutters partly closed so that he could see the bed and the door a bit ajar so that her husband could get in and so that the whole plot could be carried out without a hitch. [III, i]

The dialogue which fills the rest of the farce serves mainly to describe the character of Frate Alberigo. He is portrayed as a sensual man, intent upon satisfying his appetite. In effect, he is like any of the other beffatori who succeed by their cleverness. The fact that he is a cleric is almost insignificant because, unlike Machiavelli's intention in the *Mandragola*, Grazzini's was not to satirize the clergy. As Margherita's speech shows, the beffa is the focal point of the farce. Except for a few instances when she comments upon the clergy ("I've never liked these friars; and I wonder if I won't fall out of grace if I have dealings with them?"), it is only in Frate Alberigo's closing remarks that we feel the tremendous immorality of the man:

> If, my dear spectators, you plan to wait for our return, you're wasting your time. Because, after dinner, I plan to deliver a little sermon, showing them by various reasonings, examples, miracles and by my authority that charity is the

> most important virtue to insure a healthy soul, confirming the words of the apostle Paul, who said that one who has no charity has nothing. [III, vi]

From our discussion of Grazzini's seven comedies and his farce, *Il Frate*, it is clear that the author, although he criticized the commedia erudita, continued in the tradition of his predecessors, relying heavily on hackneyed plots and borrowing freely from the novella. Only seldom do we find any evidence that Grazzini actually rejected those traditional devices of Renaissance comedy writers which he ridiculed in his prologues and in his other writings. But while in his own comedies he respected the traditions of the erudite comedy (perhaps in the hope that his theatre would establish his reputation), he also gave particular attention to witty repartee and to slapstick. By the spirited dialogue and the visual comedy of his theatre, Grazzini revealed his interest in the new commedia dell'arte and, consequently, in a theatre which abandoned a stereotyped milieu for one of greater contemporary verisimilitude.

CHAPTER V

THE NOVELLE

GRAZZINI's greatest literary achievement is his collection of novelle, the *Cene*. In it we find a synthesis of the burlesque spirit of the poetry and the visual and linguistic humor of his theatre. In an ideal situation, the *Cene* could be considered the work of an artist whose inspiration had found its most perfect means of expression after a long period of apprenticeship to Berni and the Florentine popular poets, and the comic muse of the commedia erudita. As we know, however, there was not an ideal chronology of stylistic development toward the narrative art of the *Cene*. In fact, some of the novelle were already written by 1549 or earlier, antedating several of the comedies and much of the burlesque poetry.[1] Clearly, they were written contemporaneously with other works; and the superior artistry which Grazzini displayed in the novella is to be ascribed to his greater proficiency in the narrative form rather than to his artistic maturity.

In his well-known letter to a certain Masaccio di Calorigna (whom Verzone considered to be "an imaginary person invented by Lasca"), Grazzini speaks of the care with which he wrote the novelle; manuscripts attest to the fact that throughout his life the author revised his work, continuously editing the stories and rearranging their order.[2] But he died before completing the *Cene* to his satisfaction. And by the time the manuscripts of the *Cene* came to light and began to be edited and published in the eighteenth century, several of them had already been lost. Of the thirty novelle which were to comprise the *Cene*, only twenty-two and a portion of a twenty-third have been found.[3]

The structure of the *Cene* was undoubtedly suggested by the *Decameron.* In fact, in the 1566 catalogue Grazzini described the novelle as having been written in imitation of Boccaccio. Like the novelle of the *Decameron*, those of the *Cene* are enclosed in a framework: one winter's eve in late January, ten young people gather at the home of Amaranta, "a no less gracious and noble than rich and beautiful widow." Before supper, while the group is seated by a fire, one young man suggests that they read a selection of stories from the *Decameron.* His hostess, however, decides that they should tell their own stories: "If they are neither as good nor as beautiful as Boccaccio's, they will at least be less familiar, and for this one occasion, they will, for their novelty and variety, bring us both pleasure and a measure of instruction."[4] Amaranta's suggestion is that they each tell a story and that they return on the following two Thursdays to tell another, increasing the length of their story each week, so that "each one of us . . . will be able to prove himself by relating three different types of tales." Of the thirty novelle described by Amaranta, we are lacking most of those which were told on the third evening.

Since Grazzini repeatedly admitted his debt to Boccaccio and since the use of a framework was a tradition in large part inherited from the *Decameron*, it is interesting to consider the similarities and dissimilarities between that used in the *Cene* and that of its fourteenth-century predecessor. In both instances the storytellers are members of a leisure class: they enjoy financial security and possess a certain amount of culture. Amaranta describes the young men of her party as having "a good knowledge of letters, . . . familiarity with, not only Latin and Tuscan poets, but the Greek as well." In most cases they can therefore feel superior to the bourgeois characters who populate the novelle. Life as it unfolds within the framework remains alien to Boccaccio's young storytellers, who frolic without a care in the bucolic setting of the villa in Fiesole; it is also alien to Amaranta and her guests who, snug before a fire, awaiting a fine meal, enjoy immunity from the vicissitudes which harass the characters of the fictional, bourgeois world which they create.

But the dissimilarities between the two frameworks are by far more significant. The basic difference between them is the function which each has in relation to the entire work. Whereas for Boccaccio the frame was a necessity, a means by which he obeyed the literary canons inherited from the Middle Ages and was able, by placing his vast fresco of secular life within the framework of a pastoral setting, to excuse the licentiousness of his material, for Grazzini it was no more than a device which, at most, could give some order to the novelle. Boccaccio, as his introduction to the stories of the fourth day further illustrates, needed to justify the frivolity of his work for reasons which certainly no longer existed by the sixteenth century. Consequently, when Grazzini apologizes for his own work and seeks to justify it, he is doing no more than imitating the master:

> In truth, we are near the carnival season, a time when men of the Church are permitted to enjoy themselves. Friars play ball with each other, perform comedies, and, dressed in costume, sing, dance, and play instruments. Even nuns are permitted to celebrate by dressing as men, velvet caps on their heads, tight-fitting stockings on their legs, and swords on their hips. Why, then, should we give offense if we enjoy ourselves in telling tales? Who can honestly rebuke us for it?

As Guido Di Pino has noted, that which was an integral part of Boccaccio's masterpiece became for later novellieri a means by which to give order to their stories or to include marginal comments.[5]

To date, the most thorough study of the structural aspects of the *Cene* has been made by Giorgio Bárberi Squarotti, whose observations merit repeating here.[6] Squarotti comments first on the fact that the frame of the *Cene* is provided by a "natural scene" as opposed to the "historical scene" (the plague of 1348) which introduces the novelle of the *Decameron*. We have noted, in fact, that the festive atmosphere of Grazzini's frame recalls the evening spent by the Florentine brigate around a fire, exchanging stories. Except for the change of locale to the apartments of a wealthy widow of social standing, the evening spent by Amaranta and her guests resembles any of those familiar to the tornatella. In fact, the pleasure which the young ladies take in the more ribald novelle might well reflect the reactions of other ladies, possibly courtesans, who gathered at the residences of Tullia d'Aragona and Laura Battiferra where Grazzini and his friends entertained them with their stories. However, Squarotti's most significant comments concern the manner with which Grazzini chose to narrate his introduction to the *Cene*. His intent was not to create the relaxed atmosphere of several friends enjoying a pleasant evening, but rather to introduce the narrative technique to be used in the novelle. Already in the introduction we catch a glimpse of the linearity of Grazzini's narrative style, which brings into relief movement and detail but shuns linguistic embellishments: "Facts, pure narrative, the development of events, the precision of movement: these are Grazzini's only interests and the very essence of his novelle" (p. 502). By way of example one may choose his description of a snowball fight.

> Now, while they enjoyed themselves in song and music, the sky became overcast and it began to snow so hard that in a short time the ground was well covered. Seeing this, the

> young men ceased playing and singing, left the room and went into a beautiful courtyard where they romped in the snow. The mistress of the house, a lovely and pleasant young lady, heard them and there came to her the idea of playfully attacking her brother and his friends. She quickly called four young ladies, two her stepdaughters, one a niece and the other a neighbor . . . and said: "My dear girls, I thought that we should quickly go up onto the roof and, together, make a large number of snowballs and that we should then go to the windows of the courtyard and wage a great war on those young men who are fighting each other; they, of course, will want to battle us in turn, but, being below us in the court, they will be struck by so many snowballs that they'll be at our mercy."
>
> Everyone was pleased with her idea and they organized themselves, taking their maids with them to the terrace. On the roof they very quickly filled three trays and two large baskets with firm snowballs and stealthily went to the windows which looked out over the courtyard where the unruly young men still fought with each other. Having placed a basket or tray under the windows, they faced the courtyard, one next to the other, and, bare-armed, they began to throw snowballs at the young men. The youths were startled by such an unusual surprise, so little did they expect it. Attacked so unexpectedly and suddenly, they stood there gazing upward, unable to decide what to do. Consequently, they were soundly struck on the head and face, on the chest and all over. Seeing that the ladies were really going at it, they gathered their forces, all the time laughing and shouting, and they began the most pleasant skirmish imaginable. But the men got the worst of it for they were struck whenever they bent over, and when they tried to throw a snowball, another came and struck them. Sometimes some of them slipped and fell and were struck by eight or ten snowballs at one time. The ladies thought this was great fun and for a good twenty minutes, as long as the snow lasted, they had the most pleasant time.

The attention which the author gives to the detail of the preparations and to the strategy of the fight resembles that of an historian objectively recounting an actual battle.

Many observations which can be made on the narrative style of the introduction to the *Cene* will be valid, too, for the novelle themselves. The attention to detail and to movement, which has been termed the plasticity of Grazzini's prose, is a constant characteristic.[7] The lack of attention to the individual storytellers, the failure to give them any psychological dimension, is also characteristic of the novelle, where events, facts, and movement take precedence over the characters who, as in the comedies, are often only instruments of the action.

The stories told on the first evening, the *piccole,* the short ones, are confined to the narration of one episode, usually a beffa. For their brevity and lack of narrative elaboration, they resemble any of the several scenes in Grazzini's comedies when the beffato succumbs to the machinations of the beffatori. (See, for example, the extremely theatrical scene in *Cena* I, ii, when the pedagogue is emasculated by his ward.) The *mezzane,* the stories of the second evening, allow for greater variety in the narrative and greater contrasts in tone—from the pastoral setting of the first story, to the fantastic and prebaroque elements of Lisabetta's narrative (II, iii), and the horrible and grotesque tragedy of Tiberia and Sergio (II, v). Of the *grandi,* the stories which were told on the eve of Berlingaccio (Maundy Thursday), we only have two in their entirety. These almost exceed the limits of the novella genre in their multiplicity of events, and, in truth, foreshadow the novel of the seventeenth century.

Obviously, Grazzini did not remain faithful to Boccaccio in the arrangement of his novelle. Giovanni Grazzini considers their order to reflect a conscious effort on the author's part to demonstrate in the three *Cene* various degrees of elaboration upon the traditional novella form.[8] Many critics are of the opinion that Grazzini reached the zenith of his abilities with the narrative in its more elaborate forms. D. H. Lawrence, as we know, chose to translate the second story of the last *Cena* in order to introduce Grazzini to the English-speaking public.

But Grazzini's prose technique seems best suited to brevity. The description, for example, of Brancazio Malaspini, frightened nearly to death one evening while passing some gallows along the Arno (I, ix), surpasses in effect the series of episodes which are contained in either story of the last *Cena*. Grazzini's inability, noted in his comedies, to integrate the variety of his material, is again evident in the longer novelle, where one event follows another as in a poorly constructed novel. Length, it would seem, was a handicap for Grazzini who was most inspired in the individual comic scene; his art failed him at the moment he had to connect several of these scenes into an integral unit.

At this point, before considering the novelle, it is useful to recall an observation made earlier: Grazzini, the novelliere, cannot for an instant be divorced from the burlesque poet or the writer of comedies. By the sixteenth century the novella was a genre which had undergone a variety of influences, the most significant of which came from the theatre, and Grazzini's novelle necessarily reflect these. The novella form was only one of several—though perhaps the most suitable—which Grazzini chose to use, and his inspiration never varied. Consequently, his novelle reflect the same themes, the same interests, the same weaknesses (in structure, for example) as his other works.

There is a significant difference, however, between the world of the *Cene* and that of Grazzini's comedies and poetry. It is in the variety of tone, which ranges from the coarse humor also found in the burlesque poetry to the macabre and the tragic. This added dimension which Grazzini gave to his Florentine world is due, of course, to the facility with which the novella lent itself to portraying a variety of human sentiments and situations. And Grazzini, who sought to represent the Florence of his day, was able to infuse more life into his work by touching upon reality in its multiple aspects. Nevertheless, Giovanni Grazzini's comment that the *Cene* represent a "symphonic metaphor of life" is not exactly accurate.[9] There always remains a lack of balance between comedy and the other aspects of life in the *Cene*. It was the beffa and the comic situation which interested Grazzini most and which remain the real subject of a majority of his novelle.

The comedy of the *Cene*, reflects, in many respects, the mood of the burlesque poetry more than that of the comedies for it better evokes the spirit of the Florentine brigate. Members of the brigate, who were so often the subjects of Grazzini's verse, appear time and again in the novelle. Scheggia, Monaco, Pilucca, and others all possess the same carefree attitude toward life, shunning hard work and taking every opportunity to demonstrate their abilities as masters of the beffa:

> Scheggia and Pilucca, as you have probably heard, were clever and fun-loving companions and both adept at their trade: one was a goldsmith, the other a sculptor. And although they were quite poor, they were merry enemies of work, a smile always on their faces; and, not giving thought to anything, they lived happily. [II, iv]

The beffe which they devise are an important source of humor in the novelle, and this humor is more gross than in the drama, more indicative of the sadistic pleasure which the beffatori took in the successful outcome of a pointless practical joke. The beffato who, in the comedies, usually suffers no more than humiliation, in the novella becomes a victim of inhuman treatment. A priest, Piero da Siena, for example, is made to think that he suffers from hallucinations, and

> dazed and half out of his mind, he was led to bed where, ruminating on his problem, he was so overcome with grief and melancholy that he ate and slept very little. So that, either because of the strangeness of his misfortune or because of his melancholy humors, madness, or frenzy, or even because of the devil which blinded him, one day when he was alone in his room, he threw himself headfirst from a window which looked out onto a courtyard and, striking the ground, he was smashed and died on the spot. [I, vii]

As Michel Plaisance says, there is an obviously more sympathetic attitude toward the beffato of the comedies than toward those of the novelle.[10] The reason would seem to be that, although Grazzini always found humor in the beffa ("nothing in the world gives more pleasure, particularly to women, than an act of revenge" [I, vi]), he had to temper them for the comedies to insure a happy ending.

Despite this difference between the beffa in the comedies and in the novelle, it was always the virtuosity of the beffatori that most interested Grazzini. This becomes most evident in the *Cene* where the author is best able to describe the details of the action. Often the novelle develop as a descriptive analysis of the plans and the strategy for a beffa. As the beffatori begin to carry out their plans, Grazzini describes every detail of the action, including the reactions of the participants, whether it be the exuberant joy of success experienced by the practical jokers or the amazement and disbelief of the beffato. One of the best examples of how Grazzini studies every feature of the beffa is in II, iv, where the familiar team of Monaco, Pilucca, and Scheggia conspire with a necromancer, Zoroastro, to trick the unsuspecting Gian Simone. We might cite by way of illustration the reactions to the first of two beffe, when Gian Simone believes that he has seen the results of the necromancer's powers to bring Monaco flying from the Mercato Vecchio into his room:

> Seeing this, Gian Simone was so startled and filled with fright that he just about dropped dead. Still, he wanted to speak but couldn't; and so great and unusual was his fear that he moved his bowels and filled his pants. Scheggia said to him, "Well, Gian Simone, what do you think? Isn't this clear enough proof that, with magic, he can do whatever he wishes?" Monaco shouted: "Ah, villainous traitors! Just what's going on? Is this how you treat good fellows?" Pilucca began to comfort him, but Scheggia and Zoroastro, standing near Gian Simone and noticing that he was silent, his face ashen in color, began to wonder about him; just as

> he was about to sit down, they grabbed him under the arms and walked him about the room. Coming to his senses again, Gian Simone, trembling, began to speak. "Let's go! Let's get out of here! Oh, to be at home again!" His teeth were trembling so violently that, weeks later, he still felt the effects. Scheggia took him by the hand and silently led him toward the stairs; but he hadn't gone two steps when he noticed that Gian Simone was leaking and he realized that his pants must be full. He turned and said to him, "Gian Simone, I'd say that you have shit." "Any fool could tell you that," answered Pilucca. "Don't you smell him?" "I'm surprised that I didn't release my heart and soul," said Gian Simone. "Oh! I was just about a victim of the devil!" "I think you'd better change clothes," answered Zoroastro, "so that you don't dirty up my house. And then, we'll see each other later." So Scheggia left and Pilucca pretended to be calming him down. Gian Simone was led to his house, all the time refusing to speak but moaning and sighing. Scheggia, having knocked at his door and having locked him inside, returned to his companions at Zoroastro's house. They laughed all evening and throughout supper.

One can see from the passage quoted above another parallel between the humor of the *Cene* and that of Grazzini's other work, especially the burlesque poetry: both exploit vulgarity and obscenity to elicit the same raucous laughter that results from the duping of a fool.

Grazzini's comedy, then, is of a type which depends upon the sadistic instincts of the audience to enjoy witnessing the humiliation of an unsuspecting victim at the hands of astute tricksters. It is a comedy which is anything but subtle, and, in the *Cene*, its grossness is emphasized by the insistence upon crude language and upon tricks which physically deform the victim and render him helpless. The instinctual nature of this humor, and its appeal to the baser senses, closely aligns it with the sensual nature of the culture from which it is derived.

At times the grotesqueness of the humor in the *Cene* gains an intensity which completely changes the tone of the novella;

a comic tale becomes macabre by insisting upon the cruelty or the horror of a situation. Thus there is a close relationship between some of the humorous novelle and those few which we would call tragic: in both cases the author dwells upon the horrifying details of human cruelty almost as if the bestial nature of man was meant to be a motif of the *Cene*.[11] A novella such as I, vii, which begins with a practical joke by one priest upon another, disintegrates into a series of macabre scenes in the darkness of a church as the body of a dead girl is subjected to manhandling with the resultant madness and suicide of the beffato. Grazzini's insistence upon the details of the body as it hangs from a rope—"[Piero] saw the dead girl tied up and hanging from the bell rope by her own tresses. He immediately recognized her by her long, blonde hair and by a crown of assorted flowers on her head. With great effort, he carefully untied her, put her over his shoulders and carried her to the tomb for reburial"—is characteristic of an interest in the lugubrious which appears throughout the novelle and which, in the emphasis it places upon the visual horror, foreshadows the baroque taste for the shocking and revolting aspects of reality.

Consequently, when Grazzini abandons comedy to write novelle of a tragic nature, he continues to depend upon the visual horror of the scene to elicit the emotions of his reader. Even when he attempts to develop the tragedy of the situation by studying the dilemma of the hero, he must, in the final scenes, shock his audience. We can, of course, explain this by Grazzini's inability to handle the psychological nature of a character or to probe beyond the surface for the dramatic possibilities of a situation, but if we recall the state of Italian tragedy during this period, we can see that he also followed a literary tradition and exploited the taste for horror which the drama of Seneca had encouraged. In fact, the narrative of II, v, reads like a scenario from an Italian Renaissance tragedy (we note again Grazzini's debt to the theatre), and Tiberia's monologue is worthy of most tragedies of the period. Tiberia, the young wife of Currado, is passionately in love with her stepson, Sergio. After having nursed him during a long illness, she realizes that she is ill herself because of her unrequited love:

> "Oh you wretched and miserable creature! You sought him out and now you suffer because of him. Now that he lives, you are afflicted with grief and torment. You brought health to one who is now the cause of your infirmity; you gave life to one who is now the cause of your dying. How much better to have never been born, oh miserable one, than to live so disconsolately. And with whom are you in love? How can such a love be if you are to remain free of sin? How, without shame, can you realize your fondest desires and the hopes which so afflict you? Forget this illicit love; think of something more worthy if you wish to flee endless shame and save your soul from eternal damnation." But then, remembering the beauty, the refinement, and the charming words of her beloved, she could no longer be resolute and said to herself: "How can I not love and enjoy, how can I help but adore and honor such a noble and regal person, whose entire being, whose very acts and speech are so beautiful that they were produced by heaven, destiny, and love for my comfort, my peace and my well-being? I cannot, I must not oppose what heaven decrees. And why do I sin? I, who am young, love a young man and that is only natural. Haven't I read and heard about so many other loves which were really illicit and vile? Not only have relatives loved each other, but even brothers are known to have loved sisters, fathers their daughters. If one considers the situation well, it is clear that he need never have anything to do with me. Just what do I fear then? Why don't I tell him openly about my desire and my torment and grief? He is kind and courteous and, in addition, he is obligated to me: he has offered his services a thousand times and he has told me that his fondest desire is to serve me and to do my pleasure. Why, then, do I hesitate? Who holds me back? Why am I so slow in seeking him out? Oh, how I know that he will reproach me and grieve for my coldness and cowardice! Hearing my sighs and seeing my tears, he will, I'm sure, become saddened and compassionate. And I, my own enemy, the very cause of my own damnation, still pine and

> hesitate to reveal everything to him? Already I can see his arms outstretched to embrace me, I feel them holding me close; already I can feel his kiss upon my lips."

Although Tiberia attempts to justify her feelings toward Sergio, the moral transgression which she commits by becoming his mistress must be punished. However, in the final scene, when Grazzini has the opportunity of creating a truly tragic moment, heightened by the helplessness of the two youngsters who are tied to their bed before they are murdered, he is unable to restrain himself and describes their anguish as they are blinded and then slaughtered. The tragedy of Tiberia and Sergio is overshadowed by the gruesome details of their dying moments:

> The poor, wretched lovers, their tongues torn out, their eyes gouged, their hands and feet severed, blood rushing from every orifice of the body, were at the point of death. Nevertheless, hearing Currado's final words and hearing the room being cleared and the doors closed on them, they managed to find each other by touch. And embracing with the stubs of their limbs, their mouths close together, they grievously awaited death, holding each other as closely as possible.

Similarly, in I, v, the tragic murder of two children is exploited for the visual effect of the death scene as they fall victim to their mother's knife "like innocent lambs."

In part, the superiority of the *Cene* over the comedies and the burlesque poetry is due to the variety of tone which, as we have seen, ranges from the comic to the macabre and the tragic. We might note, however, that Grazzini did not include in the *Cene* any novelle of a sentimental-romantic nature. His narrative is dominated by his taste for the theatrical, his desire to transform his Florentine world into what Giovanni Grazzini calls the "visual and the spoken."[12] There was no place in the *Cene* for sentiments which could not be translated into action or dialogue. The best example of the author's attempt to express feelings through a dramatic situation is in II, iii, where Lisabetta degli Uberti must express her love and devotion to Alessandro by relating a dream full of movement and plastic images, giving a tangibility to her emotions.

This comment on Lisabetta's dream leads us into a discussion of the narrative style of the *Cene*, a style which in many ways reflects the art of the writer of comedy. In the novella, Grazzini makes extensive use of comic dialogue in order to capture the vivacious spirit of the Florentines, whose wit was often most evident in their conversation. (A fine example is the passage, earlier quoted, about the beffa played on Gian Simone.) In addition, the narrative technique of the novella reveals the linear, mobile, quality of the comedies in its succession of events, one rapidly following upon another. Both the speech and the activities of the Florentines—we might say, the pulse of Florentine life—were the basis of Grazzini's art in the theatre and in his prose works. In the *Cene* Grazzini was able to give an added, spatial dimension to the dialogue and these other elements of style, by describing physical reality in great detail, and by accentuating the corporeal aspect of the physical world, he brought the reality of the situation more strikingly into relief. Characters, for example, though they may lack psychological development, are usually described in careful physical detail. The portrait of Sandra in I, i, is an instance in which the author pauses over the physical characteristics of a servant girl in an attempt to convey by words the robustness of her body:

> She was from Casentino and, as you know, twenty-two years old: fairly short, but large and solidly built; a brunette with lovely, firm flesh and very good color in her face; large, watery eyes which shot out fire and protruded so that they seemed to want to jump out of her head. She was a real peasant type, a work horse who could pull anyone out of the mud.

Such attention to detail is by no means confined to the description of an individual. We have seen it applied for dramatic effect in Guasparri del Calandra's frightening experience on the Ponte alla Carraia; it intensifies the macabre tone of the beffa played on Prete Piero da Siena; it increases the horror of Tiberia and Sergio's fate at the hands of Currado.

These three elements of Grazzini's style—a concern for the nearly photographic depiction of the physical world and the anatomy, in particular, the translation into prose of movement and human activity, and the extensive use of dialogue—are evidence of the author's attempt to represent surface reality and the dimensions of the physical world. Perhaps he was limited to describing the exterior world by an artistic temperament which would not allow him to penetrate human emotions and motivations. But we should recall, too, that Grazzini's prose style foreshadows that of the late sixteenth century and that which was to be the baroque prose of the seventeenth century. Grazzini's successors often confined themselves to portraying the physical world as if they could thereby discern some meaning in the life forces. In his own way, Grazzini, by confining himself to the physical world of sixteenth-century Florence, attempted to capture the spirit of life in his people.

There is an extremely important aspect of Grazzini's prose which relates it even more closely to his other works and, significantly, to the prose style of the seventeenth century. For Grazzini, the prose medium was not solely a means of narration; it also provided an opportunity to display that verbal virtuosity which we have noted so often in his comedies and in his poetry. At times, in fact, his prose does not rise above the word-play of his burlesque rhymes:

> Neither clever episodes nor witty replies, audacious words nor witty witticisms, silly grossness nor gross silliness, neither humorous invention with a pleasing and marvelous ending, neither pleasure nor content, but rather, fiery indignation, anguished laments, mad jealousy and jealous mad-

> ness, a cruel invention with a hopeless, bestial ending, unpleasantness and grief had this time brought abundant tears to the eyes of the lovely young ladies. [I, vi]

But instances such as this are rare, for with his prose Grazzini's style becomes more refined. He combines convoluted phrases in the style of Boccaccio with a constant awareness of the value and of the effect of the individual word. Sometimes the word, both in its aural qualities and its suggestiveness, is chosen to give greater visual and tactile reality to the item described; at other times it is chosen from the repertory of Florentine dialect terms to enhance the local flavor of the prose. This is to suggest that in the *Cene*, not only do we find the polemical spirit of the author who constantly probed the possibilities of the Florentine language, but at the same time the germ of that prose style which in the following century was to exploit the word for all its implications and suggestions.[13]

CONCLUSION

Considering Grazzini's active opposition to the Accademia Fiorentina and to some of the most illustrious personalities of late Medicean Florence, it is surprising that historians of the late Renaissance have not given his work more serious consideration. Since Grazzini always remained on the fringe of academic life, antagonizing pedants and ridiculing their work, he has been neglected and written off as an interesting Florentine personality but of little consequence to the mainstream of sixteenth-century academicism. Grazzini's opinions of his contemporaries and of current literary styles are significant, however, to one who would understand the changing climate of the late Renaissance in Florence. By opposing the arid formalism of the traditionalists, Grazzini, like many of his little-known contemporaries, belongs to a counter-academic trend which looked to the daily life of the people for its inspiration. This trend involved two important developments whose significance to later literature needs examination. First, there was a lively interest in the long tradition of popular literature. In actively opposing pedantic influences upon the popular genres, while yet maintaining the purity of the spoken language in their compositions, popular writers, and particularly Florentines like Grazzini, attempted to bring a new respectability to their art. It was to appeal to the public by its reflection of everyday life, but, at the same time, its literary merit was to make it the most valuable and lasting document of contemporary Renaissance life. Intimately connected with the increasing interest in an art of popular inspiration was a vital critical spirit among the adversaries of academic life. Unlike the formal critical methods of the academicians, those of the popular writers were entirely based on the conviction that art is life and that the measure of a true artist lies in his ability to represent reality as he sees it. This was the inspiration behind Grazzini's *Cene.*

This critical spirit was accompanied by changing tastes in technique of composition. Interest in the spoken word manifested itself in literature by a preoccupation with dialogue. Grazzini's comedies and novelle sacrifice psychological penetration of characters and situations for clever and witty speech. Effects of language become one of the author's primary concerns. In a similar way, movement and the nervous activity of life are brought to the fore in an attempt to capture the life force on the written page. In this fervent attempt to portray life in art, all of life's ingredients become subject to consideration, the grotesque and the deformed as well as the humorous and the beautiful. The result in literature is a chiaroscuro and a near frenzy of movement which we might term literary "mannerism."

Grazzini's position in the development of literature during the late Renaissance is, like that of many of his contemporaries, highly ambivalent. Although it reflects many prebaroque elements of style and taste, it remains closely aligned to traditional literary tenets. In this sense, Grazzini's art, though limited by its Florentine provincialism, is an effective gauge of the changes which were taking place in sixteenth-century literature as the authority of literary tradition came into question.

APPENDIX I

GRAZZINI'S *TAVOLA DELLE OPERE*

This catalogue of Grazzini's works was discovered by Carlo Verzone in the library of the Strozzi family. It was first published by him in his edition of Grazzini's *Rime burlesche* (Florence: G. C. Sansoni, 1882), pp. cxix–cxxiv, and is reproduced here as it appeared in that edition.

La qualità, e quantità delle composizioni, e
i nomi loro particolari, fatte da me per infino a questo giorno XV di settembre MDLXVI;
e da farse in tutto il rimanente della mia vita.

Rime Petrarchesche

Sonetti, intorno a Cinquecento, con quegli composti ancora in morte d'Amici, e d'huomini illustri, e di Giovani, e di Donne bellissime.

Madrigali circa Quattrocento, con quegli composti

per Intermedi delle Commedie mie, e d'altrui.
*Sestine, due.
Canzoni, quattro.
*Canzone in morte di Carlo Quinto Imperadore.
*Canzone in morte di Donna Maria de' Medici.
*Canzona amorosa prima
*Canzona amorosa seconda
*Capitoli quattro
Stanze sopra la Gelosia
Stanze in nome di Dante, e del Petrarca
*Stanze in nome di Marcantonio Villani
*Stanze di Battaglie, cioè un libro di Romanzi chiamato *Ruggier da Risa,* ma non riscritto, nè fornito affatto com'egli debbe stare
Stanze sopra le bellezze d'una gentil Donna
Stanze in dolersi d'Amore e della sua Donna

Rime spirituali

Sonetti, da trenta.
Madrigali, intorno a quindici.
*Capitoli, uno al Crocefisso
*Stanze, la Festa di san Felice in Piazza, cioè l'Annunziazione della Vergine.
*Laude, da Quaranta

Rime Pastorali

Sonetti, intorno a Cento.
*Canzoni, due.
Sestine, una.
*Stanze, in lode d'una Ninfa.
*Stanze, Innamoramento di Ghiacinto, e di Dafni
*Stanze, Bellezze di Lidia
*Stanze, cantate da due Pastori
Madrigali, intorno a Cencinquanta, intendendovisi i Narcisi.

* An asterisk denotes those compositions which Verzone was unable to find.

Egloghe Diece

Egloga, le Nozze dell'Illmo e Ecc.^{mo} Duca Cosimo.
Egloga, Natale di Don Francesco Medici.
Egloga, Amaranta, in morte d'una gentil Donna.
Egloga, Amor di Melibeo.
Egloga, Canto di Galatea, e di Filli.
Egloga, Bellezze di Lidia
Egloga, Sagrifizio di Siringa a Venere.
Egloga, Disputa d'Amore
Egloga, Disperazion di Tirsi.
Egloga, Passione, e morte del figliuol di Dio.

Rime burlesche

Capitoli intorno a ottanta, a immitazione del Berni, ma sceltine e riscrittone da Cinquanta.
Capitolo, in lode della Salsiccia.
In lode della Caccia.
In biasimo della Caccia
Capitol terzo della Caccia
Capitol della Pazzia
Capitolo in lode delle Mele
In lode delle Castagne
In lode de i Piselli
In lode de i Beccafichi
*In lode del Sonno
In lode degli Spinaci
In lode del Sedere
In lode de i Zoccoli
In dispregio de i Zoccoli
In lode della Zuppa
*In lode de i Fichi
In lode del Pensiero
In disonor del Pensiero
In lode delle Corna
In lode de i Coglioni
In lode de i Pesceduovi
In lode del Calcio, Giuoco di Palla
In lode della Rovescina
In dispregio de i Guanti
Al Padre Varchi
A Visin Merciaio
A Cencio del Organi
Al Medesimo
A M. Pier Fagiuoli
A Messer Baccio d'Avanzati
A M. Vincenzio Guidi
In lode della Vecchiaia
In lode delle Barbe
In lode dell'ozio
In lode del Dispetto
*In lode della Maninconia
In lode di Zanni, e del Magnifico Commediai.
In lode del Giuoco del Maglio

*A M. Lione da Ricasoli
*Al Lottino Segretario
A M. Lionardo della Fonte
A Giovambatista della Fonte
A Simon della Volta
Al Padre Stradino
*A Cecco di Sandro Battiloro e M° di Scherma
In nome di Cencio degli Organi
*In lode de' Pedanti
In lode de i Poponi
In lode della Zinzera Femmina di Mondo
In lode del San Giorgio di Donatello
*In lode delle Melagrance
In lode del nome di Giovanni
In lode del Bagnarsi in Arno
Sonetti, circa seicento, tra mandati a varie persone e composti sopra diversi soggetti, e scritti in lode, e in biasimo d'alcuni Amici, o Nimici.
Canzoni, quattro.
In morte di Giuanni Falconi
In morte dello Stradino
In morte d'un Cane di M. Pandolfo Pucci
Sopra il Membro virile
Madrigli, dugento, o in circa
Madrigalesse intorno a cinquanta
Stanze, parecchi Mane
La Guerra de i Mostri
Le lodi dell'Antella, e di Ligliano
*In lode delle Stravaganze dello Stradino
*In lode della Tornatella, compagnia così detta
*La Rotta degli Aramei.
*Il Trionfo degli Humidi.
Il Lamento dell'Accademia
E Stanze altre spicciolate a due a due, e a quattro, e a sei, così burlesche come alla Petrarchesca, e Spirituali in quantità grandissima.

Prose in sul Grave

Le Cene, o vero il Trentafavole, che sono trenta Novelle dette in Firenze da cinque Huomini, e da cinque giovani Donne di verno intorno al fuoco a veglia, in tre Giovedì; che l'ultimo venne a essere il giorno di Berlingaccio: dove se ne dissero cinque innanzi, e cinque doppo cena; per essere state le maggiori, e le più lunghe; perciocchè le prime furono piccole, e le seconde mezzane, scritte, e composte ad immitazione del Boccaccio.

Commedie sei senza il Pedante che si stracciò, e arse

La Gelosia.
La Spiritata, recitate, e stampate.
La Pinzochera.
La Strega, o la Taddea.
I Parentadi
La Medaglia, o la Sibilla.

Commedie Spirituali, Quattro

*La Croce, o santa Helena.
*Santa Appollonia.
*Santa Caterina.
*Santa Orsola, e tutte improsa.

Farse, tre

*Il Frate.
*La Monica.
*La Giostra.

Comenti

Il Piangirida.
Sopra il Capitolo della Salsiccia in nome di Maestro Niccodemo della Pietra al Migliaio.
Sopra il sonetto, *Una candida Cerva sopra l'herba*
Sopra il sonetto, *Già fiammeggiava l'amorosa stella*
Sopra un sonetto
. . . .

Dialoghi, cinque

*La Girandola.
*Il Giacchio tondo, in mia difesa contro i Dotti
*Il Pater igniosce in mia difesa contro i Pedanti
*La Compieta che ragiona delle Mascherate, e delle Commedie secondo l'uso moderno

Canti, o Mascherate circa a cento tra carnascialeschi, in sul grave, e satirichi mandati per Firenze, per le case; a Nozze, a Cene, e a Conviti: con quelli ancora che non si son visti.

Orazioni due
*A Gismondo Martelli in lode della Poesia, e in persuaderlo a seguitarla.
Al Crocefisso, nel venerdì santo.

Le Satire, e le Elegie per esser poche, e in terza rima l'ho messe tra i capitoli; queste fra i Petrarcheschi, e quelle fra i burleschi.

Degli Epigrammi, e degli Epitaffi ancora che n'habbia composti assai, non ne farò memoria alcuna.

Lettere Poetiche, e notabili

L'entrata di Carlo Quinto imperadore in Firenze
*L'entrata della Moglie del Duca Alessandro Medici
*L'esequie del Duca Alessandro.
*Lettera de Tremuoti, quando furono grandissimi a Scarperia.
Lettera della Piena del Quaranzette
*Lettera della Piena del cinquanzette
Lettera del Gobbo da Pisa
Lettera del k in nome di Pietro Aretino a gli Accademici Fiorentini; e così molte altre che servono per epistole innanzi a diverse composizioni tanto in Rima, quanto in Prosa, e ancora scritte a molti Amici, delle quali non ho tenuto conto, nè fatto stima.

Scritte doppo

Stanze in dispregio delle sberrettate.
*Stanze in lode del Signor Carlo, Conte di Belgioioso.
Stanze in difesa delle Comedie in prosa.

APPENDIX II

GRAZZINI'S PRINTED WORKS

This list of Grazzini's printed works incorporates and supplements those compiled by Carlo Verzone for his editions of the burlesque poetry and the novelle, and by Giovanni Grazzini for his 1953 edition of the comedies. I have included only those works published before 1900; later editions cited appear in the Note on the Translations and the References. In listing anthologies and collections which include selections from Grazzini's writings, I have given closest attention to the earlier periods. For the nineteenth century, with the publication of many anthologies and scholastic editions, I have had to limit myself to the more important or unusual items. For those entries which I have been able to locate, I have made the appropriate indication.

For descriptions and locations of both edited and unedited manuscripts, see Verzone, ed., *Rime*, pp. lvii–xxxiv, and *Cene*, pp. xxiii–xxxv, and the contributions of Paul Oskar Kristeller in *Iter Italicum* (London, 1963), Vol. I.

Abbreviations

Verzone, ed., *Rime* Grazzini, Antonfrancesco. *Le Rime*, ed. Carlo Verzone. Florence: Sansoni, 1882.

Verzone, ed., *Cene*	———. *Le Cene*, ed. Carlo Verzone. Florence: Sansoni, 1890.
Poggiali	———. *Eglogbe ed altre rime*, ed. Domenico Poggiali. Livorno, 1799.
Moücke	———. *Rime*. 2 vols. Florence: Moücke, 1741–42.
BM	British Museum
BNP	Bibliothèque Nationale, Paris
BNF	Biblioteca Nazionale Centrale, Florence
BSM	Biblioteca di San Marco, Florence
Accademia della Crusca	Accademia della Crusca Library, Florence
BNR	Biblioteca Nazionale Centrale, Rome
LC	Library of Congress
H	Harvard University Library
P	Princeton University Library
Folger	Folger Library, Washington, D.C.
UC	University of California Library, Berkeley
UW	University of Wisconsin Library, Madison

1547

1. Rime della Signora Tullia di Aragona; et di diversi a lei. Con privilegio. In Vinegia appresso Gabriel Giolito de Ferrari. MDXLVII.

   Several other editions published during the sixteenth and seventeenth centuries. Includes one sonnet by Grazzini (Moücke, I, xxiii).

   BM BNP BNF BNR UW

1548

2. Il Primo libro dell'opere burlesche di M. Francesco Berni, di M. Gio. della Casa, del Varchi, del Mauro, di M. Bino, del Molza, del Dolce, et del Firenzuola ricorretto, et con diligenza ristampato. In Firenze. MDXLVIII.

   Reprinted in 1550, 1552. Later editions were supplemented and titles vary. Includes four ottave in the name

of Berni and two sonnets (Verzone, ed., *Rime*, pp. 79–81).
BNP (also has 1552 edition)

1549

3. Le Rime di M. Agnolo Firenzuola fiorentino. Fiorenza: Giunti. MDXLIX. [Edited by L. Scala]
Contains one sonnet by Grazzini.
BM BNP

1551

4. La Gelosia. Comedia d'Antonfrancesco Grazini fiorentino detto il Lasca. Recitatasi in Firenze publicamente il carnovale dell'anno 1550. Stampata in Fiorenza in casa de Giunti. MDLI.
Includes six madrigals by Grazzini (Moücke, I, xiv–xix).
BM LC

1552

5. I Sonetti del Burchiello, et di messer Antonio Alamanni, alla burchiellesca. Nuovamente ammendati, e corretti, et con somma diligenza ristampati. In Firenze. MDLII.
Contains one sonnet by Grazzini, "In nome di Burchiello" (Verzone, ed., *Rime*, p. 81).
BM
6. La Gelosia. Comedia d'Antonfrancesco Grazini fiorentino. Detto il Lasca. Nuovamente stampata. In Venetia per Gio. Griffio. Ad instanzia di Pietro Boselli. MDLII.

1557

7. De' sonetti di M. Benedetto Varchi colle risposte, e proposte di diversi. Parte seconda in Fiorenza appresso Lorenzo Torrentino. MDLVII.
Includes three sonnets by Grazzini (Moücke, I, vi, xxxi, xxxii).
BM LC

1559

8. Tutti i trionfi, charri, mascheaate ò canti carnascialeschi andati per Firenze, dal têpo del Magnifico Lorenzo vecchio

de Medici, quâdo egli hebbero prima cominciamêto, per insino à questo anno presente 1559. Con due tavole, una dinanzi, e una dietro, da trovare agievolmente, e tosto ogni canto, ò mascherata. In Fiorenza. MDLVIIII.

BNF H

1560

9. Il Primo libro dell'opere toscane di M. Laura Battiferra degli Ammannati, alla illustrissima e eccellentissima Signora, la Signora Duchessa di Fiorenza e di Siena. Con privilegio. In Firenze appresso i Giunti. MDLX.

Contains sonnets by Benedetto Varchi, Agnolo Allori (il Bronzino), and others. Two sonnets by Grazzini (Moücke, I, xliv, xlv).

BM (also has another edition of 1694) BNP also has 1694 edition.

1561

10. La Spiritata. Commedia di Antonfrancesco Grazini, detto il Lasca, recitatasi in Bologna, e in Firenze al pasto del magnifico Signore, il S. Bernardetto de Medici, il carnovale dell'anno MDLX. In Fiorenza appresso i Giunti. 1561.

1562

11. La Spiritata. Commedia di Antonfrancesco Grazini detto il Lasca, recitatasi in Bologna, e in Firenze al pasto del magnifico Signore, il S. Bernardetto de Medici, il carnovale dell'anno. MDLX. In Venetia, MDLXI. Appresso Francesco Rampazetto, MDLXII.

BNP BSM

1563

12. Poesie toscane, et latine di diversi eccel. ingegni. Nella morte del S. D. Giovanni Cardinale, del Sig. Don Grazia de Medici, et della S. Donna Leonora di Toledo de Medici Duchessa di Fiorenza, et di Siena in Fiorenza appresso L. Torrentino. Impressor Ducale. MDLXIII.

Contains various poems by Grazzini: one madrigal

Moücke, I, xlvii), two sonnets (Moücke, I, lv and lvi), and six madrigals (Moücke, I, xlii–xlvii).

1564

13. Oratione o vero discorso di M. Giovan Maria Tarsia. Fatto nell'essequie del divino Michelagnolo Buonarroti. Con alcuni sonetti, e prose latine e volgari di diversi, circa il disparere occorso tra gli scultori, e pittori. In Fiorenza appresso Bartolomeo Sermartelli. MDLXIIII.

   Includes one sonnet by Grazzini (Verzone, ed., *Rime*, pp. 84–85) and Benvenuto Cellini's discourse on sculptors and painters.

   BM

14. Poesie di diversi authori latine e volgari, fatte nella morte di Michel'agnolo Buonarroti. Raccolte per Domenico Legati. In Fiorenza. Appresso Bartolomeo Sermartelli. MDLXIIII.

   Includes three sonnets by Grazzini (Moücke, I, lvii–lviiii).

1565

15. Rime di diversi nobilissimi, et eccellentissimi auttori in lode dell'illustrissima Signora, la Signora Donna Lucretia Gonzaga Marchesana. In Bologna per Giovanni Rossi. Havuta prima la licentia da Mons. Leone Leonori, Vicario Generale di Bologna. Et dal R. P. Inquisitore. MDLXV.

   Three sonnets (Moücke, I, xli–xliii) and six madrigals (Moücke, I, xxxv–xl) by Grazzini.

1566

16. Componimenti latini, e toscani da diversi suoi amici composti. Nella morte di M. Benedetto Varchi. In Firenze. Con licenzia, et privilegio. 1566.

   Includes two sonnets by Grazzini, one addressed to M. Laura Battiferra, the other to Lionardo Salviati.

17. Descrizione degl'intermedii rappresentati colla commedia nelle nozze dell'illustrissimo . . . principe di Firenze e di Siena. Firenze, 1566.

   Grazzini's *Descrizione* was written to describe the 1565 production of Francesco d'Ambra's comedy, *La Co-*

fanaria, with stage sets designed by G. B. Cini. Subsequent editions of the text of the comedy were accompanied by Grazzini's commentary.
BNP

18. La Spiritata. Comedia di Antonfrancesco Grazini, detto il Lasca, recitatasi in Bologna, e in Firenze al pasto del magnifico Signore, il S. Bernardetto de' Medici, il carnovale dell'anno MDLX. In Venetia, appresso Francesco Rampazetto. MDLXVI.

1568

19. La Gelosia. Commedia d'Antonfranc. Grazini fiorentino. Nuovamente ristampata, & aggiuntovi gl'intermedi. In Fiorenza appresso i Giunti. MDLXVIII.
BM BNP LC

1571

20. Primo volume della scielta di stanze di diversi autori toscani, raccolte, et nuovamente poste in luce da M. Agostino Ferentilli et da lui con ogni diligenza riviste. Al Signor Francesco Gentile. Con licenza et privilegio. In Venetia, ad instantia de' Giunti di Firenze. MDLXXI.
Includes sonnets of Benedetto Varchi, G. B. Guarini, and Grazzini's "Stanze sopra la gelosia."

1573

21. Sonetti spirituali di M. Benedetto Varchi. Con alcune risposte, e proposte di diversi eccellentissimi ingegni. Nuovamente stampati. In Fiorenza nella stamperia de' Giunti. 1573 con licentia, et privilegio.
Two sonnets by Grazzini (Moücke, I, vii–viii).
BM UC

1579

22. Stanze in dispregio delle sberrettate. Del Lasca. In Firenze. A distanza di Francesco Dini da Colle. MDLXXVIIII.
Edition is very rare. See Verzone's discussion, *Rime*, p. xxx, n. 1.

1582

23. Comedie d'Antonfranc. Grazini academico fiorentino, detto il Lasca; cioè La Gelosia, La Spiritata, La Strega, La Sibilla, La Pinzochera, I Parentadi. Parte non piú stampate, né recitate. Con privilegi. In Venetia, appresso Bernardo Giunti, e fratelli. 1582.
BM BNP BNF LC Folger

1584

24. La Guerra de mostri d'Antonfrancesco Grazini detto il Lasca. Al Padre Stradino. Con privilegio di tutte l'opere. In Firenze, per Domenico Manzani, 1584.
LC

25. [Another edition] La Guerra de mostri d'Antonfrancesco Grazini, detto il Lasca. Al Padre Stradino. Con privilegio di tutte l'opere. In Firenze, per Domenico Manzani, 1584.
This edition is rare.

1589

26. Lezione di Maestro Niccodemo della Pietra al Migliaio [i.e., Grazzini]. Sopra il capitolo della salsiccia del Lasca. All'Arciconsolo della Crusca. Con privilegio. In Firenze, per Domenico e Francesco Manzani, 1589. Con permissione de' superiori.
BM

1590

27. Rime piacevoli di Cesare Caporali, del Mauro, et d'altri auttori. Accresciute in questa quinta impressione di molte rime gravi, et burlesche del Signor Torquato Tasso, del Sig. Anibal Caro, et di diversi nobilissimi ingegni. Al molto Mag. Sig. Lodovico Righetti. In Ferrara. Per Benedetto Mamarello. MDXC.
Includes Grazzini's capitolo, "In lode della pazzia" (Verzone, ed., *Rime*, pp. 559–64).
Six printings by 1592. BM has 1592 edition. BNP has 1591 edition and others.

1603

28. Delle Rime piacevoli del Berni, Casa, . . . Dedicate all'illustriss. Signore, il Signor Giacomo Doria. In Vicenza, per Barezzo Barezzi libraro in Venetia. Con licenza de' superiori. 1603. [3 volumes]
    Two later editions, 1609–10 and 1627. The latter has 4 volumes.
    BM (also has the two later editions)

1606

29. Lezione di Maesrtro [sic] Niccodemo della Pietra al Migliaio. Sopra il capitolo della salsiccia, del Lasca. In Firenze. Per Domenico Manzani, MDCVI. Con licenza de' superiori.
    Reprint of 1589 edition with emendations.

1612

30. La Gigantea et la Nanea insieme con la Guerra de mostri. In Firenze. MDCXII.
    Reprint of 1584 edition with a few variations.
    BM BNP

1628

31. La Sibilla. Comedia d'Antonfrancesco Grazini, academico fiorentino, detto il Lasca. Stampata la prima volta, e non recitata mai. Con licenza de' superiori, e privilegio. In Venetia, MDCXXVIII. Presso Gio. Battista Combi.
    BNP
32. La Strega. Comedia d'Antonfrancesco Grazini academico fiorentino, detto il Lasca. Nuovamente ristampata, e non recitata mai. Con privilegio e licenza de' superiori. In Venetia, MDCXXVIII. Presso Gio. Battista Combi.
    BNP

1661–1723

33. Prose fiorentine raccolte dallo Smarrito accademico della Crusca [i.e. Carlo Dati]. Nella nuova stamperia all'insegna della Stella. Firenze, 1661–1723. [6 volumes]

Contains Grazzini's letter to Varchi and two sonnets (Moücke, I, cxiv–xv).
BM
Two later editions: Florence, 1716–45, edited by Giovanni Bottari, Rosso A. Martini, and Tommaso Buonaventuri (17 volumes), and Venice, 1735 (5 volumes). Later editions located at BM UC.

1700

34. Notizie letterarie, ed istoriche intorno agli uomini illustri dell'Accademia Fiorentina. Parte prima. In Firenze. MDCC. Per Piero Matini stampatore arcivescovale. Con lic. de' sup.
Includes several poems by Grazzini.
UC UW

1714

35. Memorie istoriche della miracolosa immagine di Maria Vergine dell'Impruneta raccolte da Giovambatista Casotti lettore d'istoria sacra e profana nello Studio di Firenze. All'Altezza Reale di Cosimo Terzo Granduca di Toscana. In Firenze. MDCCXIIII. Appresso Giuseppe Manni all'Inseg. di S. Gio: di Dio. Con licenza de superiori.
Has five sonnets by Grazzini (Moücke, II, lxxxvi–viiii, vii).
BM BNP UC

1717

36. Fasti consolari dell'Accademia Fiorentina di Salvino Salvini consolo della medesima e rettore generale dello Studio di Firenze. All'Altezza Reale del Serenissimo Gio: Gastone Gran Principe di Toscana. In Firenze. MDCCXVII. Nella stamperia di S. A. R. Per Gio: Gaetano Tartini, e Santi Franchi. Con licenza de' superiori.
Has two sonnets by Grazzini (Verzone, ed., *Rime*, pp. 65–66).
BM BNP Accademia della Crusca

1741–42

37. Rime di Antonfrancesco Grazzini detto il Lasca. In Firenze. Nella stamperia di Francesco Moücke. Con licenza de' superiori. [Volume I, 1741; Volume II, 1742]
LC UC

1743

38. La Seconda Cena di Antonfrancesco Grazzini detto il Lasca ove si raccontano dieci bellissime, e piacevolissime novelle non mai più stampate. All'Illustriss. Sig. Giovanni Bouverye Cavaliere Inglese. In Stambul dell'Egira 122. Appresso Ibrahim Achmet stampatore del Divano. Con approvazione, e privilegio della formidabile Porta Ottomanna. [Florence, 1743]

1750

39. Rime oneste de' migliori poeti antichi e moderni scelte ad uso delle scuole. Con annotazioni ed indici utilissimi. Tomo primo. In Bergamo, MDCCL. Appresso Pietro Lancellotto. Con licenza de' superiori.
    Includes various sonnets by Grazzini included in Verzone (*Rime*) and Moücke.
40. Teatro comico fiorentino, contenente XX delle piú rare commedie citate da' Sigg. Accademici della Crusca. In Firenze, MDCCL. Con licenza de' superiori. [6 volumes]
    BM UC BNP
41. Tutti i trionfi, carri, mascherate o canti carnascialeschi andati per Firenze dal tempo del Magnifico Lorenzo de' Medici fino all'anno 1559. In questa seconda edizione corretti, con diversi mss. collazionati, delle loro varie lezioni arricchiti, notabilmente accresciuti, e co' ritratti di ciascun poeta adornati. [Edited by Neri del Boccia, pseud. of R. M. Bracci]. In Cosmopoli [Lucca], 1750–80 [Two parts]
    BM UW P

1754

42. Del novelliero italiano. Contenente novelle XXXI. In Venezia. MDCCLIV. Presso Giambatista Pasquali con licenza de' superiori. [3 volumes]
    Volume III contains *Cena* I, 9; *Cena* II, 1, 4, 6.
    BM

1756

43. La Prima e la seconda Cena. Novelle di Antonfrancesco Grazzini detto il Lasca. Alle quali si aggiunge una novella

della terza Cena, che unitamente colla prima ora per la prima volta si dà alla luce. Colla vita dell'autore; e con la dichiarazione delle voci più difficili. In Londra. MDCCLVI. Appresso G. Nourse. [Edited by F. Niccolò B. Pagliarini Romano]
BM BNP LC H

1765

44. Scelta di prose e poesie italiane. Prima edizione. In Londra, appresso Giovanni Nourse. MDCCLXV.
Rare

1769

45. Commedia in tre atti senza titolo [*Il Frate*], in Niccolò Machiavelli, *Opere*, Cosmopoli [Venice], 1769.

1772

46. La Gigantea, la Nanea e la Guerra de mostri. Poemi di diversi. Yverdon. MDCCLXXII.
BM

47. Il Frate, in Niccolò Machiavelli, *Tutte l'opere* . . . con una prefazione di Giuseppe Baretti. Londra, stampate per T. Davies, 1772. [3 volumes]
LC BM BNP

1776

48. Les nouvelles d'Antoine-François Grazzini, . . . Lefebvre de Villebrune, trans. Berlin [Paris], 1776. [2 volumes]
BM BNP

1787

49. Ariosto, Berni. Satirici e burleschi del secolo XVI. Venezia MDCCLXXXVII. Presso Antonio Zatta e figli. Con licenza de' superiori e privilegio.
BNP

1790

50. La Prima e la seconda Cena. Novelle di Antonfrancesco Grazzini detto il Lasca. Alle quali si aggiunge una novella

che ci resta della terza Cena. Leida. MDCCXC. Appresso G. Van Der Bet.

BM

Other editions in 1793 (BM BNP LC H), 1804 (BM), 1810 (BNP UC).

1799

51. Egloghe ed altre rime di Antonfrancesco Grazzini detto il Lasca ora per la prima volta accuratamente pubblicate. Livorno, 1799.

BM BNP LC UC

1813

52. Commedia in tre atti senza titolo [*Il Frate*], in Niccolò Machiavelli, *Opere*. Italia [Florence], 1813. [8 volumes]

BM LC

53. Serie dei testi di lingua stampati che si citano nel Vocabolario degli Accademici della Crusca, posseduta da Gaetano Poggiali con una copiosa giunta d'opere di scrittori di purgata favella, le quali si propongono per essere spogliate ad accrescimento dello stesso Vocabolario. Livorno. Presso Tommaso Masi e Comp., 1813. [2 volumes]

Contains various poems by Grazzini.

BM

1815

54. Le Cene. Milano. Per Giovanni Silvestri. 1815. [3 volumes]

BNP LC UC

1823

55. La Gigantea e la Nanea insieme con la Guerra de' mostri e le stanze del poeta Sciarra [pseud. of Pietro Strozzi], in *Poesie di eccellenti autori toscani per far ridere le brigate.* Leida [Livorno?], 1823. Presso G. Van Der Bet. [In 3 parts]

BM

56. Sonetti di Angiolo Allori detto il Bronzino ed altre rime inedite di più insigni poeti. Firenze, Magheri, 1823.

Two sonnets by Grazzini inspired by portraits executed by Bronzino.
LC

1825

57. Saggio di rime di diversi buoni autori che fiorirono dal XIV fino al XVIII secolo. Firenze nella stamperia Ronchi e C.° MDCCCXXV.
Ottave written by Grazzini to Signora Armenia.
BM LC

58. The Italian Novelists. . . . London, 1825. [4 volumes]
Includes four novelle by Grazzini.
BM

1829

59. La Strega, in *Teatro classico italiano antico e moderno, ovvero il Parnaso teatrale.* Con illustrazioni biografiche, istoriche e critiche. Edizione giusta i testi piú accreditati. Lipsia, presso Ernesto Fleischer. 1829.
BM

1833

60. Le Cene di Anton-Francesco Grazzini detto il Lasca, in *Raccolta di novellieri italiani.* Tipografia Borghi e compagni. 1833.
Rare. Verzone, ed. *Cene,* p. xviii, states that most copies were lost in a flood which inundated Florence in 1844.
BM

61. La Guerra dei mostri, in *Scelta di poemi giocosi.* Milan: Nicolò Bettoni, 1833.
UC

1839

62. Scelta di poesie liriche dal primo secolo della lingua fino al 1700. Firenze, Felice Le Monnier e compagni, 1839.
Contains various poems by Grazzini which are included in the collections of Moücke and Poggiali.

1840

63. Novella storica relativa a Lorenzo de' Medici detto il Magnifico scritta da Gio. Batista [sic] Grazzini detto il Lasca. Badia Fiesolana. 1840.

1842

64. Capitolo inedito di Anton Francesco Grazzini detto il Lasca tratto da un codice che si conserva nella biblioteca del Museo Brittanico di Londra. Faenza. Dall'imprimeria del Conti. MDCCCXLII.
    Capitolo is addressed to Raffaello de' Medici.
    BM

1843

65. Novelle scelte e lezione di Giovanni [sic] Grazzini detto il Lasca. Parma: Pietro Fiaccadori, 1843.

1846

66. Poesie italiane inedite di dugento autori dall'origine della lingua infino al secolo decimosettimo raccolte e illustrate da Francesco Trucchi socio di varie accademie. Prato, per Ranieri Guasti. 1846. [4 volumes]
    Contains various poems by Grazzini.

1847

67. Tesoro di novellieri italiani scelti dal decimo terzo al decimonono secolo, e pubblicati per cura di Giuseppe Zirardini. Paris, 1847.
    Nine novelle by Grazzini.
    BM

1851

68. Italiänischer Novellenschatz. Ausgewählt und übersetzt von A. Keller. Leipzig, 1851. [6 volumes]
    BM

1852

69. Il Frate, in Niccolò Machiavelli, *Opere minori*. Firenze: Le Monnier, 1852. [Edited by F. L. Polidori]
   Grazzini's farce is included among the works attributed to Machiavelli, but the editor expresses doubt about its authorship.
   UW

1853

70. Le Cene di Anton-Francesco Grazzini detto il Lasca. Torino. Cugini Pomba e comp. editori. 1853.
   BNP

1856

71. Rime burlesche di eccellenti autori, raccolte, ordinate e postillate da Pietro Fanfani. Firenze, Felice Le Monnier, 1856.

1857

72. Le Cene ed altre prose di Antonfrancesco Grazzini detto il Lasca riscontrate sui migliori codici per cura di Pietro Fanfani. Firenze, Felice Le Monnier, 1857.
   Fanfani intended to publish the complete works of Grazzini in three volumes. However, he published only the first two. See next entry.
   BM BNP

1859

73. Commedie di Antonfrancesco Grazzini detto il Lasca. Riscontrate sui migliori codici e postillate da Pietro Fanfani. Firenze, Felice Le Monnier, 1859.
   BM P UW
74. Lettera di A. F. Grazzini a messer B. Guasconi in Roma, in *Giornale storico degli Archivi Toscani*, III (1859), 288–94.
   UC UW
75. Opere di Benedetto Varchi. Trieste: Sezione letterario-artistica del Lloyd Austriaco. [2 volumes]

Includes sonnets exchanged between Grazzini and Varchi.
UC

1860 [?]

76. Nel fausto giorno in cui il . . . Marchese V. Pianetti e la . . . Donzella Virginia dei Marchesi Azzolino si giuravano fede maritali, questi amorosi versi finora inediti, dettati dal Lasca, come ricordo d'affettuoso ossequio G. Aiazzi . . . pubblicava. [Florence, 1860 (?)]
BM

1861

77. La Giulleria. Novella di Ant. Francesco Grazzini detto il Lasca. Parigi a spese dell'editore. 1861.
Rare; 120 copies printed (Verzone, ed., *Cene*, p. xx).

1865

78. Dell'inondazione di Firenze nel 1547. Florence, 1865. [Published by Guglielmo Enrico Saltini]

1868

79. Le Cene di Antonfrancesco Grazzini detto il Lasca riscontrate sui migliori codici; con annotazioni di B. Fabbricatore. Napoli, Società Editrice dei Novellieri Italiani, 1868.
80. Tre novelle di Antonfrancesco Grazzini detto il Lasca ora la prima volta messe a stampa secondo un codice della comunale di Perugia per cura del bibliotecario Adamo Rossi. Perugia, C. Boncompagni e C. editori, 1868.
BM

1870

81. Alcune poesie inedite di Antonfrancesco Grazzini detto il Lasca. Poggibonsi, G. Coltellini e C.° editori, 1870.
BM H

1873

82. Opere di Francesco Berni. Nuova edizione riveduta e corretta. Milan, Edoardo Sonzogno, 1873.

1877

83. Commedie del teatro antico fiorentino, scelte e annotate per i giovanetti in aiuto allo studio della lingua comune dal Prof. Silvio Pacini. Florence, Felice Paggi libraio-editore, 1877.
   Contains *La Sibilla* and *La Spiritata.*
   BM
84. I Narcisi: madrigali sopra un giovane inteso per Narciso. Florence, 1877.

1881

85. Le Canzoni dell'ova in maggio a Monteguidi: canzone a ballo. Florence, 1881.

1882

86. Le Rime burlesche edite e inedite di Antonfrancesco Grazzini, per cura di Carlo Verzone. Florence: G. C. Sansoni, 1882.
   BM P UC UW
87. Les Soupers du Lasca, ou recueil des nouvelles d'A. Grazzini . . . dit le Lasca. . . . Traduction complète et littérale. Paris, 1882. [2 volumes]
   BM BNP

1883

88. Canti carnascialeschi, trionfi, carri e mascherate secondo l'edizione del Bracci. Milan, Edoardo Sonzogno, 1883. [Edited by Olindo Guerrini]
   UC

1885

89. Contes de Grazzini, traduits de l'italien par G. G. . . . Paris, C. Marpon et E. Flammarion, 1885. [2 volumes]
   BNP

1887

90. Novella inedita di Antonfrancesco Grazzini detto il Lasca e una novellina popolare sarda. Florence: G. Carnesecchi, 1887.
   UW

1890

91. Le Cene di Antonfrancesco Grazzini detto il Lasca. Per cura di Carlo Verzone. Florence, G. C. Sansoni, editore, 1890.
    BM LC UW

1891

92. Le Rime di Tullia d'Aragona cortigiana del secolo XVI edite a cura e studio di Enrico Celani. Bologna presso Romagnoli dall'Acqua libraio editore. 1891.
    BM BNF BNR UC UW

1893

93. Canti carnascialeschi, seguiti dai canti carnascialeschi di Lorenzo de' Medici. Rome: Perino, 1893.

1897

94. Commedie di Antonfrancesco Grazzini detto il Lasca. Per cura di Pietro Fanfani. Florence: Le Monnier, 1897.
    UC

1898

95. Lezione sopra un sonetto del Petrarca. Giovanni Gentile, ed. Castelvetrano, Lentini, 1898.

REFERENCE MATTER

NOTES

PREFACE

1 Among the several useful studies which have considered the late Renaissance in Italy and which will be of interest to those concerned with the tenor of life and art in the second half of the sixteenth century are Eric Cochrane, "The End of the Renaissance in Florence," *Bibliothèque d'Humanisme et Renaissance*, XXVII (1965), 7–29, and H. G. Koenigsberger, "Decadence or Shift? Changes in the Civilization of Italy and Europe in the Sixteenth and Seventeenth Centuries," *Transactions of the Royal Historical Society*, X, 5th Series (1960), 1–18. Paul F. Grendler, "The Rejection of Learning in Mid-*Cinquecento* Italy," *Studies in the Renaissance*, XIII (1966), 230–49, discusses several *poligrafi* who "mirrored a widespread discouragement and disillusionment in Italy during the years 1535 to 1555" (p. 249) and points to the growing dissatisfaction with humanistic teachings during the late Renaissance; see also his recent study, *Critics of the Italian World, 1530–1560* (Madison, Wis., 1969). Ezio Raimondi, "Per la nozione di manierismo letterario," in his *Rinascimento inquieto* (Palermo, 1965), pp. 267–303, surveys several studies on stylistic changes in late Renaissance literature and provides, in his notes, an ample bibliography on the subject.

2 Giovanni Gentile, "Delle commedie di Anton Francesco Grazzini detto il *Lasca*," *Annali della R. Scuola Normale*

Superiore di Pisa: Filosofia e Filologia, XII (1897), 3–129.

3 Among the most perceptive studies of Grazzini's novelle see Giorgio Bárberi Squarotti, "Struttura e tecnica delle novelle del Grazzini," *Giornale storico della letteratura italiana*, CXXXVIII (1961), 497–521, and Giorgio Pullini, "Novellistica minore del '500," *Lettere italiane*, VII (1955), 389–409.

4 Among the best and most recent studies of Grazzini's theatre, see Aldo Borlenghi, "Regolarità e originalità della commedia del Cinquecento," *Studi di letteratura italiana dal Trecento al Cinquecento* (Milan-Varese, 1959), pp. 122–230; Bruno Porcelli, "Le Commedie e le novelle del Lasca," *Ausonia*, XIX, vi (1964), 33–45; XX, i (1965), 26–39; Giorgio Pullini, "Teatralità di alcune commedie del '500," *Lettere italiane*, VII (1955), 68–97; Aldo Vallone, *Avviamento alla commedia fiorentina del '500* (Asti, 1951).

5 Besides the works cited above (n. 3), see Guido Di Pino, *Antologia critica della novella italiana dal XV al XVIII secolo* (Messina, 1959), passim; Enrico Emanuelli's introduction to Antonfrancesco Grazzini, *Le Cene* (Rome, 1943), pp. vii–xxvi; Giovanni Pischedda, "Sulla Lingua della novellistica rinascimentale," *Studi medio-latini e volgari*, VIII (1960), 193–210; Luigi Russo, "Novellistica e dialoghistica nella Firenze del '500," *Belfagor*, XVI (1961), 261–83, 535–54.

CHAPTER I

1 Antommaria Biscioni, "Vita del Lasca," in *Le Cene* of Antonfrancesco Grazzini, 3 vols. (Milan, 1815), I, 10. According to Biscioni, Grazzino d'Antonio married on March 5, 1497, bringing to his new bride a dowry of 720 florins which, "for those days, was quite a considerable sum" (p. 9). Biscioni names 3 brothers: Simone, Lorenzo, and Girolamo.

2 Biscioni, pp. 4–5, lists ten members of the family who practiced the profession. Both Biscioni (p. 10) and G. B. Dott. Magrini, *D'Anton Francesco Grazzini detto il Lasca e delle sue opere in prosa e in rima* (Imola, 1879), p. 4, defend Grazzini against those who would deny him his noble lineage. Magrini states that the family was esteemed

for its "learning, nobility, and influence." Concerning Grazzini's mother, about whom little is known, Magrini adds that she, too, was of a noble family "which enjoyed the dignity of a priorship" in the Florentine government.

3 Antonfrancesco Grazzini, *Le Rime burlesche edite e inedite,* ed. Carlo Verzone (Florence, 1882), p. 103, vv. 1–3: "I am in Staggia, my homeland, the seat of my ancestors and the birthplace of my grandfather." (Subsequent references to Carlo Verzone's edition of Grazzini's poetry, the most complete to date, will appear in the text with the page reference and, where Verzone has numbered the lines, with line references also.)

4 Biscioni, p. 10, and Ad. van Bever and Ed. Sansot-Orland, "Un Conteur florentin du XVIe siècle: Antonfrancesco Grazzini dit le Lasca," *Bulletin du Bibliophile et du Bibliothécaire* (1903), p. 137. In a study of the profession of the pharmacist during the Florentine Renaissance, Raffaele Ciasca, *L'Arte dei medici e speziali nella storia e nel commercio fiorentino dal secolo XII al XV* (Florence, 1927), p. 323, lists the shop in which Grazzini worked as one of the most centrally located in Florence during the sixteenth century. Antonio Virgili stated, in 1881: "This pharmacy, which is now called the Moor's, still exists. Inside there is an inscription which notes that Lasca was a druggist in the shop beginning in the year 1521. . . . A few months ago, there was also his portrait, but it has since been removed." *Francesco Berni* (Florence, 1881), p. 521, n. 1.

5 "Just what, if not peaches, figs, and similar fruits, cause such ills and make me . . . sell enemas?" (Verzone, p. 633, vv. 91–93). It is to be noted that Verzone questions the authorship of this poem and, therefore, the validity of using it as proof of Grazzini's profession (p. 631, n.). See Van Bever and Sansot-Orland, "Un Conteur florentin," p. 137. Biscioni (p. 10) says that he was a pharmacist but that he was never officially registered (*matricolato*).

6 Piero Longardi and Piero Galdi, *Le Accademie in Italia* (Turin, 1956), p. 37, suggest this, offering as evidence unnamed chronicles of the period.

7 Biscioni, p. 12, says, "It is certain that Grazzini . . . was a serious student of belles lettres, and it seems to me that in his study he gained a knowledge of all the sciences and of

all the liberal and mechanical arts, of all that which the human intellect is capable of understanding." Magrini, *D'Anton Francesco Grazzini*, p. 4, adds: "In addition, he was a practical and speculative philosopher, studied astronomy, and was adept at improvisation, a fact which is evident from his verse."

8 Verzone, pp. c–ci.

9 Verzone, pp. 409–13, Ottave LXIX–LXXIII and pp. 385–86, Ottava XXXVI, stanzas 1–4: "Only God knows the future. . . . Everyone speaks of false prognostications: the lowliest artisan and even ecclesiastics believe in them. In all nations they should be scorned and reviled more than spies and flatterers. I'm not criticizing natural astrology, a science . . . for which I have nothing but admiration; but I am criticizing the false science of predicting future events."

10 In a letter to a friend, Bernardo Guasconi, Grazzini describes the entrance of Charles V into Florence in April, 1536, under a triumphal arch constructed in his honor and inscribed with an epitaph which Grazzini was unable to read "since it was in Latin, a language which I do not understand too well." For the complete text of the letter, see *Giornale storico degli Archivi Toscani*, III (1859), 288–94.

Although Grazzini defended his learning (Verzone, p. 101, vv. 15–17), in his poetry, too, he often alludes to his ignorance of the classical languages: "Since I was never a Greek or a Latin, I speak only with that tongue which my mother gave me" (Verzone, p. 516, vv. 16–17; see also *ibid.*, p. 93, vv. 15–20).

11 See his introduction to Grazzini's *Novelle* (Milan, 1915), p. 13.

12 For the full title of this work, see Appendix II, no. 8.

13 Olinto Dini, *Il Lasca tra gli accademici* (Pisa, 1896), p. 8, n. 1. Dini, p. 7, n. 1, cites the Codice Magliabechiana II.IV.I which contains the Codice de' Capitoli dell'Accademia degli Umidi, listing the names and the academic names of the founding members as follows:

Padre Stradino PADRE
M. Cyntio d'Amelia Romano—L'Humoroso
Niccolo Martelli—Il Gelato

Filippo Salvetti—il frigido
Simone della Volta—L'Annacquato
Piero Fabbrini—L'Assiderato
Bartolommeo Benci—Lo Spumoso
Gismondo Martelli—Il Cygno
Michelangiolo Vivaldi—il Torbido
Il Lascha—I LASCA
Baccio Baccelli—Il Pantanoso
Il Pyluccha scultore pauolo de Gei—Lo Scoglio

14 Giovanni Prezziner, *Storia del pubblico studio e delle società scientifiche e letterarie di Firenze*, 2 vols. (Florence, 1810), II, 29.

15 Cartesio Marconcini, *L'Accademia della Crusca dalle origini alla prima edizione del vocabolario (1612)* (Pisa, 1910), pp. 19–20.

16 From the Codice de' Capitoli dell'Accademia degli Umidi as quoted by Dini, *Il Lasca tra gli accademici*, p. 15, n. 2.

17 See Marconcini, *L'Accademia della Crusca*, pp. 16–17.

18 In Siena, for example, the *Congrega dei Rozzi* and several other academies came into existence at this time. See *ibid.*, p. 15, and n. 2. The quotation appears in *ibid.*

19 For one of the most complete descriptions of Giovanni Mazzuoli, see *Dino Compagni e la sua cronica*, ed. Isidoro del Lungo, 3 vols. (Florence, 1879–87), I, pt. 2, 729 ff.

20 *Ibid.*, I, pt. 2, 729–42.

21 Marco Antonio Lastri, *L'Osservatore fiorentino sugli edifizi della sua patria*, 4th ed., 16 vols. (Florence, 1831), I, 142. Lastri (1731–1811) was a Florentine ecclesiastic who spent many years of research on ancient Florentine families, laws, and institutions. The first edition of the *Osservatore fiorentino* was published in 1776–78.

22 Grazzini had used the name of Lasca as early as 1536 in the letter to Bernardo Guasconi (above, n. 10). According to the *Enciclopedia dello spettacolo*, ed. Silvio d'Amico (Rome, 1959), VI, 1252, this is the first time that the name appears. Grazzini, in a poem addressed to Benedetto Varchi, insisted upon being called il Lasca rather than Antonfrancesco or Grazzino (Verzone, p. 21, vv. 12–14). When, forty years later, he became a founding member of the Accademia della Crusca, he retained the name. At this time, Grazzini also had a device depicting a roach snap-

ping at a butterfly. Biscioni, p. 14, knew of no motto on the device but commented: "I find this device very much in keeping with Lasca's character; since his temperament leads him to a facetious and whimsical style in his compositions, [he imagines] that that fish, as is its wont, jumps from the water to catch butterflies, which, because of their irregular flight, are a symbol of the whimsicality of the human imagination."

23 Dini, *Il Lasca tra gli accademici*, p. 16.

24 Iacopo Rilli, *Notizie letterarie, ed istoriche intorno agli uomini illustri dell'Accademia Fiorentina* (Florence, 1700), I, xviii.

25 *Ibid.*, I, xix, and Michele Messina, "Anton Francesco Grazzini detto il Lasca," in *Letteratura Italiana: I Minori* (Milan, 1961), II, 1185.

26 Biagi, ed., *Le Novelle*, p. 18. Rilli, *Notizie letterarie*, I, xix, says that at the meeting of February 11, there was not a unanimous approval of a name change; the matter was in fact postponed until March 25.

27 Dini, *Il Lasca tra gli accademici*, p. 17.

28 Rilli, *Notizie letterarie*, I, xix.

29 Fornaciari, ed., *Scritti scelti*, p. iv, n. 2, describes the device, which is reproduced here as Pl. 2. The old man is the Arno River; in the background one can see the cupola and the campanile of Santa Maria del Fiore and the tower of the Palazzo Vecchio.

30 Most commentators agree that Cosimo's interest in academic life stemmed from his desire to keep close control over formally organized groups which could harbor any revolutionary feelings toward his government, and that his interest in the literary activities of the organizations was minimal. Dini, *Il Lasca tra gli accademici*, p. 16, has suggested that Cosimo, thinking that he could depend on Pierfrancesco Giambullari and Norchiati as political allies, encouraged their participation in the Academy. For further discussion, see Marconcini, *L'Accademia della Crusca*, p. 10; Guido Manacorda, "Benedetto Varchi, l'uomo, il poeta, il critico," *Annali della R. Scuola Normale Superiore di Pisa*, XVII (1903), 42; Ugo Foscolo, "Sulla lingua italiana," in *Opere edite e postume di Ugo Foscolo* (Florence, 1850), IV, 247; Agenore Gelli, "Della vita e delle opere di Gio-

van-Batista Gelli," *Opere di Giovan-Batista Gelli* (Florence, 1885), pp. viii–ix; Eric Cochrane, *Tradition and Enlightenment in the Tuscan Academies: 1690–1800* (Chicago, 1961), p. 30.

31 Biscioni, pp. 14–15, quotes from the *Libro de' Capitoli ec. dell'Accademia degli Umidi:* " . . . *because he was not called upon to draw up the 'Capitoli'* (a duty which was assigned to Cosimo Bartoli and to Giovanni Norchiati and in which it seemed only right that the cancelliere participate), *he publicly resigned the office* [italics in original]."

32 Dini, *Il Lasca tra gli accademici*, p. 19.

33 Michele Barbi, "Dante nel Cinquecento," *Annali della R. Scuola Normale Superiore di Pisa*, VII (1890), 182, describes the activities of the Accademia Fiorentina as quite dissimilar from those which might have interested Grazzini and his friends at the time the Accademia degli Umidi was founded: "it was not sufficient to read the best authors in the volgare and to practice writing after their example; it was necessary to show that the Tuscan language was capable of expressing any philosophical or astrological concept or the concepts of any other science and [to do so] as well as if it were 'Latin and perhaps even Greek.' "

34 Biscioni, p. 16, and Fornaciari, ed., *Scritti scelti*, p. vi.

35 Biscioni, p. 16. Piero Covoni's name does not appear in the first list of members of the Accademia Fiorentina. According to a letter of Grazzini to Luca Martini on February 22, 1558, Covoni had apparently remained in good standing with the Academy and was one of the censors who were to later criticize Grazzini's edition of the canti carnascialeschi. For the complete text of the letter, see *Prose fiorentine raccolte dallo "Smarrito" accademico della Crusca*, 6 vols. (Venice, 1735), V, 36–40.

36 Vincenzo Vivaldi, *Storia delle controversie linguistiche in Italia da Dante ai nostri giorni* (Catanzaro, 1925), p. 51.

37 Grazzini was reinstated in the Academy on May 15, 1566 (Biscioni, p. 16).

38 Fornaciari, ed., *Scritti scelti*, p. vii, n. 1.

39 Biscioni, pp. 16–17.

40 Van Bever and Sansot-Orland, "Un Conteur florentin," p. 139, n. 1.

41 Giambullari's treatise was entitled *Ragionamento della*

prima e antica origine della toscana e particolarmente della lingua fiorentina. The work was also known as *Il Gello.* It was first published in Florence in 1546. For a discussion of his position, see Giancarlo Mazzacurati, *La Questione della lingua dal Bembo all'Accademia Fiorentina* (Naples, 1965), pp. 113 ff.

42 Verzone, p. 151, vv. 59–64: "Poetry has gone to the dogs, and my dear Umidi will remain forever dried up and withered; without opposition, the Aramei will completely destroy the Academy."

43 Lastri, *L'Osservatore fiorentino,* I, 146, and Fornaciari, ed., *Scritti scelti,* p. vii.

Several commentators have opined that the Accademia della Crusca was unofficially formed at this time as a reactionary move against the Aramei. Lastri, *ibid.,* I, 147, states: "Lasca's sympathizers were called Crusconi and these men hoped to deceive the Aramei by founding a new academy not based on erudition and, by sound principles and examples, to establish the sure basis for the Tuscan language. Due to this, it is thought that the origin of the Accademia della Crusca goes back to 1550. But it was certainly not formed [officially] until 1582, in which year, Lasca, together with four other worthy citizens, founded it and gave it a solemn beginning."

44 See Grazzini's letter to Lorenzo Scala in Francesco Berni, *Il Primo libro dell'opere burlesche di M. Francesco Berni e di altri . . .* I (Leida, 1823), 5–10; and Vivaldi, *Storia delle controversie linguistiche,* p. 66.

45 Francesco Flamini, *Il Cinquecento* (Milan, 1900 [?]), p. 221.

46 For a description of the *sonetto caudato,* or sonnet with a coda, see Chapter III, p. 85.

47 Verzone, p. 54. Giuseppe Fatini, *Agnolo Firenzuola e la borghesia letterata del Rinascimento* (Cortona, 1907), pp. 178–79, n. 1, gives the text of a letter, previously attributed to both Firenzuola and Pietro Aretino, and now assumed to be by Grazzini, in which the author pleads to Stradino to support opposition to the attempt to do away with the letter K (Fatini, *ibid.,* pp. 23–25, and Verzone, p. cxi).

Elsewhere in his poetry, Grazzini defends the traditional alphabet, criticizing, in particular, the attempted reforms of Vincenzio Buonanni, a Florentine poet and critic, active in the academic circles (Fornaciari, ed., *Scritti scelti*, pp. 182–83).

48 The first quotation comes from Giambullari's prefatory remarks to Cosimo I in his dedication of the *Ragionamento della lingua;* the second, from G. B. Gelli's words to the son of Cosimo I, Francesco, in his preface to the *Ragionamento infra M. Cosimo Bartoli e Giambattista Gelli sopra la difficoltà di mettere in regole la nostra lingua* (Florence: Torrentino, 1551). See Dini, *Il Lasca tra gli accademici*, p. 23.

49 There is no certainty of the date of Grazzini's expulsion. In a sonnet addressed to the duke, and written after his expulsion, he speaks of the argument between the academicians concerning the proposed reforms of the alphabet as having occurred *l'altr'anno*, i.e., 1546 (Verzone, p. 70, v. 18). In his poem entitled "Lamento dell'Accademia degli Umidi," also written after his expulsion, he states that in 1547, "in the midst of water and wind, the Umidi remained dry and 'humorless' " (Verzone, p. 342, vv. 3–4). This, too, may refer to his leaving the Academy.

It should be noted here that Grazzini had great admiration for the Medici family, and to them dedicated several of his works, including his edition of the canti carnascialeschi in 1559. In his appeals to the duke concerning the Aramei, therefore, he expresses the hope that the duke had not taken offense at Grazzini's criticism of the Academy of which he was patron: "be assured that I never wrote or said a word which would detract from your glory" (Verzone, p. 70, vv. 9–11).

50 Fornaciari, ed., *Scritti scelti*, p. vii, n. 2. The poem remained unedited, however, until the nineteenth century.

51 On September 6, 1541, Grazzini wrote the following words in an introduction to a canzone addressed to a certain Giulio Mazzinghi: "I beg of you not to show this canzone of mine to certain niggardly and worthless madmen; rather, keep it away from them, hide it, remove it from the sight of the serious censors, of those severe Catos and of certain good and wise men who go about Florence with an inflated ego, their brows raised in scorn and their faces stamped with severity. Oh, my dear Giulio, may it

never fall into their hands, for if it did, the waters of the Jordan, which, in Christ, washed away all the sins of mankind, would not suffice to cleanse my hands . . . " (Verzone, p. 140).

52 Giovanni Laini, *Polemiche letterarie del Cinquecento* (Mendrisio, 1944), p. 67. Magrini, *D'Anton Francesco Grazzini*, p. 23, attributes all three poems to Grazzini, using as his proof "the style . . . the language and . . . the concepts." However, Giovanni Maria de' Crescimbeni, *Commentarj di Gio. Maria de' Crescimbeni intorno alla sua istoria della volgar poesia*, 5 vols. (Rome, 1702–22), I, ii, Chapter XVIII, 313–14, quotes from a letter written by Grazzini to Amelonghi which attributes the *Gigantea* to Benedetto Arrighi.

53 In fact, in a sonetto caudato addressed to Benedetto Varchi and to Francesco d'Ambra (Verzone, pp. 35–36), Grazzini speaks of a discourse delivered before the Academy by Bernardo Davanzati in 1550. Later, in 1564, he wrote a sonetto caudato as a commentary upon an oration delivered by Lionardo Salviati in April of that year in praise of the Florentine language. See Fornaciari, ed., *Scritti scelti*, pp. 249–50.

54 *Il Frate* was the only other play of Grazzini's to be performed during his lifetime.

55 Joseph Spencer Kennard, *The Italian Theatre*, 2 vols. (New York, 1964), I, 168. Until only recently, *Il Frate* was attributed to Machiavelli. Its interesting history has been traced by Giovanni Grazzini in a note to his edition of Grazzini's plays. The farce, entitled *Commedia in tre atti senza titolo*, was first published in 1769 as part of the collected works of Machiavelli. Later, in 1772, it was published in London with the title *Il Frate*. However, the majority of subsequent editions (until the 1902 edition of Sonzogno) continued to use the title *Commedia in tre atti senza titolo*. While preparing his 1953 edition of Grazzini's comedies, Giovanni Grazzini found a manuscript of the farce in the Biblioteca di San Marco. He considers it to be the one upon which the 1769 edition of the farce was based. He also found a listing of the manuscript as being one contained in the collection of a certain Tommaso G. Farsetti. A note by Farsetti explains that the attribution

of the manuscript to Machiavelli was a guess on the part of its editor, G. B. Pasquali, and that he, Farsetti, would have attributed it to Francesco d'Ambra. Giovanni Grazzini goes on to cite Girolamo Tiraboschi, Pierre Louis Ginguené, and Pasquale Villari, among others, as critics who, unfamiliar with Farsetti's observations, continued to attribute the farce to Machiavelli. It was possible to identify Grazzini as the author of *Il Frate* only when Verzone found and published Grazzini's catalogue of his own works which lists the farce among them. See Giovanni Grazzini's ed. of Grazzini's *Teatro* (Bari, 1953), pp. 606–11.

56 Niccolò Martelli, in a letter to Anton Francesco Doni, described the gatherings at Maria da Prato's home (*Dal primo e dal secondo libro delle lettere*, ed. Cartesio Marconcini [Lanciano, 1916], pp. 47–49). See too Gentile, "Delle commedie di Anton Francesco Grazzini," p. 8.

Vittorio Cian, "Giochi di sorte versificati del sec. XVI," *Miscellanea Nuziale Rossi-Teiss* (Trent, 1897), pp. 89–92, describes the games of chance which were played at the Florentine soirées and which Grazzini documented so well in his poetry.

57 Grazzini, ed., *Teatro*, p. 525.

58 For the *Tavola delle opere*, compiled by Grazzini on September 15, 1566, see Appendix I.

59 Gentile, "Delle commedie di Anton Francesco Grazzini," pp. 44–46. Gentile considers the prologue to be that of *La Monica* because, as he shows later in his essay (pp. 121–22), *La Giostra* was probably revised and given a new title, *L'Arzigogolo*.

60 Grazzini, ed., *Teatro*, pp. 555–56, carries the complete text of the prologue.

61 *Ibid.*, p. 577.

62 This information is given in the introduction, *Ai lettori*, to his comedy *La Strega* (*ibid.*, p. 181).

63 Gentile, "Delle commedie di Anton Francesco Grazzini," p. 57. In his *Prologo agli uomini*, published in the 1551 edition, Grazzini makes mention of the musical interludes. And in his dedication of the play to Bernardetto Minerbetti, written on February 15, 1550, he says that "twenty youths, no less noble and rich than virtuous and magnani-

mous, incurred the expense necessary for a presentation of my comedy." For both the *Prologo agli uomini* and the dedicatory preface to Minerbetti, see Grazzini, ed., *Teatro*, pp. 9–11 and p. 7, respectively.

64 See Appendix II, nos. 4, 19.

65 The fact that it was first performed in Bologna is given on the title page of the first edition, which included a dedicatory letter to Raffaello de' Medici. See Appendix II, no. 10.

66 Grazzini, ed., *Teatro*, p. 577, says that neither the occasion nor the precise date are known, but in "L''Occhiolino' del Lasca," *Nuova Antologia*, CDLXXIX (1960), 185, he states that the Bologna performance took place in 1560.

67 Grazzini, ed., *Teatro*, p. 125.

68 Before the 1582 edition of all Grazzini's comedies (with the exception of *L'Arzigogolo*, which was not published until 1750; see Chapter IV, pp. 138–39), *La Gelosia* was published in 1551 and reprinted in 1552, 1568, and 1582; *La Spiritata* was published in 1561 and reprinted in 1562, 1566, and 1582. For the edition of 1582, see Appendix II, no. 23.

69 See Grazzini's letter to Lorenzo Scala in Francesco Berni, *Opere burlesche*, I, 9–10.

70 Antonio Virgili, *Francesco Berni*, p. 521, claims that Grazzini knew Berni and, perhaps well, but there are no references in Grazzini's works to such a friendship.

Grazzini's complaint appears in the dedicatory letter to the 1548 edition published by Giunti. For the full text see also the more accessible edition of 1823, *Opere burlesche*, I, 5–10.

71 Virgili, *Francesco Berni*, pp. 517–23. Virgili also attributes the inaccuracy of Grazzini's editorial work to his fear of persecution by the Church. He states, further, that whenever Grazzini could not make sense of a line, he apparently eliminated it or interpreted it.

72 Francesco Berni, *Poesie e prose*, ed. Ezio Chiòrboli (Geneva-Florence, 1934), p. 379.

73 Chiòrboli, *ibid.*, pp. 379–80, gives examples of such changes (*dietro* for *drieto*, *tosto* for *presto*, *furo* for *furno*) and speaks of his deletions of repetitions, anacoluthons, etc.

74 Virgili, *Francesco Berni*, pp. 520–21.

75 See Verzone, p. ix, n. 1.

76 Berni, *Opere burlesche*, I, 9–10.

77 During his lifetime, Grazzini's poems appeared only in a few miscellaneous collections. See, for examples, nos. 1, 3, 7, 9, 12–16, 20–21, in Appendix II. For the most part, these poems were written in praise of a well-known contemporary.

78 See Domenico di Giovanni detto il Burchiello, *Sonetti inediti*, ed. Michele Messina (Florence, 1952), pp. 4–5.

79 See Appendix II, no. 5. See also Verzone, p. 81. In the sonetto caudato Grazzini once again seizes the opportunity to criticize the Aramei.

80 Messina, ed., *Sonetti inediti*, p. 10. Carmelo Previtera, *La Poesia giocosa e l'umorismo dalle origini al Rinascimento* (Milan, 1939), p. 261, mentions that Grazzini's comment, in his dedication, about hidden meanings in Burchiello's sonnets led to many misinterpretations.

81 For a discussion of the canto carnascialesco in the fifteenth and sixteenth centuries, see, among others, Federico Ghisi, *I Canti carnascialeschi nelle fonti musicali del XV e XVI secolo* (Florence-Rome, 1937), pp. 2–3 and passim, and Charles S. Singleton, "The Literature of Pageantry in Florence during the Renaissance," Ph.D. Diss., Berkeley, Cal., 1936.

82 For the complete text, see Il Guggiola, *Canti carnascialeschi* (Milan, 1946), pp. 11–16. The letter, one of the few sources of information concerning the canto carnascialesco, was written as a preface to Grazzini's edition of the carnival songs, 1559.

83 Singleton, "The Literature of Pageantry," p. 97, qualifies the use of the word "popular" in regard to the canto carnascialesco: "it is plain that the carnival songs of the 15th century are popular only in the sense that they are written and staged *for* the people. . . . But these earliest carnival songs have no remote, obscure or fabulous early history of mere oral tradition; and . . . they are not the spontaneous growth of the popular spirit finding voice in some minstrel of the people, but rather the play on the motifs of the popular spirit, simply their repetition, but most often their parody."

84 *Ibid.*, p. 3.

85 Olindo Guerrini, ed., *Canti carnascialeschi, trionfi, carri e mascherate* (Milan, 1883), p. 16.

86 Singleton, "The Literature of Pageantry," p. 4. See also

Charles S. Singleton, ed., *Nuovi canti carnascialeschi del Rinascimento* (Modena, 1940), p. 11.

87 The best example of such criticism is his ottava, "Sopra il compor canti moderni" ("On the composition of modern canti"), (Verzone, pp. 407–9).

88 Angelo Solerti, *Gli Albori del melodramma*, 3 vols. (Milan-Palermo-Naples, 1904), I, 22, quotes one reply to Grazzini's criticism, written, perhaps, by Buonanni himself: "Lasca, you can go right ahead, spewing forth all your poisonous [?] words; write all you want but we prefer to compose subtle and learned poems . . . we no longer want to write verses for the rabble."

89 Il Guggiola, *Canti carnascialeschi*, pp. 13–15.

90 Singleton, "The Literature of Pageantry," p. 8. The earliest collections of canti carnascialeschi, published without a date in the fifteenth century, are both entitled *Canzone per andare in maschera per carnasciale fatte da più persone*. Ghisi, *I Canti carnascialeschi*, p. 22, n. 2, says that Grazzini did not seem to know these two early editions and failed to include some of the old songs in his edition.

91 The entire text of the letter, part of which I quote here, may be found in *Prose fiorentine* (Venice) V, 36–40: "Messer Paolo dell'Ottonaio came forth and he says that those [*canti*] of his brother are in part incorrect; and he has made such an uproar in Florence that he has been advised (by the Aramei, in particular) to bring his complaint before the duke. And, through the consolo, he has had an order issued to the printer that they not be given to anyone. Of course, the case was brought before the consolo and the censors to find out about them. The censors are Gello, Piero Covoni, and one of the Segni, and the consolo is Messer Francesco da Diacceto. They prefer to trust his [Paolo dell'Ottonaio's] memory rather than the texts from which I copied and which I have produced."

92 See Verzone, pp. xviii–xix. The 1559 edition is now rare. It is missing pages 298–398.

93 *Ibid.*, p. 24.

The dispute over Grazzini's edition was to continue. Dated 1750–80, a revised edition was published in Lucca, under the direction of Neri del Boccia, a pseudonym of Rinaldo Bracci (see Appendix II, no. 41). This edition contains the poems of Ottonaio, corrected by his brother. In the preface, Bracci justifies Paolo's criticism of the 1559 edition. Antommaria Biscioni immediately responded with a defense of Grazzini's edition: *Parere del Dottore Antommaria Biscioni accademico della Crusca sopra la seconda edizione de' Canti Carnascialeschi e in difesa della prima edizione proccurata da Antonfrancesco Grazzini* (Florence, 1750), in which he states: "I'm informing him [Bracci] that, in his letter to Francesco de' Medici, Lasca never confessed to having published the canti carnascialeschi with errors; rather, in his letter he said that he *had found few books, all of them full of errors.* He added, however, that *he had been helped by his knowledge of and familiarity with verse and rhyme.* From these words, one can argue and justifiably conclude that, in his edition, Lasca used his genius and talent to attain a good reading of the canti. He was certainly capable of doing so. In regard to the errors which remained in his edition, he says in his letter to Luca Martini: *the most important* [errors] *are noted at the end: the others are of a type which can be corrected by one who understands them; one who does not will not notice them because they do not change the meaning* [italics in original]."

Bracci, in turn, answered Biscioni's defense: *I Primi dialoghi di Decio Laberio . . . sopra la nuova edizione de' Canti Carnascialeschi . . .* (Calicutidonia [Florence], 1750). However, as Ghisi, *I Canti carnascialeschi*, p. 28, says, "The result of the polemic worked to Bracci's disadvantage since his elegant edition, perhaps unjustly, did not get much recognition among Italian men of letters."

94 Enrico Carrara, *La Poesia pastorale* (Milan, 1906), p. 493. Lionardo Salviati, whom Grazzini called *saggio*, *dotto* and *leggiadro*, apparently sided with Grazzini in his various quarrels with the Aramei. See Verzone, Sonetti caudati CXLIII–CXLIV, pp. 115–16.

95 See above, note 43.

96 Fornaciari, ed., *Scritti scelti*, p. x, quotes Cesare Guasti, from the *Atti dell'Accademia della Crusca*, 1882.

97 Biscioni, pp. 26–27, and Gio. Batista Zannoni, *Storia della Accademia della Crusca* (Florence, 1848), pp. 2–3.

98 Biscioni, pp. 27–28.

99 Biagi, ed., *Le Novelle*, pp. 20–21; Fornaciari, ed., *Scritti scelti*, p. x.
100 Messina, "Anton Francesco Grazzini," p. 1186 and Biscioni, p. 32. Biscioni and other early commentators give the date of his death as February 18, 1583.
101 Messina, "Anton Francesco Grazzini," p. 1194.
102 See Luigi Razzolini and Alberto Bacchi della Lega, *Bibliografia dei testi di lingua a stampa citati dagli Accademici della Crusca* (Bologna, 1878).
103 Pietro Aretino knew of the role which Grazzini played in the disputes between the Umidi and the Fiorentini, and he may well have met Grazzini since he was well acquainted with Stradino. See Pietro Aretino, *Il Quarto libro de le lettere di M. Pietro Aretino . . .* (Paris, 1608), pp. 161–62.
104 Anton Francesco Doni, *I Marmi*, ed. Ezio Chiòrboli, 2 vols. (Bari, 1928), I, 165–67.
105 Benvenuto Cellini, *Opere complete* (Florence, 1843), pp. 557–59.
106 Paolo Emiliani-Giudici, *Storia della letteratura italiana*, 4th ed., 2 vols. (Florence, 1865), II, 74.

Dante, *Inferno*, VIII, 62, had described another Florentine, Filippo Argenti, as a *fiorentino spirito bizzarro*, and in his commentary on the eighth canto of the *Inferno*, Boccaccio defined the word "bizzarro": "I think that this word 'bizzarro' is exclusively Florentine and that it is always pejorative in meaning. Thus, we call 'bizzarri' those people who immediately and for very little cause fly into a rage and who can never, in any way, be pacified."
107 Fatini, *Agnolo Firenzuola*, p. 35.
108 See Grazzini, "L''Occhiolino' del Lasca," pp. 185–208 and p. 199 in particular.
109 Van Bever and Sansot-Orland, "Un Conteur florentin," p. 142. There are several extant bust engravings of Grazzini, four of which are contained in Georges Duplessis, *Catalogue de la collection des portraits français et étrangers . . . de la Bibliothèque Nationale . . .* (Paris, 1896–1907). Of these four portraits, one is unsigned; the others are by Caronni, F. Rosaspina, and F. Vascellini.
110 Magrini, *D'Anton Francesco Grazzini*, p. 7.
111 *Ibid.*, pp. 8 and 12.

112 Giovanni Grazzini, "L''Occhiolino' del Lasca," p. 35. See Verzone, Sonetto caudato XCII, pp. 75–80; Madrigalessa IV, pp. 249–55; Capitolo XXIII, pp. 526–29, and among Grazzini's many accusations of sodomy, see, e.g., Sonetto caudato XCIII, pp. 76–77; Madrigalessa X, p. 263 and Epitaphs I, p. 635 and XII, p. 639.

On the common practice of sodomy in the sixteenth century, especially among literary figures, see, e.g., Laini, *Polemiche letterarie del Cinquecento*, p. 276. The accusation of sodomy was a favorite theme of satirical poetry, and not only in the works of Grazzini himself.

113 See his graphic description in Verzone, Canzone III, pp. 143–48. Grazzini was also aware, as were many of his contemporaries, of the growing social problem incurred by the disease. See Alessandro Luzio and Rodolfo Renier, "Contributo alla storia del malfrancese ne' costumi e nella letteratura italiana del sec. XVI," *Giornale storico della letteratura italiana*, V (1885), 408–32.

114 For a discussion of many aspects of scapigliatura in the sixteenth century, see Lea Nissim, *Gli "Scapigliati" nella letteratura italiana del Cinquecento* (Prato, 1922).

115 G. B. Salinari, "Considerazioni intorno al Lasca," *Lo Spettatore italiano*, VI (1953), 406. See also Grazzini's own madrigal, "O sante muse," in Verzone, pp. 240–41.

116 Gentile, "Delle commedie di Anton Francesco Grazzini," p. 24.

117 See, for example, "In lode della pazzia" (Verzone, pp. 559–64, passim).

118 Indeed, Gentile, "Delle commedie di Anton Francesco Grazzini," p. 24, calls conceit "one of the essential elements of his character."

119 Grazzini, "L''Occhiolino' del Lasca," p. 187.

120 Magrini, *D'Anton Francesco Grazzini*, p. 9.

CHAPTER II

1 Francesco De Sanctis, "Storia della letteratura italiana," *Opere* (Milan-Naples, 1961), p. 413.

2 Among the many critics who have praised Grazzini for this, see Alberto Agresti, *Studi sulla commedia italiana del*

secolo XVI (Naples, 1871), p. 8; Gelli, "Della vita e delle opere di G. B. Gelli," p. xxv; Flamini, *Il Cinquecento*, p. 357; Benedetto Croce, *Poesia popolare e poesia d'arte* (Bari, 1933), p. 40; Jefferson Butler Fletcher, *Literature of the Italian Renaissance* (New York, 1934), p. 259; and Kennard, *The Italian Theatre*, I, 107 ff.

3 David Herbert Lawrence, trans., *The Story of Doctor Manente Being the Tenth and Last Story from the Suppers of A. F. Grazzini called Il Lasca*, by Antonfrancesco Grazzini (Florence, 1929), pp. x–xi.

4 Salinari, "Considerazioni intorno al Lasca," 405.

5 Such studies are too numerous to cite. But for those which give particular attention to Grazzini's works, see Gentile, "Delle commedie di Anton Francesco Grazzini"; Agresti, *Studi;* Giambattista Pellizzaro, *La Commedia del secolo XVI e la novellistica anteriore e contemporanea in Italia* (Vicenza, 1901); Alberto Agresti, "Il Negro nella commedia italiana del secolo XVI," *Atti della Accademia Pontaniana*, XXII (1892), 113–20; G. A. Galzigna, *Fino a che punto i commediografi del Rinascimento abbiano imitato Plauto e Terenzio* (Capodistria, 1899); J. L. Klein, *Geschichte des Drama's* (Leipzig, 1866–76), IV, 723–48; Giambattista Salinari, ed., *Novelle del Cinquecento* (Turin, 1955), I, 9–52; Bárberi Squarotti, "Struttura e tecnica delle novelle del Grazzini," pp. 497–521; and D. P. Rotunda, *Motif-Index of the Italian Novella in Prose* (Bloomington, 1942).

6 For this reason, the best-known work of any length on Grazzini, Giovanni Gentile's study of 1897, "Delle commedie di Anton Francesco Grazzini," is limited in scope, concentrating on the sources of plots and characters without considering originality or literary value. For a commentary on Gentile's study, see Luigi Russo, "Giovanni Gentile storico della letteratura e filosofo dell'arte," in *La Critica letteraria contemporanea* (Bari, 1954), II, 43.

7 See, for example, the important study of Pellizzaro, *La Commedia del secolo XVI.*

8 Grazzini, ed., *Teatro*, p. 465.

9 *Ibid.*, p. 188.

10 *Ibid.*, p. 187.

11 For a discussion of this inconsistency, see, for example,

Gentile, "Delle commedie di Anton Francesco Grazzini," pp. 34 ff. and Abd-El-Kader Salza, "Rassegna bibliografica," *Giornale storico della letteratura italiana*, XL (1902), 403 and passim.

12 For the polemical aspects of Grazzini's works, see Giuseppe Toffanin, *Il Cinquecento*, 5th ed. (Milan, 1954).

13 All quotations from Grazzini's plays are taken from Giovanni Grazzini's edition (Bari, 1953).

14 Grazzini, ed., *Teatro*, p. 465.

15 Galzigna, *I Commediografi del Rinascimento*, p. 11.

16 It may be that Grazzini had ambivalent feelings about the necessity of the prologue. In an interesting discussion between the "Prologo" and "Argomento" which precedes the comedy, *La Strega*, Grazzini indicates that for plot summary it is almost worthless because this is usually the function of the early scenes of the play. The Prologo, on the other hand, points out that it provides a means by which the author can speak directly to his audience. Grazzini was probably reluctant to forego the opportunity of speaking with his audience for, as Gentile points out, he is to be credited with introducing a double prologue, one addressed to the men, the other to the women in his audience (Gentile, "Delle commedie di Anton Francesco Grazzini," p. 58).

17 Grazzini, ed., *Teatro*, p. 10.

18 *Ibid.*, p. 125.

19 Galzigna, *I Commediografi del Rinascimento*, p. 9: "Theatrical entertainments were the pastime of princes and men of letters, and they were offered in the gilded halls of courts and academies to a society infatuated with classicism and scholastic rules. . . . If authors had not followed tradition, they would have been criticized by the learned men and they certainly cared little about what the common man thought. Theirs was an aristocratic art, and for them it sufficed to bring laughter to the elect societies of the Orti Oricellari or the Vatican and to be well paid by their lords. Even the less servile comedy writers—for example, Lasca—were quite reverent before Aristotle's rules, the Bible to which all subscribed."

20 Pellizzaro, *La Commedia del secolo XVI*, p. 16. On the close relationship between the comedy and the novella, especially from the linguistic point of view, see Giovanni

Pischedda, "Sulla lingua della novellistica rinascimentale."

21 Di Pino, *Antologia critica*, p. 85. Salinari, "Considerazioni intorno al Lasca," p. 406, says, on the other hand, that the comedies are only "dramatized novelle." See, too, Gentile, "Delle commedie di Anton Francesco Grazzini," p. 54.

22 Antonfrancesco Grazzini, *Le Cene*, ed. Enrico Emanuelli (Rome, 1943), p. 8. All quotations from *Le Cene* will be from this edition.

23 See the classic study of the pedant in Renaissance literature in Arturo Graf, *Attraverso il Cinquecento* (Turin, 1888), Chapter III, and also the comments of Lea Nissim, *Gli "Scapigliati,"* p. 106.

24 See, for examples, *Cena* I, v; II, v; III, i [?]. Grazzini only completed the first two *Cene*, and there is no certainty of the order in which the few extant novelle of the third *Cena* should come. See Carlo Verzone's introduction to his critical edition of the *Cene* (Florence, 1890).

25 Alfredo Galletti, "La Lirica volgare del Cinquecento e l'anima del Rinascimento," *Nuova Antologia*, CCCXLIV (1929), 291.

26 See above, n. 4, and also Salinari, ed., *Novelle del Cinquecento*, I, 32.

27 Giovambatista Casotti, *Memorie istoriche della miracolosa immagine di Maria Vergine dell'Impruneta* (Florence, 1714), pp. 162–69.

28 Jean Lucas-Dubreton, *Daily Life in Florence in the Time of the Medici*, trans. A. Lytton Sells (New York, 1961), p. 44, detected a "shadow of fear" behind Grazzini's description of magicians and sorcerers.

29 Benedetto Croce, "Novelle del Cinquecento," *La Letteratura italiana* (Bari, 1956), I, 487. Journalistic literature always remained "mere material, and it did not become form, or, to be more exact, it did not become poetic form but rather chronicle form, a collection of facts which had occurred, were thought to have occurred or which were imaginary and which titillated the curiosity and brought enjoyment."

30 Eligio Possenti, "*La Strega* del Lasca al 'Maggio Fiorentino,'" *Corriere della Sera*, LXIV (June 2, 1939), 2.

31 In fact, Giovanni Villani has opined that the plot of *Il Frate* is actually drawn from an historical event which was well

known to Grazzini's contemporaries. See Vittorio Fabiani, *Gente di chiesa nella commedia del Cinquecento*, 2nd ed. (Florence, 1905), p. 52.

32 For the most recent discussion on the influence of Florentine life in the works of Grazzini, see Bruno Porcelli, "Le Commedie e le novelle del Lasca."

33 In the comedies it is usually the servants who spend their time at the taverns. Grazzini uses the attraction of the tavern to add local color to the plays, but also to have a means by which he can dispose of his characters quickly:

"*Giannino.* What shall I do until it gets a bit later?
Carletto. Come with me to the Mercato and then we'll go to spend a while drinking.
Giannino. Where?
Carletto. Oh, to a tavern, of course; we'll spend some time at the fire and I'll pay you back a jug of wine. [*La Pinzochera*, I, ii]"

34 See Porcelli, "Le Commedie e le novelle del Lasca," XIX, 37–38.

35 Galzigna, *I Commediografi del Rinascimento*, pp. 21–22, discussed the servant in the comedies of the Cinquecento and how, in Grazzini's comedies particularly, they speak on behalf of their dignity as human beings: "In the sixteenth century. . . . masters didn't hesitate to lay hands on their servants, as Alessandra Macinghi confesses. And mistresses were particularly severe with those little oriental slaves who . . . gave them cause to worry about the fidelity of their better half. . . . It is, therefore, for this reason that Lasca's Trafela (*Spiritata*, I, i) exclaims with complete frankness, *homo sum*, . . . and that he is a human being of flesh and blood like his master. And Guagniele (II, ii) observes that 'if masters had first been servants, they would treat their own servants differently than they do.' "

36 This is, perhaps, the major shortcoming of Grazzini's farce, *Il Frate*. Much of the action is condensed into one monologue (III, i).

37 Salza, "Rassegna bibliografica," 408–9, comments on the sociological evidence provided by many comedies to support the view that during the sixteenth century, the family unit was undergoing severe corruptive influences. Others, before Salza, had made similar observations. See, for ex-

ample, Vicenzo de Amicis, *L'Imitazione latina nella commedia italiana del XVI secolo* (Florence, 1897), pp. 93–94.

38 Max J. Wolff, "Italienische Komödiendichter II. Antonfrancesco Grazzini," *Germanisch-Romanische Monatsschrift* (January, 1913), 114, states: "In one thing, however, Lasca outdoes his predecessors, viz., in the respect which he shows for the mothers. . . . In *La Gelosia* and in *La Sibilla* the mother enters actively into the action and on her own accord; indeed, in *La Pinzochera* she is even the head of the house."

39 By the sixteenth century misogyny was a fast-disappearing literary tradition. According to Vittorio Amadeo Arullani, *La Donna nella letteratura del Cinquecento* (Verona, 1890), pp. 23–24, "for the most part, satire against women in sixteenth-century drama is an expedient of art, somewhat conventional and traditional, which smacks of classical imitation." Even in Grazzini's burlesque poetry, this theme is relatively infrequent.

40 Margherita, in *La Sibilla* (V, xiii), excuses her son's seduction of Ermellina on the grounds of his inability to forestall the power of love: "his intent was not to debase her or bring her shame, but, just as all young men, he was driven by the love he feels for her." But others are more hypocritical and swathe their sensuality with phrases borrowed from the Petrarchists. Giannino, a servant in *La Pinzochera*, describes with mellifluous words the ecstasy of two lovers, Federigo and Fiammetta, but in his closing remarks, suggests that the origin of their feelings is sensual appetite (IV, vii), while Federigo, borrowing from the Petrarchists, expresses the suffering endured for Fiammetta with double entendres, the meaning of which is only too clear: "Just think of how I am being consumed by love, and yet I seem to see something new arising to disturb me. . . . This is the key that will soon bring happiness. . . . We are at her abode and the very door of my every pleasure" (IV, vii). Phrases similar to those of Giannino and Federigo were on the lips of everyone, young and old, men and women, lovers and servants. Amorality was masked with clichés borrowed from Petrarch and even from Dante. Dianora in *I Parentadi* expresses the philosophy of life of her contemporaries: "Alas! No one knows how difficult it is left only with re-

grets; not only does time flee, it flies. And it carries with it our beauty. But . . . our assets are only loaned to us by nature so that we may first use them to our own advantage and then for the good of our neighbor" (III, iii). Borrowing from Dante (elsewhere she says, "Remembering time lost, I am overcome with grief" [III, iv]) she even interprets Francesca da Rimini's lament over her guilt as another expression of carpe diem.

See Graf, *Attraverso il Cinquecento*, Chapter I, for a discussion of Petrarchism in the life of sixteenth-century society. Salza, "Rassegna bibliografica," p. 412, sees in the lover of the sixteenth-century comedy much of the superficial Platonic spirit which was responsible for so many sixteenth-century treatises on love. He goes on to say that the "uncertainty of this type of character [the lover] is derived from the conflict between the Platonic expression of love and the desire for physical satisfaction, a conflict which was common to the society of the time."

41 Salza, "Rassegna bibliografica," p. 409.

42 Pullini, "Teatralità di alcune commedie del '500," p. 95.

43 Giorgio Pullini, "Stile di transizione nel teatro di Giambattista Della Porta," *Lettere italiane*, VIII (1956), 299–310, makes important observations on the theme of gluttony in Grazzini's comedies. We may recall, too, the importance of food in Grazzini's burlesque poetry.

44 It is to be noted that none of the instances which I have cited has any significance to the main action of the comedy. Scenes of this nature slow down the action of a comedy, but provide invaluable vignettes for a study of the temperament of Grazzini's contemporaries.

45 The grotesque character of many of Grazzini's scenes contributes to what we may call the prebaroque elements of his theatre. See Chapter IV, pp. 128–29.

46 The reader can refer, as an example, to Federigo's words, in n. 40. See, too, Ignazio Ciampi, *La Commedia italiana* (Rome, 1880), pp. 51–112, for a discussion of obscenity in the sixteenth-century comedies as a reflection of the tastes of the times.

47 To my knowledge no thorough study has been made of the Florentine popular expressions in Grazzini's works. Several studies have, however, considered Grazzini's language

and have pointed to numerous ways in which the author uses his dialect, either in the comedies or in the novelle. For the comedies, see Ugo Scoti-Bertinelli, *Sullo Studio delle commedie in prosa di Giovan Maria Cecchi* (Città di Castello, 1906), in which the author compares Cecchi's works to Grazzini's, Aretino's and Francesco d'Ambra's. Useful, too, are the explanations of many of the expressions used by Grazzini in Pico Luri di Vassano (pseudonym of Lodovico Passarini), *Saggio di modi di dire proverbiali e di motti popolari italiani* (Rome, 1872), passim. See also Aldo Borlenghi, rev. of Antonfrancesco Grazzini, *Teatro* (Bari, 1953), in *Aut Aut* (March, 1953), 175–78; Aldo Borlenghi, ed., *Commedie del Cinquecento*, 2 vols. (Milan, 1959), I, 9–43; Mario Apollonio, *Storia del teatro italiano*, 2 vols. (Florence, 1958), I, 430–34.

48 Vallone, *Commedia fiorentina del '500*, p. 9, states that the comedy is closely related to the *trattato* in the sixteenth century because it is a defense of the popular idiom.

49 Grazzini "L''Occhiolino' del Lasca," p. 206.

50 Croce, "Novelle del Cinquecento," pp. 485–86. Emanuelli, ed., *Le Cene*, p. xxiv, states that in the *Cene*, historical truth or chronicle "is used only to provide greater verisimilitude for the reader."

51 Porcelli, "Le Commedie e le novelle del Lasca," XX, 28.

52 *Ibid.*, pp. 28–29. See, too, Guglielmo Alberti, "Il Lasca: lettura e digressioni," *Belfagor*, II (1947), 187–90 in particular.

53 The beffa, a subject which has titillated the imagination of many critics of the novella and the comedy as well, deserves some comment. In a recent article, "Evolution du thème de la *beffa* dans le théâtre de Lasca," *Revue des études italiennes*, No. 4 (October–December, 1965), 493–94, Michel Plaisance describes its character in the novelle. He remarks on the sadistic quality of the beffa and its function, especially when used against priests and pedagogues, as social chastisement. It is significant that he does not mention the beffa as a manifestation of Florentine ingenuity and cleverness. In this regard, the beffe in Grazzini's novelle differ from those in the *Decameron*. There is no longer the "amena spensieratezza" of Boccaccio who looked with kindliness upon the abilities of the beffatori (Pullini, "Novellistica minore del '500," p. 390). The most cruel jokes

are played on those whom Grazzini considered deserving of the punishment, priests and scholars. It is as though, aware of the Florentine penchant for the cruel joke, Grazzini was justifying its use, defending its practice upon those who merited punishment (Porcelli, "Le Commedie e le novelle del Lasca," XX, 32).

54 Porcelli, "Le Commedie e le novelle del Lasca," XX, 28–29. Di Pino, *Antologia critica,* p. 85, also points to the danger of calling Grazzini's framework a slavish imitation of Boccaccio and tradition. He sees in it an example of the theatrical and scenic quality of Grazzini's narrative. On the structural technique of the *Cene,* see Bárberi Squarotti, "Struttura e tecnica delle novelle del Grazzini," pp. 497–521.

55 See, for example, the frequency with which Church rites and exorcism are combined in *La Spiritata* and, in particular, Albizo's advice in III, iii: "Before I say anything else, I had best speak to the spirit. . . . and you must, in the meanwhile, go to a man of the church. In fact, go to Master Innocenzio at the Carmine and—now listen carefully—have him copy the *De profundis* without the gloria; when he has finished, have him stand up straight and read it aloud slowly. You must kneel at his feet and begin to tear into little pieces the paper upon which he has copied the psalm. Don't stop until he has finished his recitation. Then, get up, collect every one of the pieces, and throw them into the first fire you find."

56 Porcelli, "Le Commedie e le novelle del Lasca," XX, 33.

CHAPTER III

1 Only once in his poetry did Grazzini allude to the *Cene* (Verzone, p. 489, vv. 61–63: "Tell [Stradino] that I have written an entire day of a *Decameron* with a comment addressed to him") although there are frequent references to his comedies. Since the manuscripts of the *Cene* have marginal notes expressing his dissatisfaction with them, it is probable that only a few friends were allowed to read them and that the author intended to revise them before they were published.

2 See Chapter I, n. 77.

3 *Prose fiorentine*, Part IV, Vol. I (Florence, 1734), 73–75.
4 Periodically, miscellaneous poems, burlesque and otherwise, are still published. See, for example, Joseph G. Fucilla, "An Unedited Religious Sonnet by Il Lasca," *Modern Language Notes*, LXIX (1954), 420–21, and Costantino Arlía, "Roba di begliumori: Il Lasca," *Il Borghini*, VI, No. 23 (June 1, 1880), 357.
5 Francesco Flamini, *Notizia storica dei versi e metri italiani dal medioevo ai tempi nostri* (Livorno, 1919), p. 62.
6 Crescimbeni, *Commentarj*, p. 112.
7 Andrea Sorrentino, *Francesco Berni poeta della scapigliatura del Rinascimento* (Florence, 1933), p. 71.
8 See a treatment of the Berneschi and their influence on seventeenth-century poetry in Rodolfo Macchioni Jodi, "Poesia bernesca e marinismo," *La Critica stilistica e il barocco letterario* (Florence, 1958), 261–71.
9 For a study of similar contradictory trends in the sixteenth century, see Riccardo Scrivano, *Il Manierismo nella letteratura del Cinquecento* (Padua, 1959).
10 Compare also Madrigals XVII and XVIII, expressing a similar delight in the modern canti (Verzone, pp. 228–29).
11 See Verzone, p. 175, v. 46; p. 392; pp. 400–401; p. 544, v. 5.
12 For a discussion of the role of the intermezzi in the sixteenth-century Florentine comedy, see Orville K. Larson, "Spectacle in the Florentine *Intermezzi*," *Drama Survey*, II, No. 3 (February, 1963), 344–52.
13 The Zanni are discussed at length in Vito Pandolfi, *La Commedia dell'arte*, 6 vols. (Florence, 1957), I, 157–64.
14 Scrivano, *Il Manierismo*, passim.
15 Gino Saviotti, ed., *Rime del Berni e di berneschi del secolo XVI* (Milan, 1922), p. xiv.
16 Singleton, *Nuovi canti carnascialeschi*, pp. 6–12.
17 Laini, *Polemiche letterarie del Cinquecento*, p. 192.
18 Giovanni Grazzini, "L''Occhiolino' del Lasca," p. 193.
19 Luigi Baldacci, ed., *Lirici del Cinquecento* (Florence, 1957), pp. 338–39; Manacorda, "Benedetto Varchi," pp. 48–50, and Umberto Pirotti, "Benedetto Varchi e la questione della lingua," *Convivium*, XXVIII (1960), 527, n. 5.
20 *Egloghe ed altre rime*, ed. Domenico Poggiali (Livorno, 1799). A few poems are also to be found in earlier editions such as the *Rime* in two volumes published in 1741–42 by

Moücke. In this chapter, all quotations from Grazzini's lyric poetry and eclogues are from Poggiali's edition.

21 For a discussion of the new form, uses, and content of the Renaissance pastoral, see William Leonard Grant, *Neo-Latin Literature and the Pastoral* (Chapel Hill, N.C., 1965), Chapters VIII–XII.

22 See Poggiali, p. 37. The song develops in the following way:

I. As a diamond flashes light,
or lightning illuminates the sky,
or the sun's rays illuminate the world,
so, and more, does Lidia brighten all she looks upon.

II. The brightness of a sunrise,
or the sparkling of the waters at sunset,
or the ripples over a field reflecting the sun,
or a star sparkling in the sky,
are like Lidia's smile.

III. The fresh winds in the trees,
and the waters tumbling in streams,
and the echo of birds' songs in a valley,
are like Lidia's melodies.

IV. As a beautiful animal turns in a meadow,
or a victorious knight turns from battle,
or Diana turns to gaze upon her nymphs,
or a ship turns upon a tranquil sea,
in such a way does Lidia display her graceful movements.

V. Lidia also influences all of nature:
if she casts her glance, thorny bushes bloom;
if she laughs, wild, poisonous beasts lose their ferocity;
if she sings, winds and thunder are quieted;
if she walks, all men halt.

VI. *but*
my eyes have no clearer light than hers;
my ears only hear her;
my thoughts are only of her.

23 Sonnet LXXII, for example, has a grace which might well have appealed to Leopardi:

Silvia, non ti ricordi quando andavi

(E io con teco) dietro a i vaghi uccegli
Pigliandoci piacer sì varj e begli,
Coi diletti d'Amor tanto suavi?
Etti uscito di mente, che tu stavi
Meco presso ad un fonte, e i tuoi capegli
Di fiori e d'erba coronavi, e quegli
Occhi seren ver me grati giravi?
Ma che, lasso, dich'io? Già mai non puote
(Ch'Amore non vuol) tornarle dentro al cuore
Questo ch'io parlo in sì duro lamento.
. . . .

[Poggiali, p. 120]

("Silvia, don't you remember when you, and I in your company, chased after lovely birds, taking pleasure in the sweet delights of Love? Have you forgotten that you stood beside me near a fountain, your hair crowned with flowers and herbs, and that you turned your lovely eyes to me? But what, alas, do I say? Never again [for Love forbids it] will there return to your heart all this which I so grievously lament.")

CHAPTER IV

1 See Fortunato Rizzi, *Delle farse e commedie morali di G. M. Cecchi* (Rocca S. Casciano, 1907).
2 See Appendix I, p. 169. Laini, *Polemiche letterarie del Cinquecento*, p. 213, states that Grazzini burned the manuscript of *Il Pedante* for fear that he would be accused of plagiarizing a comedy of Francesco Belo.
3 Nino Borsellino, ed., *Commedie del Cinquecento*, 2 vols. (Milan, 1962), I, xx.
4 *Ibid.*, p. 88, and Pullini, "Teatralità di alcune commedie del '500," p. 90.
5 Aulo Greco, "Alla ricerca del Lasca," *La Rinascita*, V (1952), 293.
6 Borsellino, ed., *Commedie del Cinquecento*, I, xvi, xviii.
7 Borlenghi, review of Grazzini's *Teatro*, p. 178.
8 Flamini, *Il Cinquecento*, p. 285.
9 For a discussion of Grazzini's role in the attempt to revitalize Florentine literature and culture during the sixteenth century, see Apollonio, *Storia del teatro italiano*, I,

309; Borlenghi, "Regolarità e originalità della commedia del Cinquecento."

10 Gentile, "Delle commedie di Anton Francesco Grazzini," pp. 56–72.

11 See Gentile's discussion of the influence of Ariosto's episode concerning Ginevra di Scozia, *ibid.*, pp. 60–61.

12 *Ibid.*, p. 77.

13 For a discussion of several elements of the commedia dell'arte present in the late Renaissance erudite comedy, see Pullini, "Stile di transizione nel teatro di Giambattista Della Porta," pp. 299–310.

14 Daniel C. Boughner, *The Braggart in Renaissance Comedy: A Study in Comparative Drama from Aristophanes to Shakespeare* (Minneapolis, 1954), pp. 96–97.

15 Gentile, "Delle commedie di Anton Francesco Grazzini," pp. 101–12.

16 Pullini, "Teatralità di alcune commedie del '500," p. 89.

17 Gentile, "Delle commedie di Anton Francesco Grazzini," p. 108.

18 *Ibid.*, pp. 118–22 and Grazzini, ed., *Teatro*, pp. 599–601.

19 Grazzini, ed., *Teatro*, p. 600.

20 *Ibid.*, p. 601, and Gentile, "Delle commedie di Anton Francesco Grazzini," p. 121.

21 Gentile thinks that the most probable source is a *facezia* of Domenichi. See "Delle commedie di Anton Francesco Grazzini," p. 126.

22 See Chapter I, n. 54.

23 See the discussions of *Il Frate* in, for example, Carlo Gioda, *Machiavelli e le sue opere* (Florence, 1874), pp. 192–96; Luigi Tonelli, *Il Teatro italiano dalle origini ai nostri giorni* (Milan, 1924), pp. 125–27; Ireneo Sanesi, *La Commedia*, 2nd ed., 2 vols. (Milan, 1954), I, 369; Borsellino, ed., *Commedie del Cinquecento*, I, xxvii–xxviii and 87–88.

24 Marvin T. Herrick, *Italian Comedy in the Renaissance* (Urbana, 1960), pp. 26–27.

CHAPTER V

1 The most complete history of the text of the *Cene*, from its earliest mention by Giovanni Cinelli Calvoli (*Biblioteca volante*) in the eighteenth century, is to be found in Ver-

zone's edition of 1890, pp. ix–lxvii. More recently, Bruno Porcelli has provided some useful information for dating the *Cene* in "Le Commedie e le novelle del Lasca," XX, 26–39.

2 For the complete text of the letter, see Verzone, ed., *Le Cene*, Appendix I, pp. 329–33.

3 Grazzini lists thirty novelle in his catalogue, and speaks of the *Cene* as complete in the closing lines of III, x: "Since the Suppers are over and the stories finished and since we have brought to completion, with the help of the Almighty King of the heavens, our task. . . ."

4 As noted previously, all quotations are from Enrico Emanuelli's edition of the *Cene* (Rome, 1943).

5 Di Pino, *Antologia critica*, p. 24.

6 Bárberi Squarotti, "Struttura e tecnica delle novelle del Grazzini."

7 Concerning the *forma plastica* of Grazzini's prose, see Pullini, "Novellistica minore del '500," p. 393 and Di Pino, *Antologia critica*, p. 38.

8 Grazzini, "L''Occhiolino' del Lasca," p. 204.

9 *Ibid.*, p. 206.

10 Plaisance, "Evolution du thème de la *beffa*," pp. 491–504.

11 Giovanni Grazzini, "L''Occhiolino' del Lasca," p. 207, suggests that Grazzini was interested in showing the cruelty of reality.

12 *Ibid.*, p. 208.

13 See Pischedda, "Sulla lingua della novellistica rinascimentale," pp. 193–210, for a discussion of the Cinquecento novelle in their capacity as linguistic polemics.

BIBLIOGRAPHY

I. PRIMARY SOURCES*

Aretino, Pietro. *Il Quarto libro de le lettere di M. Pietro Aretino. Dedicate al magnanimo Signor Giovan Carlo Affaetati, gentilhuom senza pari.* Paris: Matteo il Maestro, 1608.

Berni, Francesco. *Il Primo libro dell'opere burlesche del Berni, del Casa, del Varchi, del Mauro, del Bino, del Molza, del Dolce, del Firenzuola.* Rome: Jacopo Broedelet, 1771.

———. *Il primo libro dell'opere burlesche di M. Francesco Berni e di altri.* Ricorretto e con diligenza ristampato. 3 vols. Leida: G. Van Der Bet, 1823.

———. *Le Rime*, ed. Giovanni Macchia. Rome: Colombo, 1945.

———. *Poesie e prose*, ed. Ezio Chiòrboli. Geneva-Florence: Leo S. Olschki, 1934.

Cecchi, Giovan Maria. *Commedie di Giovan Maria Cecchi premessavi una lettera intorno alla vita ed alle opere dell'autore di Luigi Fiacchi.* 2 vols. Milan: Giovanni Silvestri, 1850.

Cellini, Benvenuto. *Opere complete di Benvenuto Cellini.* Florence: Società Editrice Fiorentina, 1843.

Domenico di Giovanni. *Sonetti inediti*, ed. Michele Messina. Florence: Leo S. Olschki, 1952.

Doni, Anton Francesco. *I Marmi*, ed. Ezio Chiòrboli. 2 vols. Bari: Laterza, 1928.

Firenzuola, Agnolo. *Opere*, ed. Adriano Seroni. Florence: Sansoni, 1958.

* All works containing any of Grazzini's writings are cited in Appendix II, organized by date of publication.

Guggiola, Il. *Canti carnascialeschi.* Milan: Il Ruscello, 1946.
Martelli, Niccolò. *Dal primo e dal secondo libro delle lettere,* ed. Cartesio Marconcini. Lanciano: R. Carabba, 1916.
Prose fiorentine raccolte dallo "Smarrito" [pseud.] *accademico della Crusca.* 17 vols. Florence: Stamperia di Sua Altezza Reale, per Santi Franchi, 1716–45.
Prose fiorentine raccolte dallo "Smarrito" [pseud.] *accademico della Crusca.* 6 vols. Venice: Domenico Occhi, 1735–43.

II. GENERAL BIBLIOGRAPHY

Alberti, Guglielmo. "Il Lasca: lettura e digressioni," *Belfagor,* II (1947), 187–202.
Armstrong, Edward. *Lorenzo de' Medici and Florence in the Fifteenth Century.* New York: G. P. Putnam's Sons, 1896.
Arullani, Vittorio Amadeo. *La Donna nella letteratura del Cinquecento.* Verona: Tedeschi, 1890.
Barbi, Michele. "Dante nel Cinquecento," *Annali della R. Scuola Normale Superiore di Pisa: Filosofia e Filologia,* VII (1890), 1–407.
Biagi, Guido. *Men and Manners of Old Florence.* Chicago: A. C. McClurg & Co., 1909.
———. *The Private Life of the Renaissance Florentines.* Florence: Bemporad, 1896.
———. "Un'etèra romana: Tullia d'Aragona," *Nuova Antologia,* LXXXVIII (1886), 655–711.
Bindi, Enrico. "Della vita e delle opere di Bernardo Davanzati," in *Lo Scisma d'Inghilterra* by Bernardo Davanzati. Milan: Istituto Editoriale Italiano, [19–], pp. 11–56.
Biscioni, Antommaria. "Vita del Lasca," in *Le Cene* by Antonfrancesco Grazzini (Milan: Giovanni Silvestri, 1815), Vol. I, 3–41.
Camerini, Eugenio. "Studio," in his edition of *L'Assiuolo* by Giovan Maria Cecchi (Milan: G. Dalli, 1863), pp. 3–38.
Cantù, Cesare. *Della Letteratura italiana.* 2d ed. 2 vols. Turin: UTET, 1860.
Cian, Vittorio. *La Satira.* 2 vols. Milan: Vallardi, 1938–39.
———. "Varietà letterarie del Rinascimento," in *Raccolta di studii critici dedicata ad Alessandro D'Ancona* (Florence: G. Barbèra, 1901), pp. 23–45.
Ciasca, Raffaele. *L'Arte dei medici e speziali nella storia e nel*

commercio fiorentino dal secolo XII al XV. Florence: Leo S. Olschki, 1927.

Cinelli Calvoli, Giovanni. *Biblioteca volante*. 2d ed. 4 vols. Venice: Giambatista Albrizzi, 1734–47.

Ciotti, Andrea. "Il Cinquecento fiorentino," *Convivium*, XXIII (1955), 753–75.

Cochrane, Eric. "The End of the Renaissance in Florence," *Bibliothèque d'Humanisme et Renaissance*, XXVII (1965), 7–29.

———. *Tradition and Enlightenment in the Tuscan Academies: 1690–1800*. Chicago: The University of Chicago Press, 1961.

Compagni, Dino. *Dino Compagni e la sua cronica*, ed. Isidoro del Lungo. 3 vols. Florence: Successori Le Monnier, 1879–87.

Croce, Benedetto. *La Letteratura italiana per saggi storicamente disposti*, ed. Mario Sansone. 3 vols. Bari: Laterza, 1956.

———. *La Spagna nella vita italiana durante la Rinascenza*. Bari: Laterza, 1949.

Dejob, Charles. *De l'influence du Concile de Trente sur la littérature et les beaux-arts chez les peuples catholiques*. Paris: Ernest Thorin, 1884.

De Sanctis, Francesco. "Storia della letteratura italiana," in *Opere* (Milan-Naples: Ricciardi, 1961), pp. 3–847.

Dini, Olinto. *Il Lasca tra gli accademici*. Pisa: Francesco Mariotti, 1896.

Dionisotti, Carlo. "Chierici e laici nella letteratura italiana del primo '500," in *Problemi di vita religiosa in Italia nel '500*, Atti del Convegno di storia della Chiesa in Italia, Cologne, Sept. 2–6, 1958 (Padua: Antenore, 1960), pp. 167–85.

Duplessis, Georges. *Catalogue de la collection des portraits français et étrangers conservée au departement des estampes de la Bibliothèque Nationale, commencé par Georges Duplessis*. Paris: G. Rapilly, 1896–1907.

Emiliani-Giudici, Paolo. *Storia della letteratura italiana*. 4th ed. 2 vols. Florence: Le Monnier, 1865.

Fatini, Giuseppe. *Agnolo Firenzuola e la borghesia letterata del Rinascimento*. Cortona: Tipografia Sociale, 1907.

Flamini, Francesco. *Il Cinquecento*. Milan: Vallardi, 1900 [?].

Fletcher, Jefferson Butler. *Literature of the Italian Renaissance*. New York: The Macmillan Company, 1934.

Flora, Francesco. *Storia della letteratura italiana*. 5 vols. Milan: Mondadori, 1948–49.

Foffano, Francesco. *L'Estetica della prosa volgare nel Cinquecento*. Pavia: Frattini, 1900.

Fornaciari, Raffaello. *La Letteratura italiana nei primi quattro secoli*. Florence: Sansoni, 1885.

Foscolo, Ugo. "Sulla lingua italiana," in *Opere edite e postume di Ugo Foscolo* (Florence: Le Monnier, 1850), Vol. IV, 237–60.

Gaspary, Adolf. *Storia della letteratura italiana*. 2 vols. Vol. I, trans. N. Zingarelli. Turin: Loescher, 1887–91. Vol. II, trans. V. Rossi. Turin: Loescher, 1901.

Gelli, Agenore. "Della vita e delle opere di Giovan-Batista Gelli," in *Opere di Giovan-Batista Gelli* (Florence: Le Monnier, 1855), pp. iii–xxvi.

Gimma, Giacinto. *Idea della storia dell'Italia letterata esposta coll'ordine cronologico dal suo principio fino all'ultimo secolo, ...* 2 vols. Naples: Felice Mosca, 1723.

Gioda, Carlo. *Machiavelli e le sue opere*. Florence: G. Barbèra, 1874.

Gori, Pietro. *Le Feste fiorentine attraverso i secoli*. 2 vols. Florence: R. Bemporad & Figlio, 1926.

Graf, Arturo. *Attraverso il Cinquecento*. Turin: Loescher, 1888.

Grazzini, Giovanni. "L' 'Occhiolino' del Lasca," *Nuova Antologia*, CDLXXIX (1960), 185–208.

Greco, Aulo. "Alla ricerca del Lasca," *La Rinascita*, V (1952), 290–306.

Grendler, Paul F. *Critics of the Italian World, 1530–1560: Anton Francesco Doni, Nicolò Franco, and Ortensio Lando*. Madison: University of Wisconsin Press, 1969.

———. "The Rejection of Learning in Mid-*Cinquecento* Italy," *Studies in the Renaissance*, XIII (1966), 230–49.

Hathaway, Baxter. *The Age of Criticism: The Late Renaissance in Italy*. Ithaca, New York: Cornell University Press, 1962.

Koenigsberger, H. G. "Decadence or Shift? Changes in the Civilization of Italy and Europe in the Sixteenth and Seventeenth Centuries," *Transactions of the Royal Historical Society*, X, 5th Series (1960), 1–18.

Kristeller, Paul O. *Iter Italicum*. 2 vols. London: The Warburg Institute, 1963.

Labande-Jeanroy, Thérèse. *La Question de la langue en Italie*. Paris: Istra, 1925.

Laini, Giovanni. *Polemiche letterarie del Cinquecento.* Mendrisio: C. Stucchi, 1944.

Landucci, Luca. *Diario fiorentino dal 1450 al 1516 continuato da un anonimo fino al 1542.* Florence: Sansoni, 1883.

Lapini, Agostino. *Diario fiorentino dal 252 al 1596.* Florence: Sansoni, 1900.

Lastri, Marco Antonio. *L'Osservatore fiorentino sugli edifizi della sua patria.* 4th ed. 16 vols. Florence: Giuseppe Celli, 1831.

Longardi, Piero and Piero Galdi. *Le Accademie in Italia.* Turin: Edizioni Radio Italiana, 1956.

Lucas-Dubreton, Jean. *Daily Life in Florence in the Time of the Medici,* trans. A. Lytton Sells. New York: The Macmillan Company, 1961.

Luri di Vassano, Pico. *See* Passarini, Lodovico.

Luzio, Alessandro and Rodolfo Renier. "Contributo alla storia del malfrancese ne' costumi e nella letteratura italiana del sec. XVI," *Giornale storico della letteratura italiana,* V (1885), 408–32.

Magrini, G. B. Dott. *D'Anton Francesco Grazzini detto il Lasca e delle sue opere in prosa e in rima.* Imola: Galeati, 1879.

Manacorda, Guido. "Benedetto Varchi, l'uomo, il poeta, il critico," *Annali della R. Scuola Normale Superiore di Pisa: Filosofia e Filologia,* XVII (1903), 1–161.

Manni, Domenico M. *Le Veglie piacevoli ovvero notizie de' più bizzarri, e giocondi uomini toscani, le quali possono servire di utile trattenimento, scritte da Domenico M. Manni, accademico etrusco.* 4 vols. Venice: Antonio Zatto, 1759–60.

Marconcini, Cartesio. *L'Accademia della Crusca dalle origini alla prima edizione del vocabolario (1612).* Pisa: Valenti, 1910.

Maylender, Michele. *Storia delle accademie d'Italia.* 5 vols. Bologna: L. Cappelli, [1926–30].

Mazzacurati, Giancarlo. *La Questione della lingua dal Bembo all'Accademia Fiorentina.* Naples: Liguori, 1965.

Messina, Michele. "Anton Francesco Grazzini detto il Lasca," in *Letteratura Italiana: I Minori* (Milan: Marzorati, 1961), Vol. II, 1183–97.

Negri, Giulio. *Istoria degli scrittori Fiorentini. . . .* Ferrara: Bernardino Pomatelli, 1722.

Nissim, Lea. *Gli "Scapigliati" nella letteratura italiana del Cinquecento.* Prato: Martini, 1922.

Passarini, Ludovico [pseud. Luri di Vassano]. *Saggio di modi di dire proverbiali e di motti popolari italiani.* Rome: Tipografia di E. Sinimberghi, 1872.

Pirotti, Umberto. "Benedetto Varchi e la questione della lingua," *Convivium,* XXVIII (1960), 524–52.

Prezziner, Giovanni. *Storia del pubblico studio e delle società scientifiche e letterarie di Firenze.* 2 vols. Florence: Carli, 1810.

Pullini, Giorgio. *Burle e facezie del '400.* Pisa: Nistri-Lischi, 1958.

Raimondi, Ezio. "Per la nozione di manierismo letterario," in his *Rinascimento inquieto* (Palermo: Manfredi, 1965), pp. 267–303.

Razzolini, Luigi and Alberto Bacchi della Lega. *Bibliografia dei testi di lingua a stampa citati dagli Accademici della Crusca.* Bologna: Gaetano Romagnoli, 1878.

Rilli, Iacopo. *Notizie letterarie, ed istoriche intorno agli uomini illustri dell'Accademia Fiorentina.* First part [no more published]. Florence: Piero Matini, 1700.

Rizzi, Fortunato. "Contrasti, dissidio e melanconia nel Cinquecento," *Nuova Antologia,* CCCV (1922), 250–65.

Rossi, Vittorio. *Storia della letteratura italiana.* 9 vols. Milan: Vallardi, 1897–1926.

Russo, Luigi. *Machiavelli.* Rome: Tumminelli, 1945.

Salinari, Giambattista. "Considerazioni intorno al Lasca," *Lo Spettatore italiano,* VI (1953), 403–8.

Savino, Lorenzo. "Una polemica linguistica del Cinquecento," *Rassegna critica della letteratura italiana,* XVI (1911), 193–224.

Scaife, Walter B. *Florentine Life during the Renaissance.* Baltimore: The Johns Hopkins Press, 1893.

Scrivano, Riccardo. *Il Manierismo nella letteratura del Cinquecento.* Padua: Liviana, 1959.

Segre, Cesare. "Edonismo linguistico nel Cinquecento," *Giornale storico della letteratura italiana,* CXXX (1953), 145–77.

Spingarn, Joel Elias. *A History of Literary Criticism in the Renaissance.* 2d ed. New York: Columbia University Press, 1963.

Tamassia, Giovanni. *La Famiglia italiana nei secoli decimoquinto e decimosesto.* Milan-Palermo: R. Sandron, 1911.

Toffanin, Giuseppe. *Il Cinquecento.* 5th ed. Milan: Vallardi, 1954.

Tommasini, Oreste. *La Vita e gli scritti di Niccolò Machiavelli nella loro relazione col Machiavellismo.* 2 vols. Rome: Ermanno Loescher, 1911.

Tonelli, Luigi. *L'Amore nella poesia e nel pensiero del Rinascimento.* Florence: Sansoni, 1933.

Villani, Giovanni. *Storia di Giovanni Villani cittadino fiorentino nuovamente corretta, e alla sua vera lezione ridotta, col riscontro di testi antichi.* 2 vols. Florence: Giunti, 1587.

Villari, Pasquale. *Niccolò Machiavelli e i suoi tempi.* 3d ed. 2 vols. Milan: Editore-Libraio della Real Casa, 1912–14.

Vivaldi, Vincenzo. *Storia delle controversie linguistiche in Italia da Dante ai nostri giorni.* Catanzaro: Guido Mauro, 1925.

Weise, Georg. "Manierismo e letteratura," *Rivista di letterature moderne e comparate,* XIII (1960), 5–52.

Zannoni, Gio. Batista. *Storia della Accademia della Crusca.* Florence: Tipografia del Giglio, 1848.

III. THE COMEDIES

Agresti, Alberto. "Il Negro nella commedia italiana del secolo XVI," *Atti della Accademia Pontaniana,* XXII (1892), 113–20.

———. *Studi sulla commedia italiana del secolo XVI.* Naples: Stamperia della R. Università, 1871.

Allacci, Lione. *Drammaturgia di Lione Allacci accresciuta e continuata fino all' anno MDCCLV.* Venice: Giambattista Pasquali. [Photocopy. Turin: Bottega d'Erasmo, 1961].

Amicis, Vicenzo de. "L'Imitazione classica nella commedia italiana del XVI secolo," *Annali della R. Scuola Normale Superiore di Pisa: Filosofia e Filologia,* I (1873), 1–151.

———. *L'Imitazione latina nella commedia italiana del XVI secolo.* Florence: Sansoni, 1897.

Amico, Silvio d', ed. *Enciclopedia dello spettacolo.* 9 vols. Rome: Le Maschere, 1959.

———. *Storia del teatro drammatico.* 4 vols. Milan-Rome: Rizzoli, 1939.

———. *Storia del teatro italiano.* Milan: Bompiani, 1936.

———. "Teatro drammatico: *La Strega* del Lasca e l'*Aminta*

del Tasso al 'Maggio Fiorentino,' "*Nuova Antologia*, CDIII (1939), 478–81.

Apollonio, Mario, ed. *Commedia italiana*. Milan-Florence-Rome: Bompiani, 1947.

———. *Storia del teatro italiano*. 2 vols. Florence: Sansoni, 1958.

———. "Il Teatro fiorentino del Cinquecento," in *Il Cinquecento* (Florence: Sansoni, 1955), pp. 141–57.

Arlía, Costantino. "Una farsa del Lasca attribuita al Machiavelli," *Il Bibliofilo*, VII, No. 5 (1886), 74–75.

Bond, R. Warwick. *Early Plays from the Italian*. Oxford: Clarendon Press, 1911.

Bonghi, Ruggiero. "Le Nostre commedie del secolo XVI e un dramma francese del XIX," *Nuova Antologia*, XCI (1887), 209–24.

Borlenghi, Aldo. *Documenti sul teatro comico del Cinquecento*. Milan: La Goliardica, 1959.

———, ed. *Commedie del Cinquecento*. 2 vols. Milan: Rizzoli, 1959.

———. "Regolarità e originalità della commedia del Cinquecento," in his *Studi di letteratura italiana dal Trecento al Cinquecento* (Milan-Varese: Istituto Editoriale Cisalpino, 1959), pp. 122–230.

———. Rev. of Antonfrancesco Grazzini, *Teatro* (Bari, 1953), in *Aut Aut* (March, 1953), 175–78.

Borsellino, Nino, ed. *Commedie del Cinquecento*. 2 vols. Milan: Feltrinelli, 1962.

Boughner, Daniel C. *The Braggart in Renaissance Comedy: A Study in Comparative Drama from Aristophanes to Shakespeare*. Minneapolis: The University of Minnesota Press, 1954.

Bragaglia, Anton Giulio, ed. *Commedie giocose del '500*. 4 vols. Rome: Colombo, 1946.

Campanini, Naborre. *Lodovico Ariosto nei prologhi delle sue commedie*. Bologna: Nicola Zanichelli, 1891.

Caprin, Giulio. Rev. of Antonfrancesco Grazzini, *Teatro* (Bari, 1953), in *Il Ponte*, IX (1953), 1600–1601.

Ciampi, Ignazio. *La Commedia italiana*. Rome: Galeati, 1880.

Clubb, Louise George. *Giambattista Della Porta, Dramatist*. Princeton, New Jersey: Princeton University Press, 1965.

Creizenach, Wilhelm. *Geschichte des Neuren Dramas*. 5 vols. Halle a.S.: Max Niemeyer, 1918.

Fabiani, Vittorio. *Gente di chiesa nella commedia del Cinquecento*. 2d. ed. Florence: Bernardo Seeber, 1905.

Galzigna, G. A. *Fino a che punto i commediografi del Rinascimento abbiano imitato Plauto e Terenzio*. Capodistria: Cobol-Priora, 1899.

Gentile, Giovanni. "Delle commedie di Anton Francesco Grazzini detto il *Lasca*," *Annali della R. Scuola Normale Superiore di Pisa: Filosofia e Filologia*, XII (1897), 3–129.

Goggio, Emilio. "Dramatic Theories in the Prologues to the *Commedie Erudite* of the Sixteenth Century," *PMLA*, 58 (1943), 322–36.

———. "The Prologue in the *Commedie Erudite* of the Sixteenth Century," *Italica*, XVIII (1941), 124–32.

Herrick, Marvin T. *Comic Theory in the Sixteenth Century*. Urbana: University of Illinois Press, 1950.

———. *Italian Comedy in the Renaissance*. Urbana: University of Illinois Press, 1960.

Ingegneri, Angelo. *Della Poesia rappresentativa & del modo di rappresentare le favole sceniche*. Ferrara: Vittorio Baldini, 1598.

Kennard, Joseph Spencer. *The Italian Theatre*. 2 vols. New York: Benjamin Blom, 1964.

Klein, J[ulius] L[eopold]. *Geschichte des Drama's*. 13 vols. Leipzig: T. O. Weigel, 1866–76.

Larson, Orville K. "Spectacle in the Florentine *Intermezzi*," *Drama Survey*, II, No. 3 (February, 1963), 344–52.

Lea, Kathleen Marguerite. *Italian Popular Comedy: A Study in the Commedia dell'Arte, 1560–1620, with Special Reference to the English Stage*. 2 vols. Oxford: Clarendon Press, 1934.

Marti, Mario. Rev. of Aldo Borlenghi, ed. *Commedie del Cinquecento* (Milan, 1959), in *Lettere italiane*, XIII (1961), 241–45.

Mignon, Maurice. "Les Principaux Types de la comédie italienne de la Renaissance," in *Etudes de littérature* (Paris: Hachette, 1912), pp. 81–114.

Nagler, Alois Maria. *Theatre Festivals of the Medici: 1539–1637*, trans. George Hickenlooper. New Haven and London: Yale University Press, 1964.

Pandolfi, Vito. *La Commedia dell'arte*. 6 vols. Florence: Edizioni Sansoni Antiquariato, 1957.

Pellizzaro, Giambattista. *La Commedia del secolo XVI e la novellistica anteriore e contemporanea in Italia.* Vicenza: G. Raschi, 1901.

Plaisance, Michel. "Evolution du thème de la *beffa* dans le théâtre de Lasca," *Revue des études italiennes*, No. 4 (October-December, 1965), 491–504.

Porcelli, Bruno. "Le Commedie e le novelle del Lasca," *Ausonia*, XIX, vi (1964), 33–45; XX, i (1965), 26–39.

Possenti, Eligio. "La *Strega* del Lasca al 'Maggio Fiorentino,' " *Corriere della Sera*, LXIV (June 2, 1939), 2.

Pullini, Giorgio. "Stile di transizione nel teatro di Giambattista Della Porta," *Lettere italiane*, VIII (1956), 299–310.

———. "Teatralità di alcune commedie del '500," *Lettere italiane*, VII (1955), 68–97.

Radcliff-Umstead, Douglas. *The Birth of Modern Comedy in Renaissance Italy*. Chicago: University of Chicago Press, 1969.

Reinhardstoettner, Karl Von. *Plautus. Spätere Bearbeitungen plautinischer Lustpiele.* Leipzig: Wilhelm Friedrich, 1886.

Rizzi, Fortunato. *Delle farse e commedie morali di G. M. Cecchi.* Rocca S. Casciano: Licinio Cappelli, 1907.

Russo, Luigi. "Giovanni Gentile storico della letteratura e filosofo dell'arte," in his *La Critica letteraria contemporanea* (Bari: Laterza, 1954), Vol. II, 41–195.

Salza, Abd-El-Kader. "Rassegna bibliografica," *Giornale storico della letteratura italiana*, XL (1902), 397–439.

Sanesi, Ireneo. *La Commedia.* 2d ed. 2 vols. Milan: Vallardi, 1954.

Scoti-Bertinelli, Ugo. *Sullo studio delle commedie in prosa di Giovan Maria Cecchi.* Città di Castello: S. Lapi, 1906.

Stoppato, Lorenzo. *La Commedia popolare in Italia.* Padua: A. Draghi, 1887.

Tonelli, Luigi. *Il Teatro italiano dalle origini ai nostri giorni.* Milan: Modernissima, 1924.

Toschi, Paolo. *Le Origini del teatro italiano.* Turin: Edizioni Scientifiche Einaudi, 1955.

Vallone, Aldo. *Avviamento alla commedia fiorentina del '500.* Asti: Casa Editrice "Arethusa," 1951.

Wolff, Max J. "Italienische Komödiendichter II. Antonfrancesco Grazzini," *Germanisch-Romanische Monatsschrift* (January, 1913), 102–17.

IV. THE NOVELLE

Anon. Rev. of *Le Cene*, ed. Carlo Verzone (Florence: G. C. Sansoni, 1890), in *Giornale storico della letteratura italiana*, XVII (1891), 133–36.

Bárberi Squarotti, Giorgio. "Struttura e tecnica delle novelle del Grazzini," *Giornale storico della letteratura italiana*, CXXXVIII (1961), 497–521.

Borlenghi, Aldo. "Il *pan unto* del Lasca," *La Fiamma* (Parma), No. 8 (January 11, 1943), 2.

Di Pino, Guido. *Antologia critica della novella italiana dal XV al XVIII secolo*. Messina: A. Sessa, 1959.

Dunlop, John Colin. *The History of Fiction: Being a Critical Account of the Most Celebrated Prose Works of Fiction from the Earliest Greek Romances to the Novels of the Present Age*. 4th ed. London: Longman, Brown, Green, and Longmans, 1845.

Fiacchi, Luigi. "Sopra la seconda Cena del Lasca," *Atti dell'Imp. e Reale Accademia della Crusca* (1819), 239–48.

Francia, Letterio di. *La Novellistica*. 2 vols. Milan: Vallardi, 1924–25.

Grazzini, Antonfrancesco. *The Story of Doctor Manente Being the Tenth and Last Story from the Suppers of A. F. Grazzini called il Lasca*, trans. with an introduction by David Herbert Lawrence. Florence: G. Orioli, 1929.

Landau, Marcus. *Beiträge zur Geschichte der Italienischen Novelle*. Vienna: L. Rosner, 1875.

Passano, Giambattista. *I Novellieri italiani in prosa indicati e descritti*. Milan: Libreria Antica e Moderna di G. Schiepatti, 1864.

Petrocchi, Giorgio. *Matteo Bandello, l'artista e il novelliere*. Florence: Le Monnier, 1949.

Pischedda, Giovanni. "Sulla lingua della novellistica rinascimentale," *Studi medio-latini e volgari*, VIII (1960), 193–210.

Pullini, Giorgio. "Novellistica minore del '500," *Lettere italiane*, VII (1955), 389–409.

Rotunda, D. P. *Motif-Index of the Italian Novella in Prose*. Bloomington: Indiana University Press, 1942.

Russo, Luigi. "Novellistica e dialoghistica nella Firenze del '500," *Belfagor*, XVI (1961), 261–83, 535–54.

Salinari, Giambattista, ed. *Novelle del Cinquecento.* 2 vols. Turin: UTET, 1955.

Van Bever, Ad. and Ed. Sansot-Orland. "Un Conteur florentin du XVIe siècle: Antonfrancesco Grazzini dit le Lasca," *Bulletin du Bibliophile et du Bibliothécaire* (1903), 134–46.

V. THE POETRY

Affò, Ireneo. *Dizionario precettivo, critico ed istorico della poesia volgare.* 2d ed. Milan: Giovanni Silvestri, 1824.

Ancona, Alessandro d'. "La Poesia popolare fiorentina nel secolo decimoquinto," *Rivista contemporanea,* Fasc. XXX (1862), 352–94.

———. *La Poesia popolare italiana.* Livorno: Raffaello Giusti, 1906.

Arlía, Costantino. "Roba di begliumori: Il Lasca," *Il Borghini,* VI, No. 23 (June 1, 1880), 357.

———. "Spigolatura laschiana," *Il Propugnatore,* XVIII, Pt. I (1885), 351–69.

Aruch, Aldo. "L'Autografo delle 'Stanze Burlesche' del Lasca," *Rivista delle biblioteche e degli archivi,* XXVIII (1917), 29–42.

Baldacci, Luigi, ed. *Lirici del Cinquecento.* Florence: A. Salani, 1957.

Barbi, Michele. "Per la storia della poesia popolare italiana," in *Studi letterari e linguistici dedicati a Pio Rajna* (Milan: Hoepli, 1911), pp. 87–117.

Biscioni, Antommaria. *Parere del Dottore Antommaria Biscioni accademico della Crusca sopra la seconda edizione de' Canti Carnascialeschi e in difesa della prima edizione proccurata da Antonfrancesco Grazzini detto il Lasca uno de' fondatori di detta accademia.* Florence: Moücke, 1750.

Bontempelli, Massimo, ed. *Canti carnascialeschi di Lorenzo de' Medici e di altri poeti dei secoli XV e XVI.* Milan: Istituto Editoriale Milano, 1920.

Bowra, Sir Maurice. "Songs of Dance and Carnival," in *Italian Renaissance Studies, a Tribute to the Late Cecilia M. Ady* (New York: Barnes and Noble, Inc., 1960), pp. 328–53.

Bracci, Rinaldo. *I Primi dialoghi di Decio Laberio in risposta e confutazione del parere del Sig. Dott. Antonmaria Biscioni, sopra la nuova edizione de' Canti Carnascialeschi, e in difesa dell'Accademia Fiorentina.* Calicutidonia per Maestro Ponziano in Castel Sambuco [Florence] 1750.

Carrara, Enrico. *La Poesia pastorale.* Milan: Vallardi, 1906.

Casotti, Giovambatista. *Memorie istoriche della miracolosa immagine di Maria Vergine dell'Impruneta.* Florence: Giuseppe Manni, 1714.

Cian, Vittorio. "Giochi di sorte versificati del sec. XVI," in *Miscellanea Nuziale Rossi-Teiss* (Trent: September 25, 1897), pp. 77–117.

Crescimbeni, Giovanni Maria de'. *Commentarj di Gio. Maria de' Crescimbeni intorno alla sua istoria della volgar poesia.* 5 vols. Rome: Antonio de Rossi, 1702–22.

———. *Istoria della volgar poesia.* Venice: Basegio, 1731.

Croce, Benedetto. *Poesia popolare e poesia d'arte.* Bari: Laterza, 1933.

———. *Poeti e scrittori del pieno e del tardo Rinascimento.* 3 vols. Bari: Laterza, 1945–52.

De-Mauri, L. *See* Sarasíno, Ernesto.

Di Pino, Guido. "Giovanni della Casa e la lirica toscana del Cinquecento," *Lettere italiane,* IX (1957), 342–56.

Fiacchi, Luigi. "Sopra il commento di Maestro Niccodemo Dalla Pietra al Migliaio sul Capitolo della Salsiccia del Lasca," *Atti dell'Imp. e Reale Accademia della Crusca* (1829), 261–70.

Fioretti, Benedetto. *Proginnasmi poetici di Udeno Nisiely.* Florence: Piero Martini, 1695.

Flamini, Francesco. *La Lirica toscana del Rinascimento, anteriore ai tempi del Magnifico.* Pisa: Nistri, [c. 1891].

———. *Notizia storica dei versi e metri italiani dal medioevo ai tempi nostri.* Livorno: Raffaello Giusti, 1919.

Fucilla, Joseph G. "An Unedited Religious Sonnet by Il Lasca," *Modern Language Notes,* LXIX (1954), 420–21.

Fusco, Enrico. *La Lirica.* Milan: Vallardi, 1950.

Galletti, Alfredo. "La Lirica volgare del Cinquecento e l'anima del Rinascimento," *Nuova Antologia,* CCCXLIV (1929), 273–92.

Ghisi, Federico. *Feste musicali della Firenze medicea (1480–1589).* Florence: Vallecchi, 1939.

———. *I Canti carnascialeschi nelle fonti musicali del XV e XVI secolo.* Florence-Rome: Leo S. Olschki, 1937.

Grant, William Leonard. *Neo-Latin Literature and the Pastoral.* Chapel Hill: The University of North Carolina Press, 1965.

Grappa [pseud.]. "Commento del Grappa [here identified with Francesco Beccuti, called 'Il Coppetta'] sopra la canzone in lode della Salsiccia [attributed to Grazzini]," in *Scelta di curiosità* (Bologna, 1881), Dispensa CLXXXIV, pp. XXV–112.

Grazzini, Antonfrancesco. "Epigram: For a Dog," trans. Oliver W. Evans. *Poet Lore,* XLVIII (1942), 98.

Jodi, Rodolfo Macchioni. "Poesia bernesca e marinismo," in *La Critica stilistica e il barocco letterario,* Atti del Secondo Congresso Internazionale di Studi Italiani (Florence: Le Monnier, 1958), pp. 261–71.

Marzot, Giulio. "L'Arte di ridere nella poesia del Seicento," *Nuova Antologia,* CDLX (1954), 29–42.

Olschki, Leonardo. *La Poesia italiana del Cinquecento.* Florence: La Nuova Italia, 1933.

Previtera, Carmelo. *La Poesia giocosa e l'umorismo dalle origini al Rinascimento.* Milan: Vallardi, 1939.

Quadrio, Francesco Saverio. *Della storia e della ragione d'ogni poesia.* 4 vols. Bologna: Ferdinando Pisarri, 1739.

Rizzi, Fortunato. *L'Anima del Cinquecento e la lirica volgare.* Milan: Fratelli Treves, 1928.

Rubieri, Ermolao. *Storia della poesia popolare italiana.* Florence: Barbèra, 1877.

Sarasíno, Ernesto [pseud. L. De-Mauri]. *L'Epigramma italiano dal risorgimento delle lettere ai tempi moderni con cenni storici, biografie e note bibliografiche.* Milan: Hoepli, 1918.

Saviotti, Gino, ed. *Rime del Berni e di berneschi del secolo XVI.* Milan: Vallardi, 1922.

Singleton, Charles S., ed. *Canti carnascialeschi del Rinascimento.* Bari: Laterza, 1936.

———, ed. *Nuovi canti carnascialeschi del Rinascimento.* Modena: Società Tipografica Modenese, 1940.

———. "The Literature of Pageantry in Florence during the Renaissance." Ph.D. Diss., Berkeley, California, 1936.

Solerti, Angelo. *Gli Albori del melodramma.* 3 vols. Milan-Palermo-Naples: Remo Sandron, 1904.

Sorrentino, Andrea. *Francesco Berni poeta della scapigliatura del Rinascimento.* Florence: G. C. Sansoni, 1933.

Vaganay, Hugues. *Le Sonnet en Italie et en France au XVIe siècle.* Lyons: Au Siège des Facultés Catholiques, 1903.

Virgili, Antonio. *Francesco Berni.* Florence: Le Monnier, 1881.

INDEX